AN UNEXPECTED
JOURNEY

JOHN H. LIVENS

Publishing Services provided by Paper Raven Books

Printed in the United States of America

First Printing, 2021

Paperback ISBN= 978-1-7370034-0-3

Hardback ISBN= 978-1-7370034-1-0

TABLE OF CONTENTS

You can consider this book a family biography—a journey of survival and overcoming major obstacles. It also could be categorized as an adventure story with romantic overtones, or a testament to the unlimited opportunities and freedom offered by the United States. The underlying theme is that tangible possessions and social standing are transitory—they can be "gone with the wind." What lasts is our character, intellect, and determination to seek a better future. Faith, love, and the support of one's family make it easier to attain these goals. These are timeless values, confined to no historical period nor individual experience. Perhaps my story will inspire you to think about your own life in these terms, to reappraise the milestones along the way that have brought you to where you are today.

PROLOGUE

It was a spectacular evening in Palm Beach, enhanced by a gentle ocean breeze. Beauty like this makes one reflect on how fortunate we are to be alive. For me, life had been an unexpected journey that easily could have ended differently. I pondered why good fortune or providence had guided me to this place.

As I drove along Worth Avenue, en route to attend a dinner, I was overwhelmed by the attractiveness and ostentatiousness of the town. The buildings and streets were immaculately illuminated by numerous sparkling lights attached to palm trees that swayed in the breeze. The brightly lit windows displayed merchandise from Tiffany, Chanel, Cartier, and other well-known brands. Being there, you felt like you were in a warm embrace.

Reluctantly, I recalled the writings of Thorstein Veblen, an economist who described such displays as "conspicuous consumption." He deemed this to be one of the evils of capitalism. I could not share his view—I felt the display around me demonstrated freedom of choice in a society where individuals are not limited in pursuit of their personal goals. Perhaps the reason why the lights looked so much brighter, the colors more vibrant, the laughter more cheerful, and the joy so much more intense was because I would have been denied the opportunity to experience this had it not been for the freedom and democracy of the United States. No wonder all this meant so much more to me.

I arrived at my destination and entered the club where the dinner was being held. Even the most jaded and sophisticated people knew the building was an architectural jewel. At the entrance, I was greeted by formally dressed waiters. They directed me along passageways illuminated by hundreds of candles, augmented by sparkling lights attached to the plants bordering the pathway. Along the way, there were elaborate flower arrangements, including numerous orchids. I passed an open courtyard filled with balloons—like lights that seemed to float in the air.

Further ahead was the main dining room, which seated more than five hundred. It was bordered with tall plants wrapped in a multitude of lights. Through the back windows, the inland waterway shimmered, which in the evenings gave a special feeling. Frequently, at the press of a button, the roof opened, and one could dine underneath the stars. On special occasions, the dance floor was converted to a rink, and one could watch an ice show while dining.

I joined my friends for cocktails in an ornate reception hall, greeted by a waiter who offered me a glass of champagne from a silver tray. Cocktails were followed by dinner in an adjoining room, specially prepared for this occasion. Afterward, guests were encouraged to tell stories. My dinner companion asked, "John, do you have a story to tell?"

What could I say? I doubted that anyone in this elegant setting could relate to the story I might tell. To fully understand, you must be transposed to a different time and place. While the opulent setting was fun, I knew the transitory nature of material possessions and social standing—they could be "gone with the wind," as had been the case for my family years ago.

When you struggle for survival, you depend on faith and hope for a better future. Character, intellect, and determination are required to reach your goals; the love and support of family aid your journey.

When posed the question of whether or not I had a story to tell, I knew my current setting was inappropriate for what I had to share. So, to tell the story, I went home and started to write. I'll let you decide if my story was worth telling.

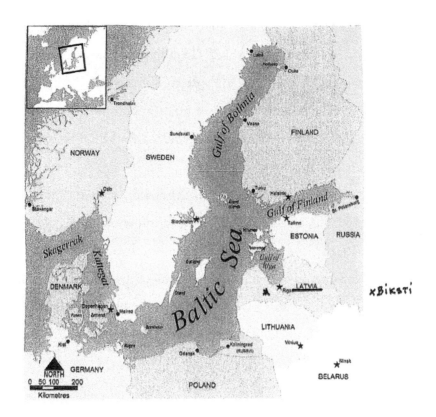

Baltic Region

CHAPTER 1

THE BEGINNING

My life began in Latvia, a small country across the Baltic Sea from Sweden. To the east, it was bordered by Russia and to the south by Lithuania and Poland. After World War II, the Eastern European countries' borders reshuffled, and Belarus replaced Poland's border with Latvia. In the thirteenth century, Riga was one of the most prosperous Hanseatic League cities, and in the sixteenth century, it was the largest city of the Swedish Empire. Latvia's favorable geographic position made it a desirable target for its more powerful neighbors—over the centuries, it has been ruled by Catholic bishops, Sweden, Poland, and Russia. Regardless of who had ultimate authority, for the seven hundred years preceding its independence in 1918, the ruling class was primarily composed of Baltic Germans.

In 1933, the year I was born, life in Riga (and Latvia in general) was booming. World War I, which had seriously damaged the country, ended, and Latvia was on the road to a prosperous recovery. This certainly was true for my parents—many of their old friends now held important positions in the Latvian government. My grandfather had passed away several years earlier and left Mother a substantial estate consisting of several small apartment buildings in Jelgava, a house and adjoining apartment buildings in Riga, and property in Biksti, which consisted of eight or nine buildings and a large manor house. After the recovery from World War I, my newly married parents led an active and happy lifestyle, including foreign travel. They took time to settle down.

My Grandparents

To better understand the influences that shaped my life, we should briefly turn to my grandparents on my mother's side.

Grandfather J Brezinskis
1862 - 1925

My grandfather was a substantial landowner. At that time, there were not many large Latvian landowners, and he frequently did business with the local Baltic German nobility who owned most of the land. He was successful in managing his property but was equally interested in life with his friends, playing cards and having fun. Late in his life, my grandfather married the daughter of a nearby, smaller Latvian landowner—a woman who would become my grandmother.

My grandmother Cornelia (we called her Oma) was more intellectual and had graduated from a language institute. She came from a large family. The most interesting person in my grandmother's family was her sister, whom we called Aunt Hance (Johanna). She wanted to be a doctor, but during the pre-World War I period, it was almost impossible for women to get a medical education in czarist Russia. So, the family sent Hance to study medicine in Switzerland and later in St Petersburg. Hance was an excellent student and frequently wrote to her relatives in Latvia. My grandmother talked about one letter her sister sent her that referred to the many students who were plotting revolution to overthrow the Czar. Aunt Hance was not interested in politics, but she attended a meeting where an articulate and aggressive agitator spoke. She was later introduced to the speaker, whom she found obnoxious. He introduced himself to my aunt as Vladimir Lenin. After completing her studies and returning home, she became one of the first female Latvian physicians. Hance went on to a successful medical career. She married another doctor, who later served as a colonel in the Latvian Army Reserve. Later in life, my path crossed several times with Aunt Hance and her family.

After my grandmother completed her language studies and served as a teacher of German and French in Russia, she returned to Latvia and married my grandfather. This seemed to be a prearranged marriage. My grandfather was interested in having a large family of sons who could take over his properties. Imagine his great distress when he could only have one child (my mother)—and a daughter at that! He

Grandmother "Oma"
Brezinski, 1872 - 1945

eventually accepted the fact, but from what I learned later, he built a house on the corner of his estate for his mistress and spent considerable time there. Thus, my mother's upbringing was left to my grandmother.

During World War I, when hostile forces approached my grandfather's estate, he told his servants to pack up fifty horses and wagons with belongings and supplies and headed to Estonia. He spent the war years in Tartu in his usual style—playing cards, having a jolly time with his friends, and occasionally sending someone who worked for him back to his estate in Latvia to ensure that everything was in order. After the war subsided, he returned and found that everything on his estate was intact—except that most of his horses were gone. Horses were essential because there were no tractors. The surrounding area at that time was controlled by renegade German troops under General Count Bermont. The war had officially ended, but Bermont wanted to put Latvia under German control and reinstall the Baltic nobility. My grandfather wanted to have his horses returned, so he organized a ball and invited General Bermont and his staff. It was a success, but another problem developed: the general was very much attracted to my mother, who was barely twenty. Because the general had a reputation as a ladies' man, my grandfather forgot about the horses and sent my mother to the city right away. The horses were eventually returned and my grandfather's landholdings prospered again.

Biksti Manor 1938

Transportation to Church

In the early 1920s, the Latvian government was established, and my grandfather anticipated that most of the large estates would be expropriated because most owners were Baltic Germans who had supported the German cause. So, he sold most of this land and purchased several buildings in Jelgava, a regional capital, as well as a house and two apartment buildings for my mother in the capital (Riga). He also acquired the Biksti estate from Baron von Ropp, with whom he had a previous business relationship (and who also wanted to return to Germany).

Years later, I would explore our house with my friends—mostly the attic and other unused spaces. One day, I pushed against a wall, and it gave way. I found two dusty metal trunks. One was full of German banknotes, starting with denominations of one thousand and going up to ten thousand Deutsche Marks. The other contained notes which turned out to be Imperial Czarist bonds. Apparently, my grandfather had not trusted the banking system. He had also opened a Swiss bank account. While ill in the hospital, my grandfather had called for a lawyer so he could list all his assets—but when the lawyer came, my grandfather felt better, and because he did not like lawyers, he sent him away. The next day, my grandfather died without ever disclosing his holdings.

The currency and bonds I found were now worthless. So, for a long time afterward with my friends, I would play blackjack and bet ten thousand marks. How transitory wealth can be!

Biksti was the place I spent my entire childhood. It included granaries, a blacksmith shop, a dairy, stables, a greenhouse, and more—

quite a place for a boy to be brought up, full of unexplored areas that made life exciting.

My Mother

Mother had a strict upbringing. Her father never allowed her to play with the servants' children. She was alone, except for governesses. Though my grandfather was initially disappointed that he didn't have a son, he came to dote upon and devoted much attention to his only child. He took her along when he bought horses and cattle and negotiated with tenants, showed her how to ride, and familiarized her with the

Mother Irma Livens
1901-1997

management of the estate. He also taught Mother various card games and how to handle firearms. Later in life, Mother continued to be an excellent card player, but she never cared for shooting.

As mentioned previously, due to my grandfather's divided attention, my grandmother Oma was largely responsible for my mother's upbringing. My grandmother had been a French teacher and was a great believer in education. So, from age six on, Mother had rotating governesses who taught her foreign languages. By age twelve, she spoke Latvian, German, Russian, French, and English. The first three she spoke fluently, like a native. I remember one time traveling with Mother in Germany when the locals asked her how things were in Berlin. (Mother spoke German with a Berlin accent because her governess was from there.)

It was a very lonely childhood for Mother. There were no other families of equal status nearby. (Keep in mind, in those days, there were no automobiles, and estates were large.) Mother told me that she sometimes felt so lonely she would crawl into the doghouse to hug her two dogs, who were her best friends—a sad story indeed!

Mother was mostly schooled at home, but eventually attended one of the best secondary schools, Academia Petrina (equivalent to a junior college level) in Jelgava. She lived with relatives, was an excellent student, and had a wonderful time. At this school, she met many young men—people who eventually became important in the Latvian government. I read a book published by one of her classmates. He refers to Mother as an "attractive, charming, wonderful person." Besides that, she came from a wealthy background, which was not the case for other classmates.

Despite her privileged upbringing, Mother was very open-minded and felt that each person should be judged on his own merits, character, values, and accomplishments rather than his social background. She had no problem with me playing with servants' children (or anyone else) because she considered all equal if they could get along. I remember her telling me the story of her early childhood—how different social groups did not mix, and how that did not always lead to a happy ending. To this day, I remember her words and am reminded that it essential to understand who we are as individuals, not our backgrounds.

To illustrate this, I'll share a story from Mother's life that left a big impression on her. This story relates to her early years, probably around 1910. Her father's estate was not too far from their neighbor, Graf (Count) von Medem, among the oldest and noblest families in the Baltics. Socially, the Baltic Germans and the Latvians did not mix, but because my grandfather was a prosperous landowner and lived nearby, he had a cordial relationship with them. Mother told me that when my grandfather went to visit the von Medems, he occasionally brought her along. While the men discussed business, Mother played with some of the von Medem children. They had several daughters and a son. Mother was particularly fond of the youngest daughter—in fact, she adored her. I am sure that this occasional friendship was a pleasant one despite their age difference; according to Mother, the young lady had an outgoing nature.

A few years later, Mother's father told her that there had been a tragic event in the von Medem family. He had to go to the funeral and wanted to take her along. This was the first funeral Mother had ever attended; she wanted to learn what had happened. Grandfather Berzinskis had only shared that the youngest von Medem daughter, Mother's favorite, had passed away. He gave no other explanation.

Mother eventually found out from Oma that the youngest von Medem daughter had fallen madly in love with a Latvian forester who worked for the family. Despite the von Medem family's objections, the two were inseparable and wanted to get married. But marrying a lowly Latvian employee was below the accepted standards of Baltic Germans, and the von Medem family was firm in its opposition. Their daughter implored them, claiming life without her beau was not worth living, but the von Medem family did not budge. So one day, she walked out onto an upper-floor balcony of their manor house and jumped off headfirst. She died instantly.

Mother was greatly saddened and disturbed by these events. This tragic love story and the social conditions that prevented their marriage seemed to bother Mother for years; and she never believed in class distinction. She treated everyone equally.

Years later, during the 1920s, all the large estates—primarily belonging to Baltic Germans—were confiscated by the Latvian government. All the von Medem property was seized, and they had little left. Shortly afterward, the von Medems departed for Germany. In the 1930s, Mother was staying with friends at an elegant Austrian resort not too far from Salzburg, enjoying the scenery and waiting for her husband to join. In the afternoon, the hotel had a tea dance with a live orchestra. Mother was sitting with her married friends. The manager of the hotel came to Mother and said, "Why don't you dance more? I can provide you a temporary partner. There is a gentleman in my employ available for these purposes, and you will find him quite agreeable for at least one dance!" He added, "You might be familiar with him because his family came from Latvia. His name is von Medem." He was from the same family who felt that their daughter (his sister) should not marry below their social level—now, decades later, the family had lost almost everything and had to earn a living in a different way.

After finishing her secondary education, Mother had no desire to return to live on her father's estate. She managed to convince her mother, who in turn persuaded her husband, to allow her to study at Heidelberg University in Germany. This was quite a departure from the sheltered lifestyle that Mother experienced in Latvia—she had never been exposed to the realities of the world. She departed for Germany and had a great time in Heidelberg, which was probably the first time in her life she experienced unlimited freedom.

After several months, she met a Romanian nobleman who was squiring her around, obviously a very romantic encounter. This apparently went on for some time, and, after a year, Mother became pregnant. This was a huge scandal that no one wanted to talk about—I only learned about it sixty years later. My grandfather told her that he did not want anything to do with this child, even though Mother's Romanian boyfriend had asked her to marry him. At that time, Mother was angry; she said that she would not marry or move to Romania, but her father demanded that her baby daughter never come to Latvia. Finally, my grandmother brokered a truce. After two years in Heidelberg, Mother returned to Latvia and left her young daughter, Silvia, behind in the care of a German family named Barth. Later, Silvia would tell me that she loved the Barth family as her own, but probably resented the fact that Mother was not there.

After returning to Latvia, Mother lived in the Riga house her father bought for her. She enrolled at the University of Latvia and continued her studies in economics. Student life at that time was very dynamic—

these were the first few years of the country's independence. She knew many of the people there through her family and her past schooling. It must have been very exciting. To illustrate: the first president of Latvia (Jānis Čakste) was my grandfather's friend, and his son was Mother's schoolmate and friend at the university. He, in turn, married one of Mother's best friends, and their friendship lasted for the rest of their lives.

During her active social life in Riga, my mother met my father. He played an early role in the establishment of the Latvian Republic and was working to reorganize their transportation system. Father was a senior member of one of the oldest student-dueling societies, Selonia, with important social and political connections. These societies were based on the German model, much like American fraternities—many graduates maintain their relationships with one another for the rest of their lives and help one another's careers along. Social life for the younger generations was quite active. When Mother got engaged to Father, my grandfather was pleased, even though he realized that her future husband had no interest in (or understanding of) the agriculture business.

In the 1930s, my parents led an enjoyable lifestyle. They lived in our Riga house and traveled abroad because of Father's work (and probably more so because of Mother's interest in traveling). Sometimes, Mother would travel ahead to Berlin or some other place and visit friends, and then would wait until Father joined after one of his business trips. After my birth, their life did not change significantly—as a young child, I was cared for by nurses and governesses.

At Biksti, my parents entertained weekend guests that were not only from Riga but also London, Sweden, and Germany. Because Father was a managing director of the Latvian Railroads, he negotiated many infrastructure contracts with international firms, which required a great deal of travel to other parts of Europe. Mother preferred Berlin and Vienna, but she also accompanied Father to London. In connection with this, I recall a story.

Mother was very prone to seasickness. One time, leaving London for France, she learned that there was a storm on the English Channel. My parents decided to board the channel ferry early so they could go to bed and have a restful crossing. Unfortunately, the moment they settled into their cabin, Mother got violently seasick for the rest of the night. When she woke up the next morning, she expected to be in Calais, but it turned out that the ship had never left the dock in Dover. Her seasickness was merely a result of her state of mind. Later in life, Mother developed an interest in Christian Science because she realized how greatly our mental attitude affects our health.

My Father

Father graduated with a degree in engineering. He studied at Riga Technical University, at St. Petersburg Imperial University, and for a short time in Germany. Like Mother, Father also spoke five languages and had a passing knowledge of Swedish. The Latvian economy and its infrastructure had been virtually destroyed during World War I and needed to be rebuilt. His language skills, combined with his academic background, made him a valuable member of the government.

Father, Herman A. Livens
(Lieven), 1893-1941
with Mother

While Father was trained as an engineer, he was very much interested in international affairs and in the government in general. He was present at the founding of the Latvian Republic on November 18, 1918—a great honor. Subsequently, he was very close to the government; in fact, when its leaders later temporarily escaped on an icebreaker ship (the *Saratov*), Father too was there. In Latvia's early years, the country was almost occupied by German troops, so the government (including Father) moved to the icebreaker to wait until hostilities subsided.

One evening after dinner on the *Saratov,* Father privately and casually mentioned to a friend that one of the leaders, Ulmanis, had poor manners that were inappropriate for someone in his position. Unfortunately, this friend told Ulmanis about Father's comments, and Ulmanis eventually became the president and one-man ruler of Latvia. On several later occasions, Father was recommended for ambassadorships, but Ulmanis always blocked these opportunities. Apparently, Father's comment had hit a soft spot: Ulmanis studied at the University of Nebraska, while Father had an elitist background and attended leading universities. Ulmanis disliked Father and held back the advancement of Father's career. Despite this, Father had an important position in the Latvian National Railroads Administration.

Father came from a small family, and we rarely saw his relatives. Mother's favorite of his relatives was a distant cousin of Father's, Mr. Garselis, who had served as mayor of Riga. He was a charming man and was close to Mother. One day, he called her from the hospital, explained that he had terminal cancer, and invited her to visit. He went on to say that she should bring a bottle of good champagne. When Mother arrived, Garselis explained that he wanted to celebrate life in the company of a wonderful friend, a friend who was going to have a bright future ahead and who would bring happiness to other people's lives. They drank champagne and shared memories. A few days later, Garselis passed away. The following years proved that death would be a familiar companion to all of us, but we could not worry—what we remember is the grace and character displayed while accepting the inevitable.

CHAPTER 2

EARLY YEARS

After my birth, Mother spent a short time in Riga and then returned to Biksti, our country place, where my grandmother and older sister Silvia lived when Silvia wasn't away at boarding school (Silvia was allowed to come to Latvia after my grandfather passed away). Mother brought along a full-time nurse who took care of me until she could hire a permanent governess. After I was settled with the nurse, Mother shuttled between Biksti and Riga. Father spent most weekends in Biksti.

Weekend in Biksti

Because the Biksti manor house was large, with ample staff, it was very easy for my parents to entertain their friends, and many now had prominent positions in the government. Besides professional people, my parents also had a wide circle of artist friends, who they also included in weekend visits to Biksti. All were young, successful, and proud of the country's independence. They had a wonderful time. It was also easy to entertain in Biksti because the manor house had many bedrooms, and help was always available. The photos on these pages display typical weekends in Biksti and Riga, where my parents spent most of their time.

Entertainment in the Riga House

My earliest memory dates back to when I was probably two years old. I remember lying in a crib in a semi-dark, stuffy nursery when suddenly, above me, there were many adult faces ogling, showing a great deal of attention. These were probably house guests to whom my parents wanted to show their new baby. Shortly afterward, all the adults left, and I was alone again in the damp nursery. I heard laughter and conversation outside. I started to cry and wail. Obviously, even as a young child, I wanted to be included. A nurse came in wearing a white, starched uniform and closed the shutters. It was naptime. So much for the temporary adult attention! Two years later, my younger sister, Peggy, was born, and there was another baby to admire. When guests arrived, I was all dressed up by Lulu, the governess, and paraded around. The adults liked to pat my head because I had almost white hair (until age ten), but after that, they left me alone. Frankly, I did not care for this display and was glad to slink off.

After a few months, my nurse (who always wore a white, starched uniform) departed. She was replaced by Lulu, who was a wonderful lady. I loved her, and she took good care of me. Unfortunately, after a year or so, she left. The reason for this was that Peggy's new governess, Elsa, did not get along with Lulu and made her life miserable. Perhaps one incident, which occurred a few years later, can adequately characterize Elsa's behavior: one day I walked into the bathroom, which had been used by Peggy, and there was an awful smell. I said, "Elsa, why don't you open the window!" Elsa replied, "You are wrong about the smell. When Peggy goes to the bathroom, there's only the fragrance of violets!" Because of Lulu's dismissal, I never cared much for Elsa, though she remained loyal to my family.

I also vaguely remember Peggy's christening—it was a big affair. There were many guests in the main ballroom at Biksti, which was used very infrequently. I was all dressed up and stood next to Father during the christening ceremony. I could not understand why many of the ladies, who all seemed to be dressed in black, were crying, but I was glad to have a younger sister to whom guests paid more attention, leaving me alone.

John H. with a nurse
1933

With father
1937

Peggy Christening in Biksti 1935

So, with Lulu gone, at an early age, I was without a governess and had limited supervision (because my parents, too, were frequently away). I was left in the care of my grandmother and the plentiful household staff. Though I was left to my own devices, I was not lonely at all. I had a good time—there were the servants' children and my best friend, the family dog, Duke (Duksis). Duke was aware that I was a child and needed attention, so he followed me around. One day, the cook gave me a chicken drumstick, and I was nibbling on it outdoors. Duke came to me and the look in his eyes said, "I am your buddy. How about sharing this?" Of course, I gave the bone to Duke—I knew I could get another from the cook.

The adults nearby saw this and laughed. "See what the dog has done to this little boy!"

I was very upset by their comment and cried. The problem was that adults just did not understand animals and how I felt about them.

Duke continued to follow me around. Later, after I had learned to swim, I went with some of the other boys to the nearby river and brought Duke. I jumped in the river and put my head under the water. Duke saw this and thought I was in trouble, so he jumped in the water and tried to push me to shore. When he realized it had been a joke, he slunk off. No matter what, Duke remained my friend. He was a large dog, a mix of German Shepherd and Great Pyrenees.

Peggy with my best
friend - 1939

Peggy and I with Father
1937

Skiing with my friend and instructor in Biksty Park - 1937

One of my favorite guests was Mr. Jansons, who was associated with the Latvian national cross-country ski team. Even though I was not yet six years old, Mr. Jansons said, "If you are interested, the time has come for you to learn how to ski." I was more than pleased. On his next trip, Mr. Jansons brought cross-country equipment and taught me the fundamentals of skiing. He was close to our family and one day mentioned, "Do you know that your family goes back for centuries? Your original ancestor was a local chief who, along with his underlings, worshiped trees. The Livonian Knights converted him to Christianity." I said that Mother occasionally dragged me to church, but I also liked trees. I soon had had enough of history and asked, "Why don't we go skiing?" Mr. Jansons instilled in me a lifelong love of skiing, which gave me many happy memories.

Another guest whom I remember was a very well-known Latvian author, Aleksandrs Grīns. His books can be compared to those of Ernest Hemingway—tales of action, war, and love. His *Blizzard of Souls* is the best known of his works; in 2019, it was adapted into one of the most popular movies ever produced in Latvia and was included in the 2020 Cannes Film Festival. After the Soviet occupation in 1941, I was distraught to read that Mr. Grins had been tortured and executed. Such was life then—and such was the dramatic change that took place in Latvia within a short period of time.

As time went on, I further explored the Biksti estate. There were several barns for storage of hay and other agricultural products. There were about six or seven families living on the estate who worked part or full time, including many children of various ages. During the summer harvest, the staff was supplemented by extra workers. I was particularly attracted to the blacksmith shop. The blacksmith worked full time for the estate and also took on outside work, so there was always action. I loved to watch him make horseshoes, shoe horses, and work on all kinds of farm implements. There were always sparks flying and fires burning.

Next to the shop lived the blacksmith's family, which consisted of his wife (who was one of our housekeepers) and his two sons. Initially, there were also two older daughters, but when they married, they moved out to their own apartments. My sister Peggy and I were very friendly with the blacksmith's youngest daughter, Irene, who was four years older than me. She spent most of her time with us at the main house. Because her mother was also there all the time keeping house, Irene essentially became part of our family. When, in 1944, we had to leave Biksti and flee to Germany, the housekeeper came to Mother and pleaded, "Our family has been working for you all these years. I'm only asking you one favor: take my daughter with you so that she can have a better life!" Mother did not hesitate, and Irene became even more a part of our family. Later, she was happily married and settled in the United States.

As mentioned earlier, there were many workers on the estate, supplemented by seasonal helpers. Most of them lived on the property. It is interesting to learn how they were compensated: the blacksmith's family, for instance, had free housing and received annually two and a half tons of wheat, one thousand five hundred quarts of milk, thirty cords of wood, and a large garden plot. The estate supplied all the material for the blacksmith's shop and paid him little cash because he could accept outside work. His wife worked as a housekeeper for a minimum of seventy days per year. She also helped with other work, for which there was extra pay.

In short, Biksti was a self-sufficient, almost feudal community with little outside interference. While Mother owned the property, the day-to-day affairs were handled by an estate manager and his assistant. Nevertheless, Mother prided herself on understanding agriculture, which she learned from her father. She made all the major decisions. Father knew very little about farming and was not interested.

One memorable event in my life was when Father invited me to travel with him to a commencement address that he was giving at a school in the western part of Latvia. As a special treat, he used the president's personal railroad car and left it at the local train station so I could go to bed there. It was hooked up to the train later that night, when I was asleep, and we traveled to the western part of Latvia that way.

As I was growing up, Father visited on the weekends, and as I got older, he encouraged me to take walks with him in the morning. This, unfortunately, meant that I had to be all cleaned and spruced up. Most of the time, at this age, I played with the workers' boys—and was usually as disheveled as them. Silvia even called me a country urchin (lovingly, of course!).

However, Father was always formal and dressed elegantly, even in the country. On these walks, he wore a three-piece suit and told me about the different trees in the forest. The problem was that he had not spent much time in the country, and I could recognize the trees even better than he could. The staff had already warned me that Father could hardly tell the difference between wheat and rye—which, of course, I knew. So, I dutifully tagged along on the walks and hoped for them to end quickly. Occasionally, Father talked about politics and government, which already interested me, even at my early age. On one of these walks, Father told me that he had special tickets for us to attend the 1940 Olympics in Helsinki, which would be a men's trip for him and me. I was really looking forward to it, but as I will explain, the future held other plans.

Growing Up

Growing up in Biksti made me independent. Most of the time I played with our workers' children and lived like they did; I frequently ate meals with their families in their somewhat primitive living quarters. During the summer, I hardly ever wore shoes, except when we had guests. There was a nearby river, and we spent a lot of time fishing and enjoying country life. I could do virtually anything on the estate with my buddies and not get into trouble. After all, my family owned the place, and no one could tell me what to do. I reached a truce with Elsa, Peggy's governess, who acted like Mother's representative in personal matters, even though the estate had a professional manager. (Ever since she ran off my beloved Lulu, she and I disliked one another.) I would no longer rant about my problems with Elsa to Mother, and she would not complain to her about my mischievous activities—An early lesson in negotiation and compromise.

A significant event for all of us took place in the fall of 1939 when Peggy and I went to school for the first time. Mother hired a local photographer to record this event and invited the workers' children, who also attended the school, to travel with us. Mother wore a fancy city dress with an elegant hat, and all of us rode in a carriage with two horses and a driver to the school, which was only a mile away. It was a simple country school, and there was no kindergarten—so Peggy, who was only five years old, joined my class.

The first day of school - 1939

The first-grade students followed a teacher from one classroom to another. By government mandate, all the pupils had to wear uniforms. It was supposed to help reduce the differences between social classes. Mother did not like this, so my sister and I were elegantly dressed. I

My buddy

had an English jockey hat and matching socks and wore a shirt and jacket, and Peggy was equally elegant with a custom hat. It did not take long for me to understand that I did not like to be dressed in fancy clothes that stood out—I wanted to be like the others and make new friends. To my mother and grandmother's chagrin, I gave up the proper outfit and only wore it when there were visitors. I just wanted to be like all the others. I always avoided fights or any violent encounter with other boys because I was taught that this was improper. My solution was to make friends with the most muscular boy in the class, who became my best buddy. If problems started to develop, he was there, and no one ever touched me. I have a photograph of one of my early buddies, and even today he looks tough.

Usually, in June, all of us went to Riga to visit Father and stay in our city house for a week. On one of these visits, my grandmother (Oma), Peggy, her governess Elsa, and I traveled by train to Riga. At the train station, Father's chauffeur met us, ready to drive us to the townhouse. As we got in the car, my grandmother said, "These large cities are full of germs, and the children should have proper gloves and not touch anything!" So, instead of going to our home, we went directly to a shop that sold children's gloves. My grandmother purchased a pair for Peggy and me. As she was making the payment, my grandmother said,

"My grandson knows the multiplication tables, and he can give you the correct figures!" The shopkeeper said, "Little boy, tell me, what is two times three?" Of course I knew the answer—the educational system to a large degree required memorizing information. That was not enough for Elsa, and she said, "Little Peggy knows more—she knows the double-digit multiplication tables!" The shopkeeper said, "What is twelve times thirteen?" Peggy knew the answer right away. It's no wonder that later in life she became a professor and, until college, never received a grade below an A. To this day, I do not know my double-digit multiplication tables!

Frankly, I did not care for visiting Riga because I could not play outdoors. Our house adjoined a courtyard that was next to two four-story wood apartment buildings, which also belonged to Mother. When I saw some boys playing in the courtyard, I wanted to join but was told that they were "townies" and should be avoided. So I spent most of my time indoors, wishing I was with my friends in the country.

In Riga, Father had a very fancy radio with multiple-wave capacity, which allowed one foreign station. Because there was no television, that was a good substitute. Occasionally, my sister Silvia and Mother took me out with them in the city, but I got bored tagging along. The only part I enjoyed was riding up and down the escalators in the department store—at that time, it was the only escalator in the Baltics.

By the late 1930s, Mother concluded that our manor house was too large, and it did not have any modern conveniences like central heating and electricity. There was another large building on our property that, at one time, had served as a fortress for the Teutonic Knights. It was a rectangular structure built around 1560, with walls about five feet thick made from stone to protect from attackers. Mother hired one of the best-known architects in Latvia to redesign the house. The builders had a great deal of difficulty ripping out one-third of the wall and replacing it with two-story glass windows, an advanced concept at that time for country living, and a state-of-the-art water heating system was installed, also very rare for the countryside. We had a man stoke the boilers full time to make sure the fire did not go out so we always had hot water and heat.

Father had a seventy-five-foot wind turbine tower built to generate electricity and charge a multiplicity of lead-zinc batteries that provided twelve-volt electric current. It was difficult to wire the building for electricity because all the walls were solid stone, so the wires had to be attached to the baseboards. A few years later, we installed a diesel generator that produced the regular two-hundred-twenty-volt current. The wiring frequently caused sparks to fly due to short circuits. I was told to look out for any and report it to the handyman, who would patch it up. The circuit breakers usually did not work. At that age, I felt that this was a very significant responsibility.

Around this time, my sister Silvia finished boarding school and spent more time in Biksti. She was a lovely person with a warm, cheerful personality, was an excellent cook, and was loved by everyone. Silvia was more than thirteen years older than me, and she helped when Mother was not around. When I had cuts and bruises, she patched me up—

there was no nearby medical care available. When I stepped on a bottle and cut my leg and there was no one to stitch it, Silvia did a terrific job bandaging it so I would not get an infection. I remember it well—I still have a scar on my foot today.

When out-of-town guests arrived in Biksti, Silvia knew I would not be well prepared, so she made sure that I took a bath, put on clean clothes, and combed my hair. I remember several occasions when she could not get the comb through my hair because it was full of hay and grit. Once the guests arrived and I had met them, after a while Silvia would nod, her signal that I could disappear. I sure was waiting for it! I felt Silvia was a perfect older sister.

While my childhood, by today's standards, might appear to be unusual, I was very happy. I knew my parents loved me, even though they were frequently away. Also, I was surrounded by other caring people, including my grandmother, sister, and our many servants.

Holidays and Celebrations

One of the more memorable events of the year in Latvia is the celebration of St. John's Day on June 23, the summer solstice. Besides Christmas, it is considered one of the most important holidays of the year. It also denotes the celebration of "name day" for everyone named John, which made it a special event for me.

Before the festivities started in the countryside, the workers on the estate—after adequately fortified with several beers—came to the manor house singing a song that went, "Ligo, ligo"—roughly translated,

"Rocking along." There were at least fifty, including their families and friends. When the celebrants arrived at our place, they put an oak wreath on my head and carried me on their shoulders to the meadow, where the celebration was taking place. There were bonfires and a barrel filled with wood and pitch that was lit and then hauled to the top of a high vertical pole. The festivities continued with more singing, beer, and cheese made for the occasion. Some of the young couples went into the forest to see whether they could find the magic fern that blossoms once a year. Of course, there was no such fern—it just gave them an opportunity to have a great time on their own. Others tried to jump over the bonfires to show their skills, but because of my age, they kept me away. Anyway, it was a great festive event for all, especially for me, because the celebration involved my name. Like the others, I wanted to stay up all night and see the sunrise, but Mother sent me and Peggy home to bed.

Christmas was also an important celebration for the family. My sister and I loved it, not only because of the beautifully decorated Christmas tree, and the many gifts. Workers from the estate selected a Christmas tree in the woods and set it in our living room. We decorated it with ornaments and specially baked glazed cookies. To the branches, we attached holders with small candles. The location of the candles was tricky because we wanted to make sure the flames did not reach the branches above and start a fire. Initially, this was not a problem, but as a tree dried out, the chances of a fire hazard increased. I was told to watch out for possible fires and extinguish minor ones.

We had a family celebration on Christmas Eve when Santa Claus (probably one of the farm hands) arrived and asked the children about their behavior during the year. That was before the distribution of gifts. Frankly, I was worried because we were told that Santa Claus knew everything. I committed my share of mischief during the year and hoped that Elsa or someone else had not squealed to Santa. Fortunately, Santa was not very well informed, and I always received generous gifts (whether deserved or not). Afterward, we ate a celebratory dinner accompanied by Christmas carols.

On Christmas Day, we had another celebration with all the workers and their families who lived on the estate. Including children, there were more than thirty people, and they all received gifts. Mother made everyone feel welcome and wanted them to know that she cared for them as individuals. Father held my hand as he read passages from the New Testament about the birth of Christ and the renewal of life. To this day, when I hear the St. Luke readings at Christmas, I think of Father and the days gone by—a lifestyle, time, and place never to be restored. It reminds me we should enjoy the full measure of everything while we are here.

Another holiday I remember vividly from my childhood is Easter. It is a significant holiday for the Greek Orthodox Church, which represents only a fragment of the Latvian population but is celebrated by all. In anticipation of Easter, eggs were covered with various designs, some quite artistic. The eggs were boiled in colored paper wrapping to give them a patina and glaze. The next step was to select not only the most beautiful egg but also the strongest. We took our egg and lightly punched it against the opponent's egg. The egg that broke first had to be eaten by the loser, which usually was not the case because the cook made plenty of egg salad. The winner went on to the next round, and so on.

In the early years, I always lost in the first round and was so sad that I almost cried. Later, one of my local buddies came to me and said that he had a plastic egg that appeared to be identical to a real egg. We made sure the egg was colored and entered the contest. We won every round but eventually had to admit the true nature of my egg. Some of the losers were not happy about it, but what can you do—I too had been a loser before! This made me learn to think outside the box and find creative solutions to problems that initially appeared to be insoluble—as long as these solutions did not cause harm and were in good fun.

One of the last significant social events in Biksti before the war began was Silvia's confirmation. Confirmation in this part of the world is equivalent to a debutante party in the United States. Usually, the celebrant is around eighteen years old.

All of us prepared for Silvia's confirmation. It was to be a grand party with a platform built outside the house with flowers, tables, lanterns, and balloons. There were many cars in the driveway—which was unusual because automobiles were rare at that time. After the ceremony at the church, there were flowers and guests everywhere as the party started. I went to the bathroom and found that even the bathtub was full of flowers—there was no more space in the vases. I briefly went to the party;

it was in full swing, but no one paid much attention to me, except for an occasional pat on my head. I retreated to my room and heard the distant sound of music and dancing. I knew that it brought happiness to Silvia, but it was not my cup of tea.

Changing Times

There were signs in the late 1930s that the world was changing. To illustrate this, I'll share a story Mother told.

At that time in Latvia, the Benjamins were a prosperous and prominent family in Latvia. Mr. Benjamin was the owner of the largest and most successful newspaper in Latvia, *Jaunas Zinas*. In the city, the Benjamins had an elegant townhouse. For their seashore residence, they hired the best Latvian architect and built probably the most attractive place on the entire Baltic coast. The Benjamins liked to entertain in high style.

In the late 1930s, my parents were invited to one of the Benjamins' festivities—an elaborate and elegant event. The gardens were beautifully lit with numerous lights, and there were flowers everywhere. The path to the Baltic Sea was lit so that one could see the dunes and the waves beyond. A large orchestra played in the ballroom, and throughout the house, there were wandering musicians. Mrs. Benjamin invited the leading soloists from the Latvia National Opera to perform. The men were in white ties or uniforms, and the ladies, too, were dressed their best. Mother said she worked with the dressmaker for weeks before the party because she wanted an exceptional dress made for the occasion.

One of the main attractions of the party was the famous Latvian fortune teller, Mr. Fink. His predictions had proven to be accurate in the past, so people valued his counsel. Because Mr. Fink rarely appeared in public, it was quite unusual for him to attend a social gathering—but this just further proved Mrs. Benjamin's strong influence.

After wandering through the house with Father, Mother patiently waited to have a turn with Mr. Fink. When she arrived, Mr. Fink was engaged in conversation with Mrs. Benjamin. Mrs. Benjamin asked Mr. Fink to tell her fortune. Mr. Fink looked at Mrs. Benjamin and said, "Madam, I cannot do that!" Mrs. Benjamin said, "I demand that you tell my fortune because you are in my house." Mr. Fink said, "I do not want to do it in this setting because it will be unpleasant, but it will be the truth." Mrs. Benjamin said something to the effect of, "I pay, so you have to do what I ask!" Mr. Fink said, "Very well, I will do it, but do not blame me for the outcome."

Mr. Fink told her,

I see that in the not-too-distant future, you will be in the dark, in a cold and lonely place. You will be close to starvation and very sick. There will be no escape and you will end your life there. Your husband will not be with you because he will have died earlier, far away. You will have hardly any friends and will be wishing for death. There is nothing that anyone can do to change this fate.

Mrs. Benjamin laughed at Mr. Fink and said that he was being deliberately ungrateful because she had pressured him, and therefore he wanted her to feel miserable. Mrs. Benjamin went on to say that she would not deal with him ever again. It is hard to imagine that this exchange took place at one of the most festive settings imaginable, where people did not seem to have any cares. Everyone at the party came to experience a wonderful time, and probably none of them were disappointed (except Mrs. Benjamin).

Unfortunately, Mr. Fink's predictions turned out to be accurate: little more than a year later, the Soviets invaded Latvia, seized Mr. Benjamin's newspaper, arrested him and his wife, and deported them to Siberia. Mr. Benjamin died shortly afterward. Mrs. Benjamin lingered on in a gulag, but eventually died from malnutrition and associated diseases.

It is interesting to note that Mr. Fink survived Soviet times; the leadership was also worried about their future, and they relied on Mr. Fink for advice. In Soviet-era Latvia, Brezhnev, Kosygin, and Khrushchev used the Benjamin house as a vacation retreat. Ironically, the Benjamin home today houses the Russian Embassy in Latvia.

As for Mr. Fink, he died at a ripe old age.

CHAPTER 3

SOVIETS IN LATVIA

As war clouds gathered in Europe, our lives in the late 1930s began to change. After the German annexation of Austria in March 1938 and the occupation of Sudetenland in May, which was approved by the Western powers, my parents ceased traveling to Europe. Foreign guests did not visit, and my parents' friends who came to make merry on the weekends now had serious discussions instead. The fun vanished.

I could sit in when the men were talking and speculating about the future. None of them liked the Soviets. Father and one of his friends were on a diplomatic mission to Moscow in the late 1920s and saw the poverty and cruelty of the secret police. I recall Father saying, "The Russians always liked to suffer; they are timid to take action until it is too late. They seem to like this fate, as Dostoyevsky portrays!"

I had heard of Dostoyevsky and was aware that the Soviets executed the tsar and most of the upper class. One of the men went on to say, "After the revolution, the secret police made you show your hands. If you had calluses, you were a proletarian. If your hands were soft, you were an exploiter and the enemy of the people!" I remembered back to when Silvia said that most of the time my clothes were dirty, and I looked like a country urchin. I concluded that this would probably make me indistinguishable from the proletarians, whoever they were.

The men also talked about Germany. They were concerned about their aggression and long-time interest in retaking control of the Baltic countries. They were also concerned about the unpredictable nature of Hitler and the character of the individuals with which he surrounded himself. This new government arrangement did not represent the best of Germany. These discussions worried me—I listened to the radio and had a fair understanding of the world. I was also an avid reader of magazines and newspapers, which further added to my concerns.

Another unexpected development that affected me directly occurred shortly afterward. Our family hired a student from Czechoslovakia to work on the estate. His sole responsibility was to remove weeds from the numerous pathways in our English-style garden. He started at one end of the garden, and when he reached the end, he started all over again. This work must have been tedious, and it was not an easy task for the nice young man who did not speak Latvian (and only poor German). I hung around with him and became his friend, and my grandmother tried to make his life more enjoyable. It looked like everything was going well, and we were looking forward to a fun season ahead. However, everything changed one day in May 1939, when the Germans invaded

Czechoslovakia. Father managed to obtain a special railroad ticket for the young man to return home through Poland.

Three months later, in August 1939, the Molotov-Ribbentrop agreement was signed. We now know that this divided Eastern Europe between Germany and the Soviets. A secret clause of the treaty permitted the Soviets to occupy the Baltic States, but it also allowed residents with a German background to leave the country and settle in Germany. In October 1939, shortly after the treaty was signed, the Soviets established military bases in Latvia.

Immediately, we noticed Russian troop trains and airplanes in the sky. Most people were becoming apprehensive and felt that worse was to come. It was disappointing to me because a year prior, Father made reservations and promised to take me to the 1940 Helsinki Olympics. I studied up on the subject and was most eager to go. Now, due to what was happening at home, the trip was canceled. Father assured me that instead, he would take the whole family to the most luxurious seaside hotel in Latvia: Kemeri. Frankly, I did not care too much about the hotel. I was looking forward to the Olympic games and foreign travel, about which I had heard so much. In June, Mother went early to the hotel in Kemeri and booked a suite in anticipation of our arrival. The day before we were supposed to leave—June 17, 1940—Soviet tanks rolled into Latvia, and our lives changed forever.

Mother immediately left Kemeri and went to Riga to be with Father. The city was in turmoil because the first action of the incoming Soviets was to release all prisoners, whether political or criminal. There were hardly any political detainees, but all prisoners were released and forced into demonstrations praising Stalin and requesting Latvia's incorporation into the Soviet Union. Later, we learned that the Soviets also brought people from Russia to participate in the demonstration and rigged the election. Mother telephoned and came briefly to Biksti but spent most of the time in Riga with Father, deciding what our family should do.

Through the Ribbentrop-Molotov Pact, the Soviets announced that all those who had German ancestry could leave Latvia for Germany by October of 1940. The ancestors of the Baltic Germans dominated political, economic, and social life in Latvia for more than seven hundred years. The Baltic Germans, to a degree, were responsible for the fact that Riga, in the sixteenth century, became one of the leading cities of the Hanseatic League. Until World War I, more than fifty percent of Riga's residents considered German their primary language. No matter who the ultimate ruler was—whether Sweden, Poland, or Czarist Russia—the Baltic Germans retained a privileged status and, for generations, yielded considerable influence at the Czar's court.

In the early 1920s, all the large Baltic German estates (like that of the von Medems) were taken over by the Latvian government, and the land was redistributed to those who fought for the country's independence. Many of the Baltic Germans left then, but those who remained had another opportunity to emigrate now. Some prominent Latvians who did not have German ancestry joined to escape communist rule. Those who left for Germany included my sister Silvia with her new husband, as well as many other close family friends. A total of sixty thousand left, or about three percent of the total population.

Because Father's family could trace its ancestry back to the late twelfth century and had intermarried with Baltic Germans, there was no problem for us to join the exodus. Moreover, both of my parents spoke perfect German; Mother studied at Heidelberg University and Father, briefly, at Göttingen. From what I later learned, Father was eager to leave, but Mother—being a loyal Latvian patriot—did not want to go. Mother also owned substantial property and was influenced by her World War I experience, when the family had left their estate with servants and fifty horse-driven wagons and spent the better part of the year in Estonia. When the fighting was over, they returned and resumed their life. In retrospect, it's not surprising. In desperate circumstances, people often cling to hope that in many cases is not based in reality.

My parents had another option to leave the country. An engineer who worked for Father under the Latvian National Railroads Administration had developed and patented a unique process that reduced calcium deposits in steam locomotives; his process was so successful that the engineer was invited by a U.S. railroad to implement it in the States. He moved to the United States and became very successful. The engineer wrote Father, thanking him for his help, and suggested that he should come to the United States as his guest to look for other business opportunities. This option gave my parents more time to make decisions. Once the nature of the Soviet occupation became apparent, Father decided to contact his U.S. friend and make plans to leave. Father sent several telegrams but received no response. Eventually, it became difficult to communicate overseas, and my parents later learned that the engineer was away for several months' in Hawaii and was unreachable. This is how our last hope to escape the Soviet regime evaporated.

Life Under the Soviets

In the countryside, life was also changing. The authorities confiscated all landholdings. Each family was allocated a few acres (*kolkhoz*); later, all the land belonged to the government (*sovhoz*), and everyone were mere employees of the farms. All the farm equipment and property, including personal furniture, belonged to the Soviets and was allocated for use by officials.

One day, the local communist party secretary arrived at our estate with two associates. They were there to take inventory of our land and property. I was curious and followed them because I did not look different from the other farm boys. The two pompous officials carried clipboards with sheets of paper. They immediately went to the stalls and stables and counted all the horses, sheep, cattle, pigs, and farm equipment. In the granary, they even checked the back storage rooms.

I was surprised that the men knew all the details of our property. When no one was looking, I asked one of the farmhands how these outsiders knew everything. He replied, "Don't you know that the local party secretary is Stein, who before was the buyer of cattle and horses in this area? This position allowed him unhindered access to most places." Then he quietly added, "Stein was probably a communist secret agent, and that was his mission all along!"

I had read in books about secret agents and subversion, but this was my first real experience with it. It made me more apprehensive about strangers and the questions they asked. Mother also warned me, "Under no conditions, if anyone asks where your parents are, are you to tell them! Your answer should always be that you do not know. The more you say this, the sooner they will identify you as a simple, not-very-bright country boy. That is what they probably were themselves!" These comments became deeply ingrained in my mind, and if asked about my parents' whereabouts, that became my stock answer. The local communists always wanted to gather more information about others and report it to higher-ups and thus gain recognition. A few years later, after the communists were long gone, when friends asked me where my parents were, my ingrained reply was still, "I don't know!" Mother would laugh and say, "Times have changed—now we can tell the truth again!"

All our property in Biksti was nationalized by the government. We were allocated a few rooms at the far end of the house. The furniture was also registered and owned by the government. The only place the officials stayed out of was my grandmother's room—she must have had a powerful argument with them.

The space we vacated was taken over by young women who joined the tractor school, which taught them how to operate agricultural equipment.

After completing the training, the young women worked on a *sovhoz* (a government-owned farm). Most of the tractor girls, as we called them, were pleasant (with a few exceptions, who were doctrinaire communists). I remember one girl telling her comrades, "Do not be bashful about use of the property owned by the *kulak* [rich landowner] capitalists—it is now yours! You do not have to be nice to them!"

I was fascinated watching the demonstrations of tractors and heavy-duty equipment and tagged along with the other boys. Because I was rather shabbily dressed and managed to avoid taking frequent baths, I looked like a local, and no one bothered me. I overheard the girls saying that it was fun to get away from their homes, but they hated attending the required Marxist-Leninist lectures. One of the girls added a disclaimer: "You can never say that loudly because you will be considered a counterrevolutionary—and you know what fate awaits you then."

Our school resumed in the fall, but it significantly changed as well. There were communist flags and posters of Stalin and Lenin everywhere; many classrooms had a "red corner" with papers listing students' contributions toward the ultimate victory of communism. We were told about a courageous student who reported his family's counterrevolutionary activities to the authorities. One of my teachers lectured about the benefits of communism and the glorious leadership of Comrade Stalin, but most of the staff just continued with their work; I sensed that most teachers were required to talk about these subjects, though privately they felt differently. Religion was described as the opiate of the people. I did not fully grasp the meaning of that but sensed fear and uncertainty in the air. Mother felt this environment was not good for us and took us out of school frequently under the pretext of poor health. Our teachers understood, and we did not attend school regularly that year.

One incident stands out in my mind—it illustrates some of the changes that took place. In school, we sat on wooden benches for two. In the row in front of me was a cute girl with long blonde hair. Her name was Rita, and she gave me the sweetest smile when I occasionally tugged on her pigtails. Sometimes, we even played together during recess. When the communists took over, life changed. One day, Rita came to me and said, "You *kulaks* have exploited us, the working-class people, for generations. Now we are going to take everything away from you, and you will be working for us!" I was amazed at the transformation of Rita, shocked by her bitterness and anger. I thought, "What have we done to deserve this? Nothing has changed except for the communist takeover!" I realized that the world had changed and would never be the same again; our old way of life had gone with the wind.

After school, I continued to play with my same friends as before, particularly one family who had five children and lived on our estate, not too far from the main house. Their accommodations were primitive, with very few rooms; the grandmother slept on top of an extension of the oven, which kept her warm. The family was hospitable, and I was welcomed (probably not surprising because they worked for us). I ate so many meals with them that the farm manager joked he should allocate them more grain, butter, and meat because they regularly fed me.

Now, when I visited the family, all the boys wore red scarves, denoting their membership in the Young Pioneer organization, a branch of the communist party. They still wore dirty clothing, but now they puffed out their chests like sparrows on a branch. Their parents talked about the benefits the communists offered, primarily our property. I was now considered a member of the capitalist class that exploited others, even though I had not done anything differently and they had been satisfied with me before. Somehow, hostility had been ignited in their hearts, and it even affected children. I felt uncomfortable, left, and never went back.

The housekeeper later told me that this family had probably been secret communist sympathizers. Even at that age, I doubted it; I felt they were simply caught up in the swirl of events and did not really know what they were doing. They were the only ones on the entire estate who did not remain loyal to our family. After the communists left, this family suddenly disappeared, never to be heard from again. This probably saved them from repercussions.

Though life carried on in Biksti, there were other indications that changes were in the wind. My grandmother loved to garden and was helped by a gardener with two assistants. There were more than one hundred apple trees, pear trees, raspberry bushes, strawberry plants, and other varieties of plants on our estate. During the winter, a greenhouse with grapes was heated by a furnace. They were so plentiful that we sold the surplus commercially.

My grandmother loved her flower gardens most of all. One time, when we took a walk, she told me, "No matter what happens to us, the flowers will bloom again and bring pleasure to all who admire them. If you are worried, just look at the beautiful blossoms—the flowers will make you feel better!" At that time, I did not fully grasp the meaning behind her profound words.

A few days later, a communist political officer came to speak to the tractor students and other sympathizers. Fortunately, we avoided being there. The next morning, when I walked outside to look at the beautiful tulip beds that my grandmother had shown me before, there were hardly any blossoms left. We learned that the same worker family with whom I visited frequently had come and collected all the red tulips. They gave a big bouquet to the speaker, and the rest were given to other officials. Red, of course, was the color of the communist party. The housekeeper told those who were cutting the flowers to first ask my grandmother, but they explained that now everything belonged to the state. To question that was counterrevolutionary.

Father's Deportation

Meanwhile, Mother spent more time in Riga with Father. He was removed from his senior position at the Latvian Railroads Administration. He was assigned to a lower ranking position and then was eventually dismissed, supposedly because of his elitist background. Also, because we occupied the whole house in Riga, the communist authorities assigned a lodger to share the place. Fortunately, he turned out to be a decent individual.

The Latvian government ceased to exist. The president was arrested and deported to the Soviet Union, where he perished. Government officials, artists, writers, and others with leadership potential disappeared into prisons and never returned. Later, after the Germans drove the Soviets out of Riga, they found thousands of people executed and buried in shallow graves near the central prison. People were living in fear and did not know what would happen the next day.

After spending time in Riga with Father, Mother returned to Biksti, where the situation had settled down with the tractor school that now occupied most of our property. After a few days with us, Mother wanted to bring us to Riga, where the situation was not good; she hoped that our presence would cheer up Father. Many friends were arrested by the NKVD (secret police) and never heard from again. Father was reluctant to spend many nights in our Riga house. At that time, most of the arrests occurred during the night. So, he took long walks and visited with friends. Mother felt the situation was now safe enough for us to be there for a few days.

She telephoned Father and told him we would arrive in the afternoon of June 13, 1941, and passed the same message along to the building superintendent so he could help—little did we know that most of the superintendents either chose or were forced to become NKVD informers. They knew all of the residents and their habits.

That morning, we packed our bags for the trip to Riga. Before our departure, Mother spoke to Oma, who suffered from diabetes and other complications. She said, "While I am feeling reasonably well today, I really want you to stay for another day." It was unusual for Oma to strongly plead that way, so to make her feel better, Mother decided to postpone our departure until the next morning. She said, "I will call my husband in Riga and tell him and the building superintendent about our change of plans." Fortunately, she could not reach anyone in Riga, and that saved our lives.

The NKVD were under the impression that we would arrive on June 13 as scheduled—they planned to arrest all of us together the next morning. Most likely, Father had not answered the telephone because he was taking one of his usual long walks through the city parks to avoid being at home. While he was away, one of his former colleagues, Mr. Zagers, also telephoned to warn him that unusual activity was taking place with the railroad—many cattle cars had been ordered and their windows were covered in barbed wire. Mr. Zagers later told Mother that his message never reached Father.

After an early dinner with our grandmother, all of us went to bed to be prepared for an early departure for Riga. I woke up while it was still dark because there was truck traffic. This was unexpected and unusual—most trucks were owned by the government and were not driven at odd hours. I could not sleep, and I saw a light on in Mother's bedroom and went there. I saw Mother talking to a housekeeper, and both looked distraught. She knew that there was a surge of traffic. Special trucks were driven by the local militia and guarded by NKVD police. Mother was worried and called Father right away.

After several attempts, the telephone in our Riga house was finally answered. It was the lodger on the line. He sounded upset, even uncommunicative, which was unusual. Mother asked for Father, and the lodger handed the telephone to him. Father shouted, "Do what you can to save the children!" As we later learned, an NKVD policeman then snatched the telephone out of Father's hand.

Mother understood right away what happened. She was surprised by Father's anticipation of such an event—he had already made an escape plan. He made an agreement with the lodger, whose bedroom was close to the entrance, that if anyone rang the doorbell during the night, it was most likely the police. The lodger was to wake Father and then slowly proceed to open the door, fumbling with the locks and thus delaying the NKVD. This action would allow enough time for Father to escape through the back of the house.

Unfortunately, when it happened, the lodger was groggy with sleep and upset by the disturbance. He forgot his agreement with Father and instead opened the door right away, and the NKVD charged into the house and immediately arrested Father.

Later, the lodger told us that the officer asked Father, "Where are your wife and children? Why are they not here?" Father told him, "I have not seen them for some time." The NKVD had planned to arrest all of us and were surprised not to find the rest of us there.

The lodger described what happened next. The policeman ordered Father to pack a small bag and prepare to leave. Father put on his favorite heavy Harrods overcoat, which he bought in London, even though it was the middle of summer; he knew he was headed to Siberia. Then the

NKVD put him in a Black Maria police van, and that is the last time anyone ever saw Father in Latvia.

At that time, we were not sure where they had taken Father after his arrest. Some people were delivered to the prisons, others to the railroad station and loaded into cattle cars. Each car was packed with more than thirty prisoners and had a small opening covered with barbed wire, which let air circulate. There were no sanitary facilities, except for a bucket in a corner. One-third of the fifteen thousand five hundred deportees were children, and many of the prisoners perished during the journey. Soon, I would experience what these cattle cars were like firsthand.

Deportees loaded into cattle cars - 1941

Once the cars were filled with prisoners, the train headed east to Siberia. After more than a week of travel, Father's group of prisoners was transferred to river barges pulled upstream to their destination—a gulag so remote that it was inaccessible by roads. There was no opportunity to escape. The prisoners had to cut lumber and meet a prescribed quota; if they failed, their food rations were reduced. Not surprisingly, malnutrition and associated diseases took a heavy toll. It worsened when the German army occupied a larger part of Russia; the food supply diminished, and many more died. Very few ever returned.

During World War II in Eastern Europe, death was a frequent companion for many. The Nazi genocide exterminated about six million, primarily Jews and those opposed to Hitler. It was indiscriminate murder, regardless of age or nationality. After the war, the Israelis successfully pursued those responsible for these heinous crimes and brought them to justice.

The Soviet crimes were equally grave, but they essentially got away with it. As war raged around us, in Latvia, we knew little about the extent of these crimes. We observed that some people simply disappeared. It is estimated that during Stalin's regime, close to twenty-five million Russians perished. Slightly more than half were war casualties, but the rest were political prisoners. While the Nazi crimes have been widely publicized, little is known about the Soviet atrocities. The primary Soviet method for disposing of people was to deport them to gulags and let them die from malnutrition and associated diseases. The results were the same as the Nazi genocide, but the public perception was not—the Western press described Stalin as a gregarious Uncle Joe. Fortunately, this image was finally shattered in 1972 when Solzhenitsyn published *The Gulag Archipelago*.

Decades after their crimes, most Nazi war criminals were dead or in confinement; however, with very few exceptions, Soviet war criminals fared well. Former members of the secret police, the NKVD, continued to serve in prominent positions of the Russian government. Others benefited financially by laying the foundation of the oligarch economy.

It wasn't until the 1960s that I learned the details of Father's death from one of the few survivors, a man who was imprisoned with Father in the same gulag. After his release, he was briefly allowed to visit his family in the United States. Mother called me and said that a former acquaintance of Father's was in the Boston area. To learn more, she invited him to dinner. Mother warned me that the reason this man was temporarily released for a visit to the United States was probably that he served as an informant for the NKVD. I did not take this seriously and planned a brief visit.

He told us that the winter of 1941 was among the coldest ever, and the freezing weather arrived early in Siberia. In the barracks, there was minimal heat, which made the conditions even more unbearable. Every morning, there were inmates who had died during the night— most of them knew they would die sooner or later, and Father and his friends came to the same conclusion. Suffering from malnutrition and other sicknesses, they realized that death was close, so they traded their wedding rings and other belongings to one of the guards for half a bottle of vodka. Three of them went outside the barracks, sat on the steps, and drank a toast. They linked their arms and were found this way the next morning, frozen to death.

We heard rumors of Father's death a year after he was deported, but this was the first confirmation. While it did not come as a surprise, the circumstances were gruesome. I was proud that despite the inhumane conditions, Father faced the adversity with dignity and died as the gentleman he was. He was with his friends, with whom he shared the joys of life, and they were together for their last moments. Father's last thoughts probably were about his family and whether or not we survived after his warning. I wish I could tell Father that his actions saved our lives—and allowed me to write these lines. Perhaps he looks down from above and knows.

In the 1990s, when Latvia became independent again, the NKVD archives were briefly opened. My attorney gained access. He managed to find my family file, which listed all the details of Father's arrest and deportation to the Siberian gulag. He told me that the NKVD had followed our family life and activities in the United States until the 1960s. They had records of our addresses, occupations, and other information about us.

The attorney also gave me documents about Father's arrest and a rehabilitation certificate issued by the new democratic Latvian government. The charges were that Father was "a dangerous social element" due to being a large landowner, real estate owner, and member of the governing class by serving as the Managing Director of the Latvian railroads. Of course, none of the former officials responsible for these false charges were ever prosecuted; they lived out their retirement in comfort in Moscow.

This first major deportation was followed by others. During the Soviet occupation of Latvia, the country lost ten percent of its population due to deportations to Siberian gulags, and there was a similar number of war casualties. Some, including my family, managed to escape to the West.

These experiences showed me that events that seem inconsequential at the time can change your life forever—they certainly changed mine. Even though we make our plans, the ultimate outcome is not up to us. I sometimes speculate how my life would have changed if events on that fateful night had unfolded differently, and Father had survived. The forgetfulness of a sleepy lodger changed my life, and I still wonder why. I have not found a satisfactory answer—it's beyond human comprehension. My understanding is that we must do our best and hope for a positive outcome.

Fleeing the Soviets

After Mother's brief telephone conversation with Father during his arrest, she knew the NKVD would be looking for us because they were surprised not to find us in the Riga house. Fortunately, communication in those days was not very good, which gave us the opportunity to escape.

Mother quickly packed her bag, kissed us goodbye, and said she was going to search for Father. She took the first train to Riga, and we stayed behind while the housekeeper served us a quick breakfast and packed our bags. Then my sister, the housekeeper, and I headed for the nearby railroad station, about half a mile away. We took the back way. We left the house and walked through what had been our formal garden, bordered by many apple trees; in the past, the path through the garden had been meticulously maintained, but now weeds sprouted everywhere. The communist world was different—and one could see it plainly!

After three hundred yards, we found the gate that led from the garden into a copse of trees and then to an open field. We followed a narrow path through a beautiful, verdant meadow full of fragrant grasses and wildflowers. Only a year before, Mother had driven a two-horse mower through this field to cut hay. She wanted to demonstrate her agricultural skills—that she could do the work of ordinary farmhands. Now, we walked through the same field looking over our shoulders to see if our departure was noticed. Life had changed quickly for us! I felt good that at least I did not have to wear my city clothes (a blazer, shirt, necktie, and knee socks). Our housekeeper had told us to dress simply so we would not stand out from the crowd. That was fine with me.

As we approached the railroad station, our housekeeper had us wait while she got the tickets. She did not want us to be seen at the station because we would be recognized. We stood some distance away. When we heard the engine whistle, all of us rushed to the platform and boarded the train. We were in third class for this trip—in the past, we always had premium seats. It was a traditional European train with separate cubicles seating up to six. We looked for a compartment with the fewest number of passengers but could not find one and had to sit with others. That was fine with us because we did not know anyone anyway.

I had taken this train many times before, but now it felt different. People were nervous, quiet, and constantly looking over their shoulders.

Everyone was aware of the numerous arrests during the previous night, and they trusted no one. After almost two hours, our train arrived at the Jelgava railroad station. We got out and walked to the terminal, but I lagged behind. Another train caught my attention, a few tracks down, which consisted of cattle cars with small windows covered by barbed wire, guarded by NKVD troops. The cattle cars were full of people shouting through the small openings. They pressed their faces against the barbed wire and shouted names or messages—I can still hear the sound of their desperation. Something unusual was happening, and even at my young age, I knew it was related to the recent arrests.

Our housekeeper noticed that I stayed behind. She came back, grabbed my hand, pulled me forward, and said, "Do not do this again or all of us will be in trouble!" I asked, "I have never seen people in cattle cars—who are they? Why do they have to shout? What is happening?" But our housekeeper just pulled me by the hand and said, "Don't look back and don't ask questions like this. Forget you ever saw this!" As long as I live, I will never forget the scene of the prisoners in the cattle cars, calling out to others and patrolled by the NKVD police.

From the railroad station, we arrived at my great-aunt Hance's house, where we visited before. While we were welcomed into her home, I sensed tension in the air, not only because of the many arrests that had taken place the night before but because our presence seemed to add to the concern. It became clear to me, even though I was barely eight years old (and my sister six), that we were wanted by the authorities and that anyone helping us would be punished. Despite these concerns, we spent the night at Hance's house.

Early the next morning, Aunt Hance said, "Children, it is not safe here anymore. The building supervisor and others know who you are. I will arrange for you to leave right away." Shortly afterward, we were whisked off to another friend's home and spent the night there. Both of us slept in the study that adjoined the living room. I could not fall asleep, so I overheard the heated conversation among the adults. They were concerned not only about the arrests that had taken place but also about those that were likely to follow. By sheltering us, they took a risk, but they were still willing to help us, even though we were "toxic." We were on the NKVD's wanted list, and anyone sheltering us would be handled accordingly. Furthermore, by now, the neighbors knew who we were.

The next morning, we were told that it was not safe again, and so we would be delivered to another location where no one would know us. The housekeeper took us by the hand and said, "Just follow me in the crowd, and no one will notice you. As we pass an open entryway. several blocks before the new location, we will duck in the doorway—the door will not be locked, and we will go to the second floor, where you will be staying." We entered the apartment, and an elderly lady greeted us and explained that she was a teacher at the local high school. She had no family and was willing to help us. She told us,

I leave for school every morning and come back in the afternoon.

I cannot change this routine because people will grow suspicious,

so you must fend for yourselves while I am away. No one else will come to the apartment—that would be suspicious. If the doorbell rings, do not answer, because people know I am not at home. When I leave, I will shut the curtains, and you cannot open them or people will know someone is here.

It was quite an order for two young children to spend the day quiet and alone in a strange apartment, but we knew that others were trying to do their best to help us. We did not dare open the curtains, but I sometimes peeked through the creases and saw soldiers and police in the street below. We felt relatively safe and had adequate food.

Shortly afterwards, on June 22, we heard that the Germans attacked the Soviet Union. The war began, and the German army was rapidly moving toward Latvia. A few days later, a housekeeper from Biksti arrived to bring us home. There was chaos in the street, and train service was erratic, as many of the communist functionaries fled to the east and troops moved toward the front. Fortunately for us, the police were concerned with their own fate, and no one bothered with children.

Eventually, we arrived at the Biksti railroad station and walked home. Halfway to our house, another helper came running toward us and shouted, "Do not come home! The communists are still here, and we do not know what they are going to do to you." We decided to go instead to a nearby barn—it was some distance from the main house, and it looked safe. I had played there before, and it felt good to be back.

Suddenly, Elsa (Peggy's former governess) came up and shouted, "You cannot go to the barn! When the communists leave, they may burn the barn down, and then there will be no escape for you." The safest place for us was the granary, a solid stone building. We climbed a ladder to the attic, where extra supplies were stored. One of the maids brought us blankets and food, and we made ourselves comfortable. We settled in below the terra-cotta roof and heard a great deal of activity below, with people packing and fleeing. We hoped they would not come in the granary. As a safety precaution, the housekeeper took away the ladder, which was necessary to climb to our hiding place—this way, if anyone came into the granary, they were unlikely to find us. This was stressful for Peggy, and she started shaking uncontrollably. I tried to appear brave and said, "Please stop shaking! Let us get some sleep and see what happens tomorrow." We eventually fell asleep.

During the day, Elsa brought more food, books, and cards, but we still had to spend the day in the granary attic, which was close to the main house. We could hear people in the yard shouting and packing their gear, but no one knew where the Germans were coming from, nor to where they should flee. Frankly, this made me feel better because now the others were scared too. I could hear airplanes, distant artillery fire, and explosions coming from the direction of the Biksti railroad station.

One morning, we woke up, and everything was quiet. The housekeeper brought back the ladder, and we climbed down to find everything peaceful—except for trash everywhere. There was no more tractor school; all the students and equipment were gone. The housekeeper said that instead of fighting, the communists and their fellow travelers quickly fled to the east in advance of the German troops. The household staff was busy cleaning up and preparing the rooms so that we could move back into our house.

End of the Soviet Occupation

Later that same afternoon, trucks with German soldiers drove by. The locals waved at them and sometimes threw flowers. We felt safer because the communists were gone, but we still did not know what the future held for us. Locals gathered and talked about the Soviet occupation. One story remains vivid in my mind.

The teller of the story was a farmer with a place adjoining a forest. He had been a member of the Latvian National Guard (*Aizsargi*), an organization that hated the communist authorities. Fearing arrest, as a precaution, he spent occasional nights in a nearby barn that adjoined the woods. He did so on June 13, 1941, the same night Father and about fifteen thousand five hundred other Latvians were arrested and deported to Soviet gulags in Siberia. While sleeping in the barn that night, the farmer heard a car pull up to his house; it contained NKVD agents who were looking for him. In the morning, when he returned to his house, everything was quiet. No one came to greet him. The NKVD had arrested his wife, his two children, and their grandmother, deporting all of them to Siberia. No wonder this man was furious and vented his anger on any communists he could find. But now, they were all gone.

This event was not unusual. Later, the newspapers carried a story revealing that when German troops overran parts of neighboring Lithuania, some of the local communists did not manage to escape. The people were so angry that when they caught them, the communists were clubbed to death in the streets, in plain sight of all.

Karl, who lived on the estate, was the eldest son of our head housekeeper; his father was the blacksmith. Both of his parents, two of his sisters, and a younger brother all lived on the estate and worked for the family. Karl was angry with the communists because they denied him admission to a trade school when he refused to join the party. Also, one of his closest friends was arrested and deported. Karl said that his mission from now on was to fight communists, no matter where they were. He joined a Latvian military unit that served with the German army and fought all the way to Leningrad and then back to Latvia. He was wounded several times and awarded both iron crosses, which initially was unusual for a non-German. One time, when Karl was recuperating on leave, he left early for the front. His mother said that while Karl loved his family, he felt that his true brothers were the men with whom he fought, and he wanted to be with them to share their fate. Later, he died in action as a hero.

Shortly afterward, we heard that Mother survived the communist era and was returning to Biksti. Knowing Mother's determination, I was not surprised that she survived—with her will and faith, no one could hold her back. We were ecstatic to see Mother because now she was our sole base of support and stability. We understood that Father had been deported and knew that we would never see him again.

A few days later, Mother arrived in a horse-drawn carriage and told us about her journey. Trains were running only on some segments of the railroad because the rest had been blown up, so she had continued her trip with a horse-drawn carriage that she borrowed from a friendly farmer. The farmer warned Mother of the dangers of traveling through the woods—they were full of Russian deserters ready to seize any means of transportation that would help them move east. Mother was determined to go on—a friend had given her a pistol that she kept in her lap underneath a blanket. Nothing was going to hold her back from her journey to us!

She told us what happened after her arrival in Riga, where she had gone to learn more about Father's fate. Mother did not want to be seen near our house because people might recognize her, but she talked to the lodger and a neighbor who witnessed the arrest and deportation of Father. It was very risky to be seen there, so she wore a disguise that included a wig and eyeglasses. Mother tried to stay with several friends. She spent most of her days walking around the streets and parks, rather than burdening her friends, but she asked to stay in their apartments during the night. Fewer and fewer people, however, were willing to accommodate her because of the risk of arrest. She wondered how long this would continue but decided to persevere. Some friends told her, "Irma, you cannot hide any longer. The NKVD has your husband, and now they will get you and the children. Would it not be better to give up so that you could be sent to the same camp as your husband?" Mother continued to hide, but it became increasingly difficult because she did not want to endanger her friends. However, her perseverance and courage saved our lives.

Mother was eventually introduced to a family that she did not know well (they had friends in common). She was not known in this neighborhood, so this couple could offer her shelter for a while. The woman was of Russian descent, and her husband was an academic. They had an apartment in the center of the city. Mother received a warm welcome and felt safe and comfortable. The hostess, however, did not feel well the next morning. Mother offered to go get some medication because the husband was at work. She walked downstairs, made her way through the lobby, and was stopped by NKVD agents entering the building.

They asked Mother, "What are you doing here, and where are your papers?" Mother quickly replied, "I came to visit my sick friend upstairs. She needs medicine right away, and I am on my way to the pharmacy!" The NKVD man demanded, "Show us where your friend is!" Mother had no choice but to lead them upstairs. She quickly went to the bed of the sick lady and said, "My friend, I do not have the medicine yet because the people downstairs insist on knowing what your situation is!" The woman grasped the situation when she saw the police. She played her role well, crying out, "*O Bozhe moi*! I feel sick! Please hurry! Get medicine right away before things get worse!" The two police officers stepped into the bedroom and saw the wailing woman. It did not take much to convince them that she was seriously ill, and they let Mother go without asking again for any identification papers. Mother left the building and had to look for another place to stay. Life was getting more difficult every day. She wondered how long she could sustain this hide-

and-seek existence. Here was another narrow escape thanks to her quick thinking and courage. No doubt, if the NKVD had arrested Mother, my life would have been very different.

Fortunately for her situation, it was only a few days later that the Germans attacked the Soviet Union. Their success meant the end of the communist era. It brought hope for freedom. Mother felt more secure and decided to visit one of her old friends, one of the few who dared to welcome her. Both ladies felt that the Soviet occupation was coming to an end and decided to celebrate by frying eggs for breakfast.

As they were sitting down for the meal, the air raid siren sounded, and they heard artillery fire. They left the uneaten eggs on the kitchen table and headed for shelter. Some of the explosions were very close, and the whole building shook. When it was over, both women went upstairs. The kitchen and the table with fried eggs was no more. The apartment had sustained a direct hit. They went back to the basement shelter and waited.

After several hours, everything was quiet, and they went out to the street. All the communists were gone. Mother still did not dare to return to our house, so she looked for a place to spend the night. Many of the buildings in the city were abandoned. Mother met her cousin, who told her, "I know of a safe place to stay. No one will be looking there!"

The building he showed her was the residence of the archbishop of the Russian Orthodox Church in Latvia. His place looked elegant and inviting and had not been ransacked. Mother entered it and stretched out in his large canopied bed, where she slept soundly for the first time in many weeks. The next day, she went back to our house. The lodger had disappeared, the door was unlocked, and the place had been ransacked. Most of the furnishings, clothing, and artwork was gone. However, all Mother's shoes were left because her size was so small that the shoes were useless to others. Now, Mother's priority was to join us in Biksti.

In the summer of 1941, the German army drove the Soviets out of Latvia. It was a relief because it ended a bloody year in which two percent of the population was eliminated. This feeling did not last long, however, because soon the Germans installed their administration headed by Nazi party functionaries. The previously nationalized property was restored, but there were strict quotas for the delivery of goods. People were arrested as "Bolshevik collaborators"— it turned out they were mostly Jewish. The Jewish people had already suffered under the Soviets, losing the same percentage of their population as the native Latvians; now, again, they were persecuted. There was no reliable information—people simply disappeared and were never heard from again. In the countryside where I lived, there were no Jewish people, and we had no firsthand knowledge. But we heard rumors about ghettos and other atrocities.

In this environment, there was little that one could do. There was a communist underground, but who wanted to support them? The previous year, they eliminated a large share of the population and had plans to continue this process. After World War II, another seven percent of the Latvian population was deported.

Western allies were always a shining beacon of hope, but they were fighting on other fronts and displayed little interest in Eastern Europe. That was further demonstrated when President Roosevelt virtually ceded Eastern Europe to the Soviets at the end of the war. It took almost fifty years for my native country to regain freedom.

In Latvia, there were idealists seeking freedom and self-determination. The head of this movement was Konstantīns Čakste, an old family friend and the son of the first president. But the Germans arrested Cakste, and he died in a concentration camp.

There was little one could do except strive for survival and hope for miracles, as most do in desperate circumstances. Church attendance was up, and many read the Bible to search for spiritual guidance. At age eight, I was concerned, but not greatly worried. I had confidence that my parents always did their best to ensure our survival. I was not interested in reading the Bible, nor in going to church—instead, I played with my buddies and occasionally engaged in mischievous activities. After all, we had to adapt, enjoy life, and make the best of it!

CHAPTER 4

GERMANS IN LATVIA

On June 22, 1941, Germany attacked the Soviet Union. The troops swiftly overran Soviet defenses and occupied most of Latvia by early July. In Biksti, our only contact with Germans was seeing trucks full of soldiers moving east and occasionally stopping briefly.

The Germans were well organized and already selected a governor of Latvia, as well as regional representatives to manage the country. All were members of the Nazi party, and their purpose was to see that the economic output was for the war effort; everything else was secondary. The police also rounded up the remaining communist sympathizers and eventually the Jews. I did not understand the latter because I had never met a Jewish person. Mother commented that it was not Christian (nor civilized) to single out a group for punishment. She was surprised that the Germans, who were considered highly cultured, would sink to that level. Still, there was no reliable information about these issues, only rumors, and people were primarily concerned with their own survival.

One of the Germans' first official acts affected us directly: all landowners were notified that ownership of their properties, which had been nationalized by the communists, was now returned to them. Depending on the size and composition of their properties, however, all landowners were obligated to deliver a quota of grain and other farm products to the government at a fixed price.

My first personal contact with the new regime was the arrival of a German army captain of the Veterinary Corps. He came to requisition horses, which were the primary means of the German army's transportation system. At the same time, we required horses for farming because there were no tractors. Without an adequate number of horses, farm output would decline, and all of us would suffer.

Mother understood this and wanted to make sure that the German army captain was welcomed and included in family dinners. We wanted to gain the officer's goodwill so he would not requisition many of our horses. It was relatively easy to make him comfortable—he was an outgoing, pleasant person and probably wanted to be back in Bavaria drinking beer, rather than fighting with the "Prussians," whose cause he did not particularly care about. The captain had to be cautious about expressing his sympathies, but we understood him. Also, he had a car and a driver and was able to offer transportation to Mother and her friends from Riga. After several months, the captain's mission was completed, and he went to the eastern front. We were fortunate because very few of our horses were taken.

My sister Peggy remembers another similar incident concerning Arianna, a young university student, who came to our farm as a "summer intern." (A new law required all university students to spend their summers working on farms.) Arianna was blonde and cheerful and wore dresses with a cinched waist. She immediately took on the job of greeting the government inspectors who made unannounced visits to the estate.

The inspectors came to take an official inventory of our livestock and other farm animals, and this inventory list became the basis on which levees for meat, wool, eggs, and other dairy products were assessed. When the inspectorate arrived at our place, instead of letting him go straight to the barn, Arianna would greet him and invite him into the house for a glass of schnapps and some cakes. The inspector would gladly accept such an invitation, especially when offered by an attractive young lady. After a visit and some drinks, he would head to the barn to carry out his duties. Surprise, surprise—the number of animals in the barn was quite small. During the inspector's refreshment period, the farmhands had driven a large part of the cattle herd, sheep, and pigs to some distant, out-of-sight pasture and then the inspector dutifully recorded the number of animals in the barn.

Mother felt this was an appropriate time for me to improve my language skills, beginning with German. Because she spoke five languages from an early age, she knew that the best way to acquire a new language is to have individual instruction from a tutor. So, Mother hired a German teacher from Riga, Mr. Grasis, who spent the summer with us. He was a grave-looking teacher who believed that to properly learn a foreign language, one had to start with its grammar. After a few sessions, I found this boring and disappeared into the countryside. Mr. Grasis was not too upset because he was eager to enjoy summer in the country with his young son, who had come with him. A few weeks later, however, everything changed when my interest in learning German was piqued.

Mother was frequently away, and when she returned, the first person who approached her was Elsa, who reported everything that was going on—solely from her own perspective, of course. As the reader is already aware, I did not like Elsa because she was responsible for firing my beloved governess Lulu many years prior. If I was present when Elsa reported, she immediately switched to German: "*Die Kinder* [the children]..." She did not want me to understand what she said. I did not like this—I wanted to make sure that if I had gotten into some mischief, it was accurately reported.

I went to my neglected German teacher Mr. Grasis and said, "I did not like German grammar, nor I do I care to learn how to speak the language, but now I want to understand everything! Can you help me?" Mr. Grasis replied, "That is an odd way to learn the language, but perhaps your interest will continue. Let us try!" From then on, I went out on walks with Mr. Grasis and asked him to describe what was going on in the area and then translate German into Latvian. We continued to do this on a regular basis, and soon I could understand basic German. I did not tell anyone about my efforts. Months later, when Elsa was giving her confidential report to Mother in German, I hung around and understood most of what was said. Knowing German also helped me later in life, as you will see.

Because railroad schedules were erratic due to military traffic, visitors to Biksti frequently tried to obtain a ride with military or civilian cars passing through the area; usually, these belonged to government officials or to the German military. One day, Mother telephoned and said that she was getting a ride to Biksti with German officers. I eagerly awaited her arrival. Later in the day, a large Mercedes pulled up, and a uniformed chauffeur in military uniform jumped out and opened the rear doors; Mother exited along with two other officers. Quite a show!

As was customary, Mother invited the two officers in for tea to thank them for their efforts. These officers were different from others I had seen—they were clad in immaculate black uniforms with highly polished boots. In the house, when introduced to my grandmother, they clicked their heels and were very courteous. Mother introduced me to them and offered them tea and cake. I moved to the corner of the room and heard part of their animated conversation.

The officers asked Mother how she survived the communist occupation, and she told the story. She mentioned the tractor school and what had happened to our lives. Their next question was, "Are any of the former communists or their sympathizers still here?" Mother replied that all of them had escaped, except the technical director of the tractor school, who was now in charge of the machine shop. One of the officers said, "*Gnädige Frau, wie schreklich* [Honorable lady, how terrible]! *Diese Untermenschen* [These subhumans]..."

Then they casually added, "After we finish the tea, we will go out and shoot the remaining communist." Mother was upset and tried to talk them out of it. She said that the technical director was essential to the maintenance of the estate, so we could deliver all the required goods to speed up the defeat of communism. The officers eventually relented, saying that because she was the hostess, they would honor her wish. They clicked their heels and departed.

After this experience, Mother never again accepted a ride from German military personnel. Apparently, the officers were from the SD, the security section of the SS, whose primary responsibility was to track down communists and other undesirables.

Life in Biksti

Following the Soviet occupation, life in Biksti returned to (almost) normal. Fields were cultivated, crops were harvested, and in the fall, animals were slaughtered. We were required to deliver produce and meat to the authorities to meet pre-established quotas. The meat was preserved, either by smoking or storing it in salt brine in the cold cellar. Food was preserved in a cold storage place underground that was covered by a twenty-five foot thick layer of soil. On top, there was a large woodshed that provided additional insulation. In the winter, ice blocks were cut from a nearby lake and brought by sleighs to the underground storage area, which was the size of a large living room. The ice was covered with sawdust and lasted almost a year. Occasionally, a block of ice was chopped off and brought to the food closet in the main building that served in place of a refrigerator.

Overall, the food supply was good, and everybody ate well. There were always fresh eggs, chickens, vegetables, dairy products, and all kinds of fruit during the season. The city dwellers, on the other hand, experienced food shortages and cherished an invitation to spend the weekend with us in the country. There was a labor shortage because all men between the ages of eighteen and forty-five were drafted to serve in Latvian units that fought with the Germans against the Soviets. To alleviate the problem, Germans brought to the area several cattle cars full of Russian prisoners of war. They were haggard, undernourished, and miserable. The POWs were happy to be temporarily assigned to our estate, rather than languishing in a German camp where they could barely survive.

The local authorities allocated the POWs to various farms. We received two, Ivan and Timofei. Ivan was a young former student, and Timofei was an older schoolteacher. Both turned out to be trustworthy, reliable workers. I was not comfortable having POWs around and asked the farm manager, "What will prevent these POWs from escaping? We have no guards!" The manager laughed and replied, "They have a better life here than they had before, and the front is hundreds of miles away. Furthermore, if the Soviets catch them, they will probably be shot!" I was satisfied and made friends with the two men, who quickly learned

Latvian. Mother was not required to pay them a salary, but her attitude was, "Why should they be treated differently from others if they do the same work?" She paid them accordingly.

Shortly afterward, a happy event occurred in my life. My older sister Silvia returned from Germany, where she had lived during the Soviet occupation. When she was with us in Biksti, the house again was full of cheerful laughter, and all kinds of delicious fragrances came from the kitchen, where Silvia made her specialties. She divorced her first husband and moved into our house in Riga. I looked forward to her visits or a trip to Riga. A few years later, Silvia remarried. We had a big celebration in Biksti. Kris Caune, her second husband, went on to become a Methodist minister and served a small parish in Wisconsin. Silvia was a kind, happy person who served her family, her church, and her God with joy. Her children and grandchildren have flourished. Mother was away frequently, and I worried what would happen to me and my sister if she did not return. Considering the circumstances, that seemed a valid concern—Father was no more, our grandmother was practically an invalid, and our experience with the Soviets showed us that it was difficult to rely on others. Without Mother, our life would be over. One time, as Mother was leaving for Riga, I ran up to her and said, "Please stay! We want to spend more time with you." She replied, "I am invited to a birthday celebration in Riga and have tickets for the theater." I insisted, "I want you to be with us!" Looking back, this was probably a test on my part to see how much Mother loved us. She replied, "You and your sister are the most important people in my life. If you want me to stay, I will call and cancel everything to be with you!" Mother did as she promised and stayed with us. From that point on, I never doubted Mother's love. I knew that she would make any sacrifice for us. This assurance stayed with me for the rest of my life and was proven again many times later. As I write these notes, I still feel that Mother's spirit is with me.

Life returned to a "normal" routine. The war was hundreds of miles to the east. In 1943, the German advance stalled, and people became more apprehensive. I continued to play with the other boys on the estate—there were many places to explore. Most boys at this age played hide-and-seek, but in our case, we were really looking for places to hide in an emergency. It took us several days, but we dug a tunnel under a hay pile in a barn. The tunnel was about thirty feet long and ended with an opening. It was hard work because the tunnel was very narrow, and there was hardly any oxygen. After we completed the job, my friend said that we were now safe, and no one could find us. An adult could not crawl through the narrow tunnel. I said that was fine, except that all one had to do was light a match and the whole barn would be gone. Clearly, this project did not work, and we had to find a new hiding place.

We found a new location near the rafters on top of the stable, near the hatch that led to the roof, where a thirty-foot metal tower stood with a wind rotor that drove the water pumps for the animals below. My buddy said, "Let's climb on top of this tower, and we can use it as a good observation post for our hideout!" We climbed on the roof and up the small metal rungs near the wind rotor. We were at least seventy-five feet above the ground, and I was getting apprehensive. Once we reached the top, I told my buddy, "Let's get down fast before somebody sees us and we get into trouble!" My friend replied, "I'm afraid! I can't move!" I told him, "Don't look down! Look up, and I will guide your foot to the next rung." I could barely do it. Fortunately, we got down safely, but a farmhand saw us, and we got into serious trouble.

Our next project to prepare for anything that might come our way was to build simple pistols out of discarded rifle shells. Gunpowder was our only missing piece, and the essential ingredient was sodium chloride, of which we had very little supply. My friend came up with a solution and said, "Why don't you ask one of the city ladies to bring some sodium chloride?" I said, "What do I tell her?" He went on to recommend, "Tell her that sodium chloride is medicine for your mother." I fell for it and asked for the substance.

A few weeks later, the same lady returned to visit us and brought me sodium chloride. She said that the pharmacy had told her many little boys asked for the product because they were making gunpowder. The nice lady said, "I hope you do not get in trouble. I will not do this for you again!"

I felt poorly about this, but we went on to mix our gunpowder. It worked, but one day, unfortunately, we had an explosion in my room with flames and fumes shooting out. No one was hurt, but I was punished.

I was put in the corner of a room far away from others. I was upset and started to cry. Fortunately, the pleasant lady guest, who was our visitor, saw me and brought me a sandwich covered with honey. It made me feel better immediately. Elsa, however, noticed what was going on and took the sandwich away, and my punishment continued. I always fondly remembered this lady, who was a very well-known Latvian actress. When in Riga, she generously provided us with theater tickets. This lady, in my opinion, was a terrific person not only because she helped me but also because she could pretend to be another person or even an animal—you never knew who she really was. From that point on, I liked people who were involved in the performing arts.

In the fall, Peggy and I attended the local elementary school, which was now a short distance away—in our old manor house. The pictures of Lenin and Stalin were gone, replaced by a portrait of Hitler. No one cared about politics, though. Schoolwork was easy for me, but I never got straight As until I went to school in the United States. If a boy got all As in school in Latvia, he was considered a sissy and was excluded from the group.

My sister Peggy always had all As or A+s, and she made the same grades for her behavior and deportment. The latter grades were important because if you got a lower grade, the headmaster called your family. I also had good grades, but my behavior rating hovered near the minimum— and the only reason it did not drop lower was probably because the school was on my family property, and some of the teachers lived in our buildings. I wanted Peggy to get involved in playing with me and the boys—but no success! The same was true for athletics and other mischievousness. Still, despite her refusal to join in my extracurricular activities, I always dearly loved my little sister.

Because the school was on my family property, I was familiar with the surroundings and knew many things we could do during recess. One early-spring day, I invited my friends to a nearby stream to demonstrate my new boat, a discarded hog trough. We pushed the boat into the river and jumped on some of the ice floes to be near it. The results were not surprising—one of the boys fell into the water, and we had to jump in to help him out.

After that, recess was over, and a school assembly was called. All of us stood at attention in the main hall (our former ballroom). As the headmaster spoke, I looked around and saw puddles of water pooling underneath me and my friends. I knew that spelled trouble, and it sure came!

The teacher called us in and asked what had happened. One of the boys replied, "Teacher, we were running to make the assembly and fell into a puddle of water. We had no time to dry off." The teacher said, "A good story, but I do not believe a word. I know Johnny [me] has been going to the nearby river, which is off-limits. As punishment, you will be kept in school after classes, but this time it's going to be more serious!" This was not a big deal because it had happened before, but clearly, I did not know what she meant by serious.

After classes were over, the three of us stayed behind, and the teacher came in with three hymnals. She picked out a religious hymn at random and said, "You will memorize this and not horse around. You will not leave this room until you can recite it word for word!" She left the room. When she came back later, she said, "How are things going? How many more hours will you need?" I raised my hand and said that I could recite the hymn. The teacher was surprised when I recited it correctly and did not miss a word. She said, "One would think Johnny is a regular churchgoer and has sung the hymn before. But I know that is not the case!" I was free to go.

The next day, my pals, who had spent several more hours at school, would hardly talk to me because of my early departure. I realized that my friends were more important and decided that the next time I was punished, I would stay after school if they did. It did not take us long to get into trouble again. This time, when the teacher handed out the hymns to be memorized before we could leave, she said, "Since Johnny got off easily last time, I have a special assignment for him today." With this, she handed me the hymnal book in German. I was in real trouble because my German was not that good. Fortunately, the teacher had turned the page to Martin Luther's favorite hymn. I went ahead and memorized it. My anxiety level must have been very high because even today, almost eighty years later, I still recall the opening stanza:

"Ein fester Burg ist unser Gott, eine gute Wehr und Waffe…"

A Mighty Fortress is our God, a good defense and weapon…

I memorized the hymn, but I stayed with my buddies until they were let go. I concluded that one never could know the kind of punishment the teacher would come up with next time and decided it was wiser to stay out of trouble. In a sense, she achieved her objective. However, with this experience, I gained more than I first realized—it showed me that it was very easy for me to memorize text, even without fully understanding it. This was of great help later in life, especially when I started school in the United States with minimal knowledge of English.

Loyalty to one's friends represents an important characteristic of our family. I did not know that I had to demonstrate it at an early age, and perhaps for a somewhat dubious cause, but I stuck with it. It is not only our family but also our friends who made our life worthwhile—without them, we would not be here.

There were many fun things to do, and my favorite activity in the winter was skiing. Mother had the local carpenter make several skis and brought the bindings from Riga. I had had ski instruction before and loved the sport. Now I was trying to introduce my sister Peggy to skiing—an utter failure. Silvia, too, had limited interest, but fortunately one of my buddies loved it. In the winter, we skied across the frozen fields and meadows. It was beautiful, tranquil, and picturesque. One day, we skied to a village more than five miles away and took a shortcut through the woods. There were no trails, so we had to make our own through trees covered with snow. The scene looked like a beautiful Christmas card. We stopped, built a fire, and ate our sandwiches.

By the time we turned back, it was late afternoon and approaching dusk. (In Latvia, it gets dark around 4 PM.) We were getting tired and now skied on the road back to the house. A farmer who knew us drove by with a horse and sleigh and yelled, "It is late, and you boys are cold—grab the rope I throw you, and I will pull you home!" It was great fun to ride behind a trotting horse! It was dark when we got home, but no one seemed concerned. They knew that we were familiar with our surroundings and would not get lost. Despite the uncertainties of wartime, it was fun to grow up in such an environment.

As previously mentioned, I grew up with little supervision. Thus, I was involved in all sorts of mischievous activities, as many boys are. Despite this, I knew my limits and stayed within them. Because there were many options, I had to make decisions and take responsibility for what I did. That freedom encouraged me to develop my individual judgment.

Despite the war, life was pleasant in Biksti. I played with my friends, attended school, and became an avid reader of any books I could find; our school did not have a library, and there were not many books published in Latvian. In my parents' study, I found a series of books by Mr. Grins, the friend of my parents. This was when I came to appreciate his writing.

My favorite author was Henryk Sienkiewicz, a Polish writer, who is best known for his Nobel prize-winning book *Quo Vadis*, which was later made into movies. I liked his other books much better—books that dealt with the seventeenth-century Polish/Lithuanian battles with the Tartar invaders. The author wrote so vividly that when I read, I could almost see the text as a movie. I also read books in German by Karl May, who wrote about the Wild West and the righteous Native American Winnetou. To my great disappointment, I found out years later that Karl May had never left Germany and had written all the books there. When I ran out of reading material, I borrowed books from one of the ladies who visited us—these dealt with the biographies of Rembrandt van Rijn and Leonardo da Vinci. While I read them, they were boring.

Mother Remarries

In 1943, Mother announced that she was going to marry Christian Ulmanis. He had visited Biksti several times before. I knew that Father perished in the gulags in late 1941. The wedding was scheduled to take place at Christian's farm, about twenty-five miles north of Biksti.

Christian was different from Father, who was well educated, sophisticated, had held senior government positions, and was well connected through many parts of Europe; Christian was the youngest son of a well-to-do farmer. His family could only afford to provide one of their boys a higher education—his older brother attended a Czarist military academy and, after graduation, served in the military. Later, he joined the Latvian Army, fought for its independence and was killed in action as a hero. Christian was drafted into the war and fought for Latvian independence as an enlisted man. Subsequently, he rebuilt the family farm into a successful enterprise, primarily by growing seed crops. Christian was respected in the region and involved in many civic activities. He also served as head of the local agricultural cooperative bank.

It was a relatively small wedding at Christian's home. It took place in May 1943. After the formal affair was over, I was sitting in a corner room reading. Two of Mother's friends came in and did not see me there. One of the ladies said, "Irma [Mother] is marrying below her social level. She does care for Christian, but the utmost in her mind is the welfare of her children. One needs a strong man to help a family through difficult times!" In retrospect, that was probably a correct assessment.

I got along fine with Christian and enjoyed hunting with him. With his agricultural knowledge, Christian reorganized the Biksti estate, which began running as well as ever. One year, we produced so many sugar beets that a whole freight train was required to deliver them to the refinery. After the harvest, the fields were an ideal habitat for hares, which we hunted with a dog.

One could not cross the German authorities, as we learned from a friend of Father's, Mr. Zagers—he was the one who tried to warn Father before his deportation, but unfortunately, his phone call never reached Father. Mr. Zagers was a brilliant economist and briefly served as the director of economics of Latvia under the German occupation. This position is comparable to the U.S. Secretary of Commerce, but without any policy-making powers. Shortly afterward, Mr. Zagers became dissatisfied with the German policy and resigned. This conflict put Mr. Zagers at odds with German authorities.

A similar situation happened to Mother's childhood friend, who was the son of the first president of Latvia. This gentleman, after a disagreement with the German authorities, was sent to a Nazi concentration camp and perished there. Mr. Zagers wanted to maintain a low profile, and my stepfather's country place was a suitable location. Mr. Zagers had two children; his son, who was close to my age, became a good friend with whom I shared many adventures in Biksti.

Wartime

Even though war raged on, life in Biksti remained the same, except for carriages filled with refugees passing through, heading west. The threat came from the Soviet troops, who were advancing from the east, through Lithuania to the Baltic Sea. Still, the war was more than one hundred miles away.

By July of 1944, the German central front, for all practical purposes, collapsed. Many family friends had left Riga for Germany while the railroad connections were still intact. My parents talked about the various options available to us but did not make any decisions. They continually said, "We have to do the best for the children and their future!" Naïvely, people still hoped for peace, for Allied intervention, and for the restoration of normal conditions—whatever that meant. It was an unrealistic dream—the sort that often occurs in desperate circumstances, which we were facing.

In late July of 1944, Soviet forces severed land connections from Latvia to Germany. We were surrounded by Soviet troops, with only the Baltic Sea to the west. The only viable option was to travel to Germany by ships that regularly sailed between the countries, bringing military supplies and returning with wounded soldiers and refugees. Only much later, I learned the extent of the danger to which we were exposed.

To gain a better understanding, one must look at the history. On July 20, 1944, just before noon, Lieutenant Colonel Claus von Stauffenberg entered a conference room to participate in a meeting with Hitler and his staff. It took place in Hitler's field headquarters, *Wolfsschanze* [translated Wolf's Lair] in East Prussia. Von Stauffenberg carried a briefcase full of explosives and positioned it under the conference table, near Hitler. He set the fuse and quickly departed. Moments later, another officer found that it was in his way and pushed it further under the table, behind the oaken support base. Hitler also moved a few steps further away. The briefcase soon exploded—four of the officers were killed or died shortly afterward, but Hitler was unharmed. If Hitler had been killed, World War II would have quickly ended—a blessing for most. But not for us because German troops would have withdrawn from Latvia. We would have been left behind in Soviet hands.

This demonstrates how little control we really have over our lives and how unpredictable and capricious events can be. Developments that are just over the horizon and beyond our comprehension can change our future forever. We never know why or when this will occur. We can only do our best, no matter the circumstances. We should be grateful every moment we are here and hope that our luck will continue to stay with us.

One day, we learned that Jelgava, a provincial capital about fifty miles away, had been overrun by the Soviets and was burning. In the distance, we could see dark clouds of smoke rising. The war was closing in.

I felt anxious with danger growing and no definite plan of action. Because I was barely eleven years old, there was very little that I could do. Even so, I had unshakable confidence that Mother and my stepfather would always do their best for us. I sought relief in being outdoors in the fields with my friends. Summer days were full of the fragrance of freshly cut hay and the ripening of harvest. The cycle of nature moved on as it had forever, while we humans suffered from uncertainties that we created ourselves. No wonder the tranquility of the outdoors appeals to me so deeply.

One beautiful morning, the sky was clear, and the sun shone brightly on the fields where I played with friends. There could not have been a more perfect setting. Suddenly, one of our farmhands came running and yelled, "You have to rush home right away. Your parents are packing, and you will have to leave shortly! The Soviet tanks have broken through to Dobele (fifteen miles away) and are advancing!" I ran home.

When I arrived, there was panic, and no one knew when or where the Soviet troops would come. My parents quickly collected some items and dumped them in a farm cart that accommodated a sizable load. In the past, we traveled in a carriage drawn by two specially trained horses (Dolly and Daisy) with a coachman. When Mother traveled alone, she used a carriage pulled by a single horse. This time, everything was loaded in a farmer's cart with no suspension, drawn by a single workhorse. We bounced along the dirt road not knowing what to expect and left Biksti behind. I felt sad—I had spent a happy childhood there and hoped to return.

Our goal was to travel to Christian's place, collect additional belongings, and then move west, away from the front. To expedite the trip, Christian called one of his farmhands and arranged a halfway meeting so we could have fresh horses and another carriage. Our wagon would go back to Biksti. This was going to be a dangerous trip, but our loyal former-POW Timofei volunteered to accompany us. It was a terrifying experience! When we entered a forest and came out the other end, we never knew what to expect. Would there be Soviet tanks? Soviet soldiers? Communist partisans or German troop reinforcements? There were hardly any other refugees on the road, and those we met were as uncertain and confused as us. We continued our journey and reached the agreed-upon meeting place, where we transferred the baggage, ready to move on. Latvian people tend to be undemonstrative, but Timofei hugged Mother, kissed her on both cheeks, and said, "May God be with you and guide you to a safe place"—unusual words from a former Soviet soldier!

At dusk, we arrived at Christian's house; the place was in chaos. There were refugees everywhere, coming and going, and no one knew what was going to happen next. All we knew was that the Soviet troops were advancing and had met very little resistance. Our only encouragement came from the uninterrupted flow of traffic on the main highway nearby; if traffic was moving, we knew the Soviets were not close.

Mother put us to bed, and she and Christian started to pack up another cart. I could not sleep, and suddenly the traffic flow and noise on the highway stopped. That could only mean one thing—the Soviets were coming. I looked up and saw Mother on her knees praying. She was a religious person, but she did not talk much about her faith. To see her praying under these conditions was most unusual. After a while, she calmly got up and with new energy continued packing. I sensed that danger was imminent. In my mind, I visualized what would happen if the Soviets caught up with us. Frankly, this was one of the most terrifying moments of my life.

I went downstairs and saw a single automobile coming down the gravel driveway. It belonged to an old German major who was quartered at Christian's house. He jumped out of the car, greeted Mother, and said, "Madam, you have to leave soon—the Soviets are nearby!" The major went to his room to pack his bags. I talked to the driver, who had given me car rides before. The young soldier was nervous—he pointed to the back of his car and said, "A way back, we passed the Soviet outpost. They tried to stop us, but the major ordered me to drive on and accelerate. We just zoomed away while they were shooting. As you can see, they were bad shots and only put a few bullets in the back of the car!" The German major finished packing and quickly departed.

Christian asked one of his Russian farmhands to hitch the horse so we could leave right away. The farmhand, a former Russian refugee, was hesitant to help. He said we should wait until the Soviets came. Of course, we knew what that meant. Christian did not put up with it—he took his shotgun, loaded it with buckshot, and pointed it in the direction of the help. The man hitched the horse quickly. It seems to be ingrained in Soviet character to only respond to threats.

Later, we learned that Soviet troops occupied Christian's house later the same day—mere hours after we departed in the early morning. Some of the others were late in leaving and were overrun by the Soviets, who shot two of the remaining male refugees.

From Christian's place, we headed directly to the nearest provincial town, Tukums. Christian kept his valuables in the Farmers' Cooperative safe because one could not trust the banking system in those days. He wanted to retrieve them before we moved farther west. On the road, we passed a company of disheveled German soldiers. They must have come from medical leave or other non-combat roles—they represented the reserve that the major mentioned earlier. Even I could see that they did not amount to a military force that could stop the Soviet advance. Seeing them, I understood the threat was real and imminent.

When we arrived in Tukums, the manager opened the building so Christian could access the safe. Christian entered the building, and a few minutes later, he came out with a bulging briefcase. Christian always kept this briefcase close by, so I never saw its contents. I assumed it included cash as well as gold coins. This made our life better in the years ahead.

We traveled west, away from the advancing Soviets. Our progress was slow because the horses pulled our two fully loaded wagons on unpaved dirt roads, but at least we moved forward. No one knew how far the Soviets were behind us, but we heard their advance was bogged down, having outrun their supply lines. This delay allowed the Germans to bring in replacements. While all of this sounded good in theory, we knew we had barely escaped and danger was close. We knew that if the Soviets caught up with us, our trip would not lead back to our family estate but rather to Siberia, from where few returned. No wonder my stepfather urged the horses forward as rapidly as possible.

Our sudden departure eliminated another escape option my parents considered. It was possible to reach Sweden by bribing local fishermen to take refugees in their boats. This was a risky undertaking, however—the Latvian coast was patrolled by German police and the Baltic Sea by the Soviet Navy. Those caught trying to leave were imprisoned. Moreover, the Baltic Sea tended to be stormy; many fishing boats crowded with up to ninety refugees sank, and the passengers perished. Despite this, more than four thousand Latvians managed to escape to Sweden, though no one knows how many drowned at sea. We did not have the means to get to the fishing ports quickly, from which such escapes were possible. In the end, it did not make much difference because Mother was quite familiar with Germany, and my sister lived there.

After traveling all day, we took a side road to a remote farmhouse. Christian asked the farmer for overnight shelter. The farmer told him, "Too many refugees have been here. I cannot offer anything. Just move on!" Christian replied, "You know well when the Soviets come, they will seize all your property. Why not help your countrymen in need?" The farmer looked at Christian and said, "You can stay in the barn and use water from the well, but that is all." That was fine with us because we had ample food, and there was hay for the horses.

Before going to bed, I considered how rapidly our circumstances had changed. Not long before, we offered shelter to refugees—now we were asking for help. In the past, our family could render aid to others and ask for nothing in return—today, we were in a different position and had to ask help from a farmer reluctant to offer it. As I thought about this change, lines from the New Testament came to my mind: "It is more blessed to give than to receive."

I decided that when I grew up, I did not want to ask others for material help and, in a sense, become dependent and subservient. These were not my family's values. I wanted to be able to give, rather than receive. This was a rather lofty goal for an eleven year old. Despite some struggles along the way, I believe I reached it. With these thoughts in my mind, I stretched out on the hay bed Mother made. The pleasant fragrance of hay reminded me of the many happy days I spent playing in our meadows.

The next morning, my parents drew water from the outdoor well. We washed, ate breakfast, and continued our journey. We spent nights in barns or any other lodging we could find. Food was never a problem because we carried ample supplies with us. Toward the end of our trip, we saw well-equipped German troops moving east and knew that the front would hold.

After two days, we arrived at our destination—the home of Christian's friends, the Zeidenberg family. Mr. Zeidenberg was the chief regional forester, an important position because most of the forest was government property, with lumber an important export. The Zeidenbergs warmly welcomed us in their spacious house and provided comfortable accommodations. The house, the Stackeldam Mansion, previously belonged to a noble Baltic German family.

After our adventurous journey, this was temporary tranquility. We also felt encouraged that the Germans had the elite division, *das Großdeutschland*, preparing a major offensive. The front was now stabilized, and there might be a chance that we could return to our homes. I had fun because I became a friend of the older Zeidenbergs' son, who was my age. We maintained this friendship for years to come.

Life settled into a routine, if that is what one can call it while war still raged around us. At least the Soviet attacks stopped, and the Germans were ready to start a major offensive.

One day, I saw Mother crying—a most unusual occurrence. I walked up to her and asked what was wrong. I expected to hear bad news about an impending crisis or disaster. Instead, Mother explained, "Here I am, forty-four years old, and I now have to do laundry for the first time in my life. I've never had to do it before. I do not know how, and I'm embarrassed to ask!" In those days, there were no washing machines—but it was another crisis that Mother overcame. If needed, she could adapt to any circumstances. I knew that all of this was a significant change in her lifestyle, and it was not going to get better. Mother was always willing to sacrifice anything for the benefit of the family. We were indeed lucky to have her in our lives.

To supplement our menu, we frequently added venison. Even though it was early in the hunting season, soldiers were hunting deer, and Mr. Zeidenberg felt we should do the same. I went on one of these hunts and asked my stepfather why the hunters were bringing submachine guns in addition to their regular shotguns. He replied that there was danger in the woods: groups of communist partisans. We arrived at our hunting location, which was a clearing in the middle of the woods. Suddenly, one man shouted, "Look at the men across the field!" There was a group of well-armed men, who we recognized as communist partisans. We did not want to get involved in any battle and departed as quickly as we could.

In early August 1944, the German counter-offensive made progress. The Soviet troops were exhausted. The Germans made quick progress by liberating Tukums, near my stepfather's place and, later, in August, Biksti. Also, the encirclement of Riga was broken, so my sister could join us.

By the middle of September, it was safe enough to return to Biksti. We thanked the kind and generous Zeidenberg family and started our return journey. It took several days by horse and wagon from one barn to the next, but finally we approached our home.

We did not know what to expect. Was our grandmother still there? Our helpers? Were the buildings still standing? How many perished? With these thoughts in mind, we decided to stay at a friend's farm not far away and continue the next day. As we approached his farm, we could see nothing. Barns had been burned to the ground, and buildings had collapsed from artillery shells. There were no human beings nor animals in sight. Our apprehension grew, and now we had to continue our journey toward Biksti.

As we approached our home, we saw that most of the buildings were standing but did not know the extent of the damage. As we drove into the courtyard, everything seemed to be intact, except for some shell holes in the stables. German soldiers were everywhere, and the household staff greeted us with joy. We found accommodations in the main house, even though it was full of soldiers sleeping on the floors. Oma had again protected her room as her territory—it didn't matter what the tractor schoolgirls wanted, nor the Soviet troops who had been there before, nor the German soldiers who were there now. It was a very happy reunion for all!

The next morning, we learned what had happened during the Soviet occupation; Irene (our close friend and the daughter of the head housekeeper and blacksmith) updated us. Irene was only fifteen years old, but she was fearless and loyal to our family.

She told us that as soon as the Soviet troops occupied Biksti, they rounded up all the men and lined them up against a wall to be shot. A local woman named Olga, a Ukrainian refugee who was taking care of Oma, fell on her knees and, in the name of the Holy Trinity and all the saints of the Russian Orthodox Church, begged the troops to spare the men. The Soviet political officers were devoted communists and confirmed atheists—in their eyes, religion was the opiate of the masses and therefore inconsequential. Olga's pleas based on her faith did not have much effect.

She went on to say that if they shot the men, others would starve because not enough agricultural products could be made available for a quick Soviet victory. The political officer understood and said "*Khorosho* [Okay]." He relented and instead ordered that the traitors among them would meet their fate, but the others could go. He singled out the two former Russian POWs, Ivan and Timofei; they were shot on the spot. Everyone else survived the Soviet occupation.

Then, I noticed that my loyal friend, the family dog, Duke, did not greet me. I asked a maid, and she reluctantly told me the story. When the Soviet troops occupied Biksti, one of the Russian soldiers, while talking to my grandmother, casually took out his pistol. Duke protectively snarled and was shot. Sadly, I went to Duke's gravesite, and tears welled in my eyes. I experienced again the ravages of war and the cruelty that accompanied it. These circumstances hardened my attitude, but I could not comprehend why a defenseless animal had to suffer the mayhem created by humans. Duke's demise continued to bother me. Later, I summoned enough courage to ask a minister, "Do dogs also go to heaven?" I received a noncommittal answer. I still had hope, and I wanted Duke to know how much I cared.

The following day, with my friends, I walked around the estate. They showed me what had happened in our absence. The German attack had been quick, and they suffered one casualty. My pal showed me the shallow ditch where the soldier died next to his machine gun. Several Russian soldiers also were killed on the property as they fled. One of them took a wagon with a horse and drove down a tree-lined road. He did not know, however, that his own troops mined this road. There was a massive explosion, and the wagon with the horse and soldier were blown to smithereens. We saw shreds of clothing and other debris high in the trees. Then, a farmhand shouted—"Get back! There are still mines around!" We carefully backtracked. A short time before, we had safely played on the same grounds—now everything changed. During war, one never knows where safety and security resides.

On our property, one Russian soldier had been severely wounded. His troops left him, and the Germans just left. The wounded soldier, lying in a ditch, cried out in pain for days, but no one dared to approach because there were mines, and people did not want to be caught helping an enemy.

Our old manor house was now a military hospital. After a visit, Mother came back shaken and said, "There are so many young men, some of them boys, badly wounded. The tank crews are burned, and they suffer so much!" She asked the cook to scrape together whatever flour and other ingredients he had to bake pastries, and she got some fresh milk and served the soldiers to lessen their pain.

I continued to explore the surroundings and talked to the soldiers— they were friendly and relieved not to be at the front, which was only about seven miles away. They assured me that their positions were well fortified and that the Soviets were not planning a major offensive for at least a month. Having heard this, I felt better.

One day, a strange-looking German army van arrived and extended several antennas. The crew parked the truck in a remote place and were very secretive. I was curious and walked to the van. Unexpectedly, a large German Shepherd jumped at me and almost bit me. This was no pet, but a real attack dog. A sergeant opened the door and shouted, "Get away from this vehicle and do not come back!" I asked another soldier about the van. He explained that it was part of an anti-partisan unit that monitored transmissions and pinpointed their locations, which afterward would be attacked. The soldier added that this was one of the toughest jobs in the army. The partisans did not take any prisoners. Instead, they shot them. The Germans also shot most partisans as spies.

One day, my buddies and I noticed local auxiliary policemen guarding two husky men in leather jackets cutting firewood. The policemen were elderly, well past draft age, but looked unusually alert. I asked one of them who these men were and what they were doing. The guard told me, "They are Soviet partisans who parachuted behind the lines. The Germans captured them a few days ago after they had wounded a soldier and killed others." I asked, "Why are they cutting firewood?" The guard answered that after the Germans captured the men, they asked the local police to put them to work before they were shot later in the afternoon. Given the conditions, this made sense. Nevertheless, my buddies and I moved to play somewhere else.

There were occasional dogfights in the air, and it was almost entertaining (like a video game today). When a plane was shot down, in most cases, it was Russian. We saw a parachute floating down not too far away, and a German car with a machine gun raced toward the landing spot to capture the pilot. Later, the car came back without a captive. I asked the soldiers what had happened. One said, "We wanted to capture the pilot, but his parachute floated toward the forest where there are partisans. We won't go near it, but we opened with a machine gun. Hopefully, we hit the pilot or the chute, but we are not going to investigate because it is too dangerous!" Such was life near the front lines.

Carriages full of refugees continued to pass our place. They asked for permission to spend the night, fodder for their horses, and food. Most of the refugees were Latvians from not too far away who had only traveled a few days. They were healthy and well fed and made plans to travel to Germany or further west to avoid the front. Only rarely did Russians pass through, and when they arrived, they looked emaciated, tired, and desperate. They had traveled hundreds of miles with their horse-drawn wagons from Russia through a foreign country (Latvia) that was not welcoming.

I remember one of these Russian refugee groups stopping to ask for help. As the front approached, the Russian refugees left the Soviet Union. They did not want to live again under the brutal regime, even though their future was uncertain. It was sad because the Germans did not help, and the local people had many refugees of their own. The Russian refugees had little hope for a better future, though some tried to escape to Germany.

Mother was touched by their plight and arranged shelter, as well as fodder for their horses. The Russians said they suffered through a long journey and had no food or supplies. Mother provided them with food, even though it was scarce. The next day, they asked for permission to stay longer because they had no other place to go and wanted to recuperate. At that time, Biksti was crowded with the military and other refugees, so it was difficult to keep the Russians for a long time. Mother was sympathetic and knew that their future was bleak—the Germans did not want them, and if the Soviet troops caught up, the women and children would be deported to Siberia. The men would likely be shot.

The refugees appreciated Mother's compassion and, upon their departure, gave her a silver icon. The Russians said that this icon protected them and saved their lives during the Soviet regime. It guided them to a safer place. They hoped that the icon would also bring good fortune to our family. The Russian refugees knew that their luck had probably run out. I have kept this icon, and it reminds me of compassion during turmoil. The tranquil face of Jesus portrayed in the icon brings peace to all who long for it.

Departure from Latvia

Days went by, and the war moved closer. The Latvian capital, Riga, fell to the Communists on October 13th, 1944. A few days later, the first major Soviet offensive began—fortunately, it did not make much progress. Fierce fighting flared up along the front. Being so close, we could hear artillery fire and even distinguish different guns. Stalin's Organ (*Katyusha*) rocket launchers were the most feared. We again hoped that we would be able to return to Biksti soon, even though we had to consider leaving.

Horses were required to cultivate the land, but several of our horses were requisitioned by Latvian troops to move their equipment to the front lines. Before leaving, the commander said we could get our horses back, but we would have to come pick them up. Our close pal and the daughter of the head housekeeper, Irene, volunteered for this task. Mother said the horses were not essential, but Irene, only sixteen years old at the time, insisted. She departed in a carriage drawn by the worst nag we could find so that it would not attract much attention. The following is how Irene tells the story:

> *After traveling for several miles, I arrived at the forest just before the main frontline. The soldiers were surprised to see me, but when I asked for their commander, they obliged when they learned my brothers were also soldiers. To get the horses back, I had to get permission from their commander, a captain, who was in the frontline bunker. The soldiers went on to say that it was impossible right now to go to the frontlines because of Russian sniper activity. It could only be done after dark, when supplies were brought in.*
>
> *I waited and eventually reached the frontline bunker and the commander's quarters. He was surprised and friendly. He said, "You can have the horses, but first have something to eat!" I accepted his invitation, but suddenly artillery and mortar fire erupted. The explosions were close, and the whole bunker shook. An alarm*

sounded, and an orderly rushed in and shouted that the Russians were attacking. The captain told me to rest on his bunk and gave me his trench coat. The captain ordered, "Do not let anybody in the bunker until I get back." I stayed in the bunker, shaking, while small arms fire blasted all around. Later, the captain returned and said, "This was one of the Russian probing attacks. We gave them a bloody nose, and a few of my men were wounded. The front is stable now, but you should spend the night here before departing!"

Irene did as she was told. The next day, she was back in Biksti with all the horses. Irene was a close pal of mine, and after this, I never saw her afraid.

We had to leave Biksti, and my parents resorted to an old-time practice of burying their valuables. We took paintings out of the frames and rolled them up in oil cloth. Custom-made china was carefully packed with silverware and other valuables. One had to bury this treasure trove in a safe place, not seen by anyone else. One evening, my parents went to a forester's cottage and buried the treasures in a barn because it had a clay floor and could be covered with hay. No one could see evidence of the hole. Another lot we buried in the floor of one of our buildings.

When Mother and I visited Biksti almost fifty years later, she discreetly asked about the forester's cottage. The answer was that it had been the location of a fierce battle zone, and everything was destroyed and leveled. No one even knew where the buildings had been. The other building now had apartments with solid floors. If we were to look for our treasures, everyone would tear the place apart, and nothing would be left. Mother and I decided to drop the matter. We did not need these treasures—our lives were rewarding without these material goods.

Before our departure from Biksti, we were overjoyed to see Silvia join us after escaping from Riga. Now the whole family could travel together. We packed two wagons and were ready to leave when our head housekeeper ran up to Mother and begged her to bring Irene with us so that she could have a better future. Mother obliged. Irene had spent most of her time with us, being our playmate for years. She was almost a member of the family. Irene threw her belongings into the cart, and we were off. Our objective was to go back to the Zeidenbergs' place, where we stayed before, and then to Germany. It would be the "usual trip," traveling from barn to barn and asking for accommodations.

With our belongings packed into two horse-drawn carts, we were ready to depart Biksti for a long journey to the port city of Liepāja and then on to Germany. All of us were sad, and many had tears in their eyes because we were leaving behind our grandmother and the lifestyle that had served us well for so many decades. Still, we were fortunate to have all our family members with us (including Irene).

Mother warmly hugged Oma, who could not join us due to her poor health. We left her in the care of our loyal helpers, Elsa and Irene's mother. We knew they would do everything possible to make Oma's life pleasant— they had already proven that during the prior Soviet occupation. I was distressed not only because Oma stayed behind, but also I was leaving behind my buddies, with whom I shared so many adventures.

Despite this, I knew we were doing what was best for us. Our parents frequently said, "We have to do this for the children's sake, so they can have a better future!" In the last moment, I even gave a hug to Elsa, who had never been my favorite. Those left behind called out, "You will be back as soon as before! The war will be over!" We hugged them and said, as in the past, that we would be back in a few months. In my heart, I knew this was not going to happen.

After we left, there was heavy fighting in the area, but the front remained a few miles from Biksti. When artillery fire began, Oma, with her attendants, went to the basement. The old Biksti Manor house was built around 1560 as a small fortress, with stone walls about four feet thick. As the shelling abated, Oma and Elsa emerged from the cellar and went to the kitchen. They did not realize that the Soviet troops had broken through and were nearby. One of the soldiers outside noticed movement in the kitchen and threw in a hand grenade. Elsa covered the grenade with her body to save Oma and was blown to pieces. Oma was severely wounded and died on the way to the hospital.

All of us who knew Oma and Elsa missed them. As I grew up, Oma was always there, but her health was so poor that she rarely left her suite, except to pursue her love for gardening and beekeeping. Life would have been different without her low-key presence. While Elsa and I did not get along in the beginning, now I feel differently. I wish I could thank Elsa for her loyalty and devotion to the family. She made the ultimate sacrifice.

On our way to Liepāja, we encountered a problem. We had tied our thoroughbred Arabian horse, who was Christian's pride and joy, to our main carriage. It was a beautiful animal. One of the soldiers with the HiWi band on his arm saw the horse and tried to grab the reins. These were cruel soldiers—former Soviet POWs—who served as auxiliaries in the German army. The Germans viewed them as second-rate soldiers, and Russians shot them or shipped them off to gulags when captured. When the soldier reached for the Arabian horse, Christian pulled out his 9-mm pistol and was ready to use it. The two soldiers opened the breaches of their rifles and inserted cartridges. It looked like there was going to be a shootout. Just in time, a German officer shouted and ordered the soldiers to lay off—still a very close call! Again, too much of a concern over horses.

When we got to the Zeidenbergs' home, they had already left. The place was full of refugees, and we could barely find accommodations. A few days later, Mother and Christian drove to the main embarkation port of Liepāja to look for transportation to Germany. We got passage on a ship, the *Santa Rosa*, that was sailing in two days. While Mother was eager to leave, two days did not provide enough time to get everything ready for departure. Our parents opted to take the next ship, the *Bucharest*. We learned later that Russian bombers damaged the *Santa Rosa* as she crossed the Baltic Sea.

On November 4, 1944, we repacked and got ready for the next phase of our trip. Even though Germany was attacked from the East as well as the West, and cities were regularly people who told me of the search committee no bombed, it represented more safety and the only way for us to escape the Soviets. Our baggage went into two horse-drawn carriages. Our six family members—my stepfather, Mother, sisters Silvia and Peggy, Irene, and I—sat on top of our belongings.

With apprehension, we approached Liepāja, the main port that was still free in Latvia. Ships from Germany delivered supplies and evacuated the wounded and the refugees. The front was less than fifteen miles away from Liepāja, but fortunately, it was well defended by entrenched veteran troops. The city was ringed by numerous antiaircraft batteries, mostly crewed by boys aged fifteen to seventeen under the supervision of veterans. Regularly, the Soviet bombers attacked Liepāja, but the intense anti-aircraft fire was effective. The defenders claimed to have shot down more than two hundred planes.

As we entered Liepāja, there was a bombing raid. Immediately, the sky filled with bursts of anti-aircraft fire. We hurried to shelter in an abandoned building. Irene turned to me and said, "John, you don't seem to be scared!" Bravely, I replied that a soldier told me that the safest place to be was the Russian bomber's target. Their aim was so bad, they never hit the mark! Fortunately, it was only a brief nuisance raid. After we left the shelter, I found jagged pieces of anti-aircraft shrapnel, but I later discarded them because of their sharp edges.

When we arrived at the dock, the scene initially looked chaotic. The area was covered with horse-drawn carriages loaded with personal belongings, accompanied by anxious adults and crying children. Everyone was hanging onto their possessions and wanted to board the ship. Despite this activity, the loading process was efficient. My stepfather talked to the crew, and shortly afterward, our belongings were loaded

Leaving Latvia

onto the ship. We then had to wait until our documents were processed. I lagged behind the adults and curiously watched the process.

Suddenly, there was a cry, "People fell off the dock into the water!" I immediately looked around and did not see my parents, but my sisters were there—it occurred to me that if my parents perished, there was no one else who would take care of us. We would be abandoned! How would we survive? A terrifying moment indeed. Fortunately, I soon saw my parents waving and was glad to join them as we waited to board the ship.

We sat on top of our possessions before they were loaded into the ship's cargo hold. Ships sailed only in darkness, so we waited for night. I went to the deck and saw the whole dockside covered with empty farmers' carts and forsaken horses. The horses seemed to sense that they had been left behind by their masters, who they had faithfully served. You could hear them crying out. It did not last long, as soldiers came along to collect them. Our horses and carriages were not among them because my stepfather paid a nearby farmer to take care of them "until we come back." Even at an early age, I knew this could be only a dream or an illusion.

Our ship, the *Bucharest*, sailed after dark to avoid Soviet bombers based on nearby Lithuanian airfields. The pilots did not like to fly at night. By morning, we would be farther away, and the bombers would probably find more lucrative targets. The real danger came from the Soviet submarines that patrolled the Baltic coast. They had already sunk several ships. After we left the safety of the harbor, a German naval destroyer joined us.

As we left, I stood on the deck and saw the Latvian shores disappearing in the darkness. There were no lights anywhere, due to a mandatory complete blackout. Some of the refugees started to mournfully sing the Latvian national anthem: "*God bless Latvia...*" They left all their material possessions behind and knew that their lives had changed forever— as had ours! I also understood that tangible possessions are not that significant and can be replaced. We still had our family, limited freedom, and intangible values, which no one can take away.

I stood on the deck in total darkness while the stars in the sky shone brightly. No blackouts affected them because they were guided by other forces beyond human comprehension. I recalled a few lines from a Dostoyevsky poem I heard in school:

"The darker the night, the brighter the stars.
The deeper the grief, the closer to God!"

I thought the first part was accurate, but I did not want to get close to God in heaven yet because I had not given up on life on earth—I felt it was bound to get better from here! I knew that we could, however, use some help as we sailed through these dangerous waters. In the past, we had had many close calls, yet we survived, so I knew there must be some guiding hand above looking out for us. I believed it would not leave us now.

With these comforting thoughts, I went below the decks, stretched out on the baggage, and fell sound asleep. Little did I know, a few months later, a former cruise ship—the MV *Wilhelm Gustloff*, overloaded with refugees—would be sunk by a Soviet submarine. About nine thousand and four hundred people perished, half of them children—the greatest maritime disaster in history. While all of us know about the sinking of the *Titanic*, the number of lives lost there was only one thousand five hundred and forty—tragic indeed in peacetime, but wars change everything—even our perspective of human life.

In the late morning, we could see land. It represented safety, but we wondered how good it was because the Soviet troops were rapidly advancing from the east. Nevertheless, it was safer than where we were before. I reflected on the recent events and asked myself, "Why are we here, at this time and at this place?" We had many options to escape earlier, before the situation deteriorated. We had been lucky that the steadfastness of my stepfather, with the support of Mother, helped us overcome almost insurmountable obstacles. Without them, we would not have survived. Now we faced a new reality.

We left Latvia, or more accurately its Western province (known as the Courland Fortress or Pocket), on November 4, 1944. The Courland Fortress encompasses an area of about three thousand five hundred square miles, bordered on the west by the Baltic Sea. It had been cut off from the rest of Germany by Soviet troops. To gain a better understanding of the conditions from which we escaped, one has to take a brief look at the historical background.

In the late summer of 1944, the rapid Soviet Army advance reached the Baltic Sea and surrounded about nine hundred thousand German troops, which included about fifteen thousand Latvian soldiers. The size of the defended area gradually shrank. To eliminate the resistance, the Soviets staged six major attacks, employing about two million men. The fighting was fierce, and casualties mounted—no wonder the area was called the "Courland Cauldron." During the six months of fighting, it is estimated that the Soviets incurred three hundred fifty thousand casualties, and the defenders incurred around one hundred thousand. By the end of the war, two hundred and two thousand of the defenders were captured and very few returned.

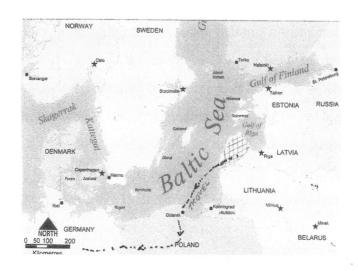

Eastern Front
1 August 1943 – 31 December 1944

☐ to 1 December 1943
☐ to 30 April 1944
☐ to 19 August 1944
☐ to 30 August 1944
☐ to 31 December 1944

The Soviet Offensive - 1944-45

To put the severity of the fighting in proper prospective, it can be compared with the ten years of the Vietnam War, in which the U.S. casualties reached one hundred fifty thousand soldiers.

Even though the fighting in Courland was horrific, it allowed more than one hundred thousand people to escape the Soviets. We were among the lucky ones.

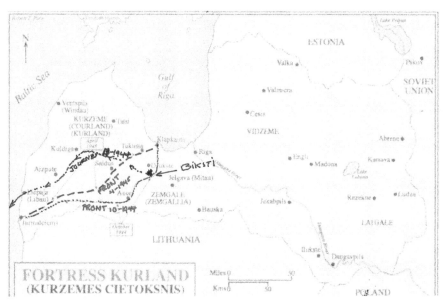

The Courland Pocket / Our escape route

CHAPTER 5

REFUGEES

On November 5, 1944, we stood on the deck of the cargo ship *Bucharest* as it entered the port of Gotenhafen, at that time part of Germany. Between World War I and World War II, due to the Versailles Treaty, it had been carved out of German Prussia and given to Poland. The Poles developed *Gotenhafen* (the Polish name for the city is Gdynia) as their main Baltic Sea port, but during World War II, it served as the German supply base for troops in surrounding Courland, plus provided reinforcements for the eastern front. The port and the city were both full of bustling activity.

Gotenhafen was a dreary town—leaden clouds hung low over the city, and the air was full of heavy drifting smoke. Soldiers and refugees crowded the streets. The activities of the harbor were well organized, and we were loaded promptly into trucks and brought to a nearby refugee transit camp.

The transit camp was one of the worst places I have ever seen or stayed. The facility was previously used as a POW transfer point, *tor*

Stargard Stalag. The camp was surrounded by a high chain-link fence topped with two layers of barbed wire. There were HiWi troops (former Russian POWs serving as German Army auxiliaries) guarding the gate—they were known for their cruelty, ingrained in them from their Soviet army days. All the barrack windows and doors were wide open, and the air was heavy with chemical fumes. The camp personnel explained that before our arrival, the barracks had been sealed and pumped full of gas to eliminate the vermin and bed bugs. Now the place was being aired out in anticipation of our occupancy.

Inside the barracks, there were triple bunk beds with no padding or straw. The latter was all right because at least there was no hiding place for bed bugs. The chemical gas had done its job—the floor was littered with dead bed bugs. A woman with a bucket swept up the bugs, and her bucket was a quarter full. She said, "How can we sleep? The bed bugs will eat us alive!" Her friend replied, "Put the legs of the bunk in a container of water. The bugs will drown when they try to climb!" A more knowledgeable man chimed in, "That will not work because bed bugs climb up on the ceiling and then drop on you!" That was bad news for me because I had the upper bunk. At night, I could not fall asleep—I expected diving attacks from numerous bed bugs. Nothing happened—the gas killed all insects and permeated the woodwork. The next morning, one could not even see a live fly, and we still smelled the chemicals.

We had no choice but to settle into our new miserable surroundings. There were showers and some food. The latter was not an issue for us because we still had our supplies. No one knew what was going to happen next—where we would go or when. We had no control over our lives, nor our future. A helpless feeling, only moderated by the fact that at least we were farther away from the Russian front.

The next day, Mother said that even though we could not change our surroundings, that should not prevent us from trying to feel better about ourselves. With that, she headed into town. Using our documents and appropriate bribes, Mother had no trouble exiting the camp. Mother's destination was a beauty salon. In the afternoon, she returned with a new hairdo and finely manicured hands. An uplifting sight!

Because there was nothing else to do, the next day, Mother took me to town with her. It was full of soldiers in transit, German refugees fleeing from East Prussia, and dour-looking Polish residents. They had the right to feel that way because this had been their country. The town of Gotenhafen itself was not that much better than the camp.

A few days later, we were loaded into a freight train of cattle cars. The cars had doors on rollers, about twelve feet wide, and near the top of the roof, there were three by three foot openings for fresh air. There were no electric lights, no heat, and no sanitary facilities—a bucket in the corner served that purpose. There were four other families in the car with all their baggage, and we were ready to go. I was happy to get away from the camp and travel west.

Our journey 11.19 44 – 6.19 45

Despite our primitive surroundings, we were comfortable. We had a five by four by four foot chest and several sacks of personal belongings, including food. There were smoked hams, sausages, and dry bread and butter that were spoiling. Mother also brought along two antique Persian carpets purchased in Istanbul many years before. Back in Biksti, when one of the rugs was being rolled up, I asked the helper, "Because there is a space in the middle, why not roll the rug around my cross-country skis? It will make no difference, and no one will know!" So, I also had my cross-country skis with me as we traveled. We also brought along a bicycle, just in case we had to continue our journey on foot. With all this stuff around us, our parents made up a nest for us near the ceiling, where we were cozy and comfortable, and could play cards to pass the time.

A steam locomotive was hooked up, and we chugged on our way, but no one knew where we were going. We traveled for hours until we pulled up to a railroad siding and waited for another locomotive or instructions on where to go next. Our journey continued with frequent delays to destinations unknown. After a few more stops, we learned that our direction was south—deeper into what had been Poland but was now annexed by Germany. Considering the hostilities between these two countries, this was not a desirable place to be!

After more delays, we traveled westward away from the Russians and, hopefully, away from danger. It turned out that this was not the case— our new destination was Berlin, one of the most dangerous places in Germany at the time and the favorite target of Allied bombers. We knew that the train would stop overnight in the railroad yards, a prime bomber target. To make the danger even greater, there were not enough air raid shelters to accommodate a trainload of refugees. More danger came from the shrapnel of the exploding anti-aircraft shells that came from the batteries ringing the city. As we approached Berlin, it was suddenly quiet. Everyone was scared. This was the second time in my life when I felt terrified. (The first time had been in Latvia, when the Soviet troops almost overran my stepfather's home as we were leaving.)

Our overnight stop in Berlin turned out to be relatively peaceful. There was a brief air raid warning, but no bombs fell. That night, another target was bombed. In the morning, we turned south, away from Berlin, hoping for greater safety. But safety was elusive because

Allied dive bombers roamed the skies and strafed troop trains and their locomotives—the pilots had no way of knowing whether the train was full of soldiers or refugees.

Life on the train for us children was not too unpleasant, and we got used to the steady, rhythmic rumble, the click-clack on the rails, and the steam clouds from the locomotive. We knew that every click took us farther away from the Soviets. Adults talked and quietly sang Latvian folk songs to lift their spirits. We played cards and read a few books that people brought.

As we moved farther south, the countryside looked more prosperous. The farms and villages were neat, and there were few signs that there was a war raging nearby. We were given food at railroad stops, but because we had our own supplies, hunger was still not an issue. There were ingenious ways to supplement our menu. A man from our car made friends with the locomotive engineer. This man took a metal canister to the engineer, who released steam and boiling water from the engine and filled up the container. Now we had hot water for tea! It was an unusual journey to say the least.

By that time, we had been on the train about a week. We headed for Bavaria, with a stop in Nürnberg. One morning, the train suddenly stopped outside the city because an air raid was in progress. We were not in the target area, though, so there was no danger. It was quite a sight to see large formations of Allied planes overhead, puffs of smoke in the air from exploding anti-aircraft shells, and smoke rising from the bomb explosions. The raid was short, but the train stood still for hours before moving. Finally, we arrived at the Nürnberg station, and we understood the reason for the delay. Workers on the track were filling in numerous bomb craters. Some of the damaged rails looked like twisted spaghetti and were rapidly being replaced. The crews worked professionally and methodically—it was a task they performed many times before. We were given hot food and wondered how the Germans could recover so quickly from such frequent disasters. When the train left Nürnberg and headed south, we were happy to leave the city behind.

In Germany and on

The train finally arrived in Treuchtlingen, a small and charming Bavarian town untouched by the war. We thought it would be safe to be in a small town of less than ten thousand inhabitants and of no military significance. Shortly after we left, Treuchtlingen was bombed, and ten percent of the people were injured or perished. In the midst of war, no one knows where safety exists!

All of us from the train were housed in a local high school. The space was full of cots, but there were hot showers, which was a pleasant change from our long journey. We had not taken a bath for more than a week!

Mother felt that this was the right time for us to strike out on our own. We had the necessary documents and more than adequate cash. The value of the *Ost-Mark*, used in Latvia, was the same as the *Deutsche Mark* in Germany. The problem was that the stores were empty, and virtually all purchases required coupons issued by local authorities; we had none. My pregnant sister Silvia, whose husband was in the army, left for Heidelberg—the same place she was born when Mother was a student at the university. Silvia had lived with a local family for years before returning to Latvia. This family, the Barths, were like second parents to her. We were happy for Silvia and knew that she would be in good hands.

It was difficult to extricate from the refugee group because no housing was available. Mother and Christian went to the *Bürgermeister's* office (town hall) to obtain a permit for rental rooms. It was almost impossible because there was no space available. These conditions did not faze Mother, and after a few appropriate gifts to the right people, we found accommodations.

We were assigned two rooms in an immaculately clean German inn with beautiful down comforters. There was a bath across the hall—after that, we felt like we had been reborn. We also had food coupons. In the evening, we went to a restaurant to have a simple meal, which was all we could have. Of course, there was plenty of low-calorie beer, which Christian enjoyed—if anyone tried to ration beer in Bavaria, it would lead to an immediate revolution!

After a few days of pleasant rest, we moved on. My parents wanted to be in a relatively safe location where we could find comfortable shelter. They selected Marienbad (*Mariánské Lázně*), Sudetenland, now part of the Czech Republic, a well-known European spa town where my grandmother had enjoyed a brief stay. We were fortunate to cross paths again with our family friend, Mr. Zagers, who we sheltered from the German authorities in Latvia after he resigned from his senior government position. This shows how important good friends are in uncertain climates. He moved earlier to Marienbad and was there to return our favor.

Early one morning—with our baggage checked and a first-class railroad ticket in hand—we said goodbye to Treuchtlingen and headed for Marienbad. It was a pleasant and uneventful journey through picturesque countryside. We passed through beautiful Bohemian hills and forests intermittent with cultivated fields ready for winter. A German hunter with his dog joined us in the carriage. The hunter said he was going home after having shot a hare. It was just like life had been for us years before, and it felt like a clock had been turned back. We knew this was not the case, though—danger lay ahead.

In the early afternoon, we arrived in Marienbad. We proceeded to the hotel, which was more than a mile outside the city. One of the first things I noticed while driving to the hotel was the many soldiers hobbling through the streets on crutches, some with empty pinned-up sleeves where arms had been before and others with shoulders still in casts. They were from military rehabilitation hospitals, which had taken over the hotels. Despite their injuries, the soldiers looked happy, probably because they were recovering and not fighting at the front. We knew that Marienbad was a hospital city untouched by bombers—that was why we were there.

After a short ride with all our baggage, we arrived at our destination, Hotel Waldfrieden (Forest Peace). By that time, we had traveled many miles on many different modes of transportation and checked our bags on the train to Marienbad, yet we never lost a piece of baggage. Despite the war, efficiency remained paramount in Germany.

The hotel was luxurious—beautifully located and surrounded by a wooded area. Its peacetime clientele had been upper-crust people seeking a cure from the local healing waters. We had two rooms, one for my parents and one for Peggy, Irene, and me. After our experience, it was hard to believe that such a lifestyle still existed, almost untouched by the war. Again, we enjoyed a bath, and Mother unpacked my best clothing, including a jacket, shirt, and necktie—things I had not worn for ages. Then, we were ready to go downstairs to the dining room.

In the dining room, Herr Ober (the maître d'hôtel) met us and directed us to a table. Here, the old traditions still prevailed, and the maître d' wore a white tie and long black coat. I looked around the dining room and saw tables set with fine tablecloths, polished silver, and glittering crystal glasses. The dining room was not full but included a few German officers on leave with their families, important-looking civilians, and a few other lucky refugees like us. Among them were Mother's friends from Latvia.

The waiters wore black tie attire and were elderly and slow moving because all of the young men were serving in the military. Mother studied the menus carefully and placed the orders. Price was never an issue, but number of required coupons determined what we could order. There were coupons for a slice of bread, margarine, and meat, but not for vegetables. After a while, the waiters sauntered up with our main course and served it in impressive style. After setting the plate in front of us with a great flourish, the waiter removed the shiny metal chafing cover, and we were ready to eat. I looked at my plate and saw a boiled potato, some steamed vegetables that look like wilted asparagus, and a microscopic piece of meat that was almost impossible to cut or swallow. Regardless, we considered ourselves most lucky to be in that place.

The length of our stay in the hotel was limited to a few weeks while we looked for more permanent accommodations. Mother again went to the city officials. I do not know what passed hands, but shortly afterward, we were assigned an apartment. It was a former pension called Haus Helgoland. We had the entire third floor with two bedrooms, a living room, a kitchen/dining area, and an alcove where Irene had a cot. The living room had a balcony overlooking the street and the forest beyond.

The food situation was deteriorating, despite the ration cards. The supplies we brought along from Latvia were nearing exhaustion, and our diet was getting worse. Mother believed that it was a priority for children to eat well because as they matured, their health could be permanently impaired. She did everything possible to make sure we had a reasonably good diet.

To accomplish this, Mother went to the countryside and negotiated with the farmers. From experience, we knew that farmers always had extra food—for the right price. I never learned about the financial arrangements, but occasionally, we had access to fresh milk, bread, eggs, and, even more rarely, some smoked meat. My responsibility was to visit the farmers, collect the food, and bring it back to the house. The round trip was fifteen miles, which I did not mind because we had a bicycle.

Occasionally, on the return trip from the farmers, the bicycle would be loaded with supplies. This made it hard to pedal uphill, particularly if the wind blew in my face. My solution was to wait for a slow-moving truck and hang on with one hand to its tailgate, so I could be pulled up the hills. The downhill segment was trickier, independent of the speed of the truck. Despite these difficulties, I went regularly to fulfill my task of bringing food from the farmers.

Even though food remained scarce, due to my parents' efforts, we never felt famished. One day, I commented to Irene, "This is a somewhat unusual and spicy sausage." Irene replied, "I heard it's made from horse meat!" That did not deter me—it tasted fine.

One wintry day, Irene and I wandered the streets of Marienbad and saw crowds lined up in front of a small structure. If many people were gathered in front of a building, it usually meant there was a store that had received food shipments. This building, however, turned out to be a Greek Orthodox Church. We were brought up in the Protestant tradition but were curious and managed to get inside. The priests wore elaborate robes, chanting and swinging censers of billowing incense. Parishioners in the pews prayed fervently, with their faces turned toward heaven. It was a strange feeling to see their calm devotion while uncertainty reigned outside—one could feel an immeasurable power giving peace to the people. I did not grasp its full meaning, but I sensed there was a spiritual force making it possible.

While war surrounded us, life in Marienbad remained peaceful. To pass the time, I befriended Latvian neighbors on the floor above us. Frequently, this couple invited me to come along on their walks through the woods, where they looked for mushrooms or just enjoyed being in nature. I did not know much about mushrooms but collected ribbons of aluminum-coated chaff dropped by bombers to jam radar. No matter where you were, there was always a reminder that war was not too far away. It turned out that the husband had been a famous actor in Latvia, and when he departed, he gave me an autographed photo.

Winter came, and there was no school. I had a lot of free time, so one day, I decided to go skiing. I had my cross-country skis, and I put them on my shoulder and climbed a mountain. No one bothered a twelve year old who walked through the woods by himself. At the top, I put on my skis and schussed down along the walking trails. It did not take long before I rapidly accelerated and could not stop—I had only cross-country bindings and could not control the skis. My only choice was to fall in the bushes before I hit a tree. On the way down, I had several tumbles but eventually arrived safely. It was a thrilling adventure. I realized that my equipment was inadequate and left it behind. Still, I always loved the sport.

One spring day, I went fishing and caught three large carps. When Mother saw the catch, she was ecstatic and prepared a feast for all of us.

Our neighbors complimented me and told me I was a skilled fisherman, but I knew I was only lucky! I did not care for the carp because there were too many bones. I would have preferred the horse sausage, if it had been available.

Even as the war continued unabated around us, we felt we lived in an oasis of peace. One of the reminders of the war raging on was seeing the sky full of Allied bombers cruising leisurely to their designated targets and leaving behind a spider web of contrails. There was no anti-aircraft fire or German fighter aircraft. It was like a gigantic parade in the sky.

In the latter part of February 1945, an unusually large formation of bombers passed above us. Later, we learned that the Allies destroyed the beautiful German city of Dresden, which had no military value. Close to sixty thousand people perished, almost the same as in Hiroshima. We were concerned because Mother's Aunt Hance moved to Dresden after leaving Latvia, but we were overjoyed when a few days later, Mother's aunt and her husband arrived, each with a single satchel in hand. That was all they could save from the burning city.

According to Mother's uncle, who besides being a physician was a retired army colonel, the conditions in Dresden after the bombing were horrific. Buildings were tumbling down, the asphalt on the streets was burning, and people were covered with phosphorus from the incendiary bombs and, with their hair burning, jumped into the river—phosphorus fires cannot be extinguished with water. Most buildings in Germany had sacks of sand to put out the fires. No wonder so many perished during this unnecessary and destructive raid. We were fortunate enough to live in a major city, but this experience so shook up our relatives that shortly afterward they left for Germany. They eventually settled in Australia, to be far away from any possible mayhem.

I also had a stark reminder that the war still waged. One day, while sitting in the living room near the window, I heard a tremendous roar and machine-gun fire. I ran to the balcony and saw a low-flying P-51 aircraft complete a strafing pass and soar away into the blue sky. The next moment, I saw the wingman follow the same pattern, flying down the street about two hundred feet from me, with blazing machine guns aimed at an abandoned trailer truck. For a split second, there was a tremendous roar as the plane zipped by. I was not scared because the aim was down the street, but I was impressed by the awesome display of power. I can see this incident in slow motion, as if it happened yesterday. I went outside and saw the street pitted with bullet holes. This did not look to me like a serious air attack—the pilots were probably just having a good time. It looked like it was more fun to fight in the air than slug it out on the ground. This later influenced my decision when I had to select a branch of military service.

Soon, signs indicated that the war was coming to an end. The Soviets rapidly advanced from the east, and the Third United States Army, under the aggressive leadership of General Patton, came from the west. We worried who would reach Marienbad first—if the Russians, then we'd have to escape again, or our road would lead directly to a Siberian gulag.

At the last moment, the Germans put up a stiff resistance and stopped the Soviet advance about ten miles away. The American troops occupied Marienbad, and we felt relatively safe.

I headed downtown to see the American soldiers. They were relaxed and stood around a few Sherman tanks, chewing gum and ogling girls. For them, the war was over, but probably not for us. Under the American occupation, Czech officials appeared from nowhere. Initially, they were considerate and doubled our food rations. Later, however, the officials urged us to return to Latvia, which was now under Soviet rule—but we knew very well what awaited us there. Luckily, the American troops stayed in Marienbad.

A month later, our family friend, Mr. Zagers, who befriended an American officer, told us that the U.S. troops would leave the area under Soviet/Czech control. Mr. Zagers already made plans to leave Marienbad for Germany. Afterwards, he traveled to the United States, where he became a well-respected professor at Gettysburg College. This time, we took Mr. Zagers's warning seriously and made plans to leave for Germany before it was too late. My parents contacted a man who previously smuggled people to Germany for substantial compensation. This man assured us that at the crossing, the Czech border guards, whom he bribed, would just wave us through.

All of us were loaded into a truck. Mother sat in the front with the driver and I, with the rest of the family in the back with our belongings. We approached the border with some trepidation and became concerned when the Czech guard requested documents—it turned out that the border guards bribed by our driver were not on duty. I heard a heated conversation in German. The new guards pointed to our documents and said, "You are from Latvia, which is now 'free' under the Soviets, and you are going home. The Soviet Army has requested that all refugees from Eastern Europe go to their collection point, which is in the next town, for transportation to the east!" We knew that meant a one-way ticket to Siberia.

Mother told the guards that we wanted to go to Germany to be with other family members (my sister Silvia). The Czech guard shouted, "Just turn around and head back. One of my men will accompany you to the Soviet post!" Fortunately, an American MP Sergeant sauntered by and asked in broken German, "Was ist los?" [What is going on?] The Czech guard launched into a lengthy explanation. Mother interrupted and said in English, "Sir, we are trying to go to Germany to be with our family in the American Occupation Zone!" The sergeant was startled to hear good English and yelled to the Czech guard, "Let this lady and her family through! You're causing a traffic jam!" Mother thanked him, and we were on our way to the American Occupation Zone in Germany.

What I learned from this experience was that, while we achieved our objective of safety in war-torn Europe by settling in Marienbad, there is nothing permanent when turmoil rages around you. One must be prepared for surprises and be ready to move on at any given time. Fortunately, we recognized this and moved on.

CHAPTER 6

AFTER WORLD WAR II

Weiden

After escaping from Czechoslovakia, our first stop in Germany was Weiden in der Oberpfalz. This Bavarian town's population was less than thirty thousand—and that included at least ten thousand refugees.

Post-World War II Germany was in turmoil—close to twenty million people were displaced. Most of them were Germans who were expelled from the East by the Poles and the Czechs. These refugees left their homes with very few possessions and received limited government assistance. We were more fortunate because refugees from formerly occupied countries were helped by the United Nations Refugee Relief Administration (UNRRA), which assisted with housing and food (mostly U.S. Army surplus).

During this post-World War II mass migration, Latvia was particularly hard-hit. About one hundred forty thousand escaped to Germany, and several more thousands escaped to Sweden via fishing boats. The escapees represented the better educated, more elite segment of the population—those who were most threatened by the new Soviet occupation. Another one hundred thousand served in the German army, and close to thirty thousand were captured by the Allies. The rest remained in Courland or were casualties. If one includes the death toll during the Soviet occupation, Latvia lost close to twenty-five percent of its population. This portion was rapidly replaced by ethnic Russians.

I recall that the press extensively covered the atrocities committed by the Nazis. They killed close to six million innocent people, and various governmental agencies aggressively brought the perpetrators of these heinous crimes to justice. They received their well-deserved punishment. At the same time, the press referred to Stalin as Uncle Joe, a friendly figure who helped the Allies win the war in Europe. Hardly any mention was made that Stalin was responsible for the death of more than twenty million people—three times the amount of people who perished during the Holocaust.

With naïve perceptions like this in the press, we did not feel secure about our future, even though the war was over—some refugees were forcefully repatriated to the Soviet Union, which meant the gulags. However, we felt relatively safe in the American Occupation Zone because we knew that the United States stood for freedom and was not intimidated by aggressive Soviet moves. We had not heard of anyone forcefully repatriated from the American Occupation Zone and knew that the Americans stood fast on their principles (rather than just talking about them publicly, as others had done). Early on, my admiration of the United States grew.

Our fears of forced deportation to the Soviet Union were reinforced by events in Sweden. The Swedish government, which views itself as the moral compass of Europe, forcefully deported one hundred and fifty Latvian and Estonian soldiers to the Soviet Union. The soldiers, after the end of the war, sought refuge in a neutral country—yet were forcefully returned to the Soviet Union. They knew well what they could expect there, so many chose instead to commit suicide in a gruesome fashion.

More than forty years later, the Swedish government apologized. To restore its reputation as a country upholding high moral principles, the government invited the survivors to Sweden. Few accepted, most of them had perished.

Similarly, a British commander in Austria turned over several thousand Cossack soldiers to the Soviets. They fought with the Germans against communism. The Cossacks are a fiercely independent ethnic group that served with distinction in the Czar's Army. Again, many of them committed suicide rather than be shipped to the gulags, never to return.

In the American Occupation Zone, we were only twenty-five miles away from the Czech border—a country turned over to the Soviets. Even though we had comfortable accommodations and adequate food, we needed to look for another location that offered more safety.

Lauingen

In late summer of 1945, with the help of the UNRRA, we moved from Weiden to an attractive Bavarian town called Lauingen. Located on the left bank of the Danube, it was virtually untouched by the war. It also had a small contingent of American troops, which gave us a feeling of additional security.

Our accommodations in Lauingen were pleasant. We had an apartment in the center of town that had formerly been occupied by the assistant headmaster of the local high school. Food was available from the refugee camp managed by the UNRRA, which also provided additional food coupons if necessary. Still, everything was rationed, and currency was basically useless.

Altogether, our stay in Lauingen was a relaxing interlude, but we wanted a more permanent residence that also offered schooling. I had already missed more than a year of school, which was concerning to Mother, who highly valued education. My parents searched for another location under the UNRRA's jurisdiction. The camps would assure us adequate shelter and a basic supply of food, but this time with a school.

The husband of one of Mother's old friends had been elected as the head of a Latvian DP (displaced persons) camp in Kleinkötz, Bavaria, not far from Günzburg. This camp housed several hundred Latvian refugees who planned to start a school. The new location would bring us closer to our friends and give us some permanency. Because we were late arrivals, our housing was not going to be great, but that was the least of our concerns. So, in late fall of 1945, we left Lauingen for Kleinkötz.

Kleinkötz

The camp at Kleinkötz formerly housed German troops and workers that serviced a nearby ammunition depot hidden in the woods. It consisted of several large barracks, as well as regular housing for the officers.

We were assigned a single large room in one of the barracks. The room accommodated the five of us and measured about thirty by thirty feet with little privacy. My parents unrolled their oriental rugs and hung them from the ceiling, thus creating their private space. I slept in the opposite corner of the room in the upper bunk, and my sister Peggy slept below me. Irene slept in the other corner of the room in her cot.

There was a pot-bellied stove in the corner that provided heat in the winter, and we used it to cook to supplement the meals we received from the central kitchen. In front of the window, there were two tables and chairs, which served as a dining area and a place for us to do our schoolwork. At the end of the barrack building, there were showers and other sanitary facilities.

Today, housing like that offered at Kleinkötz would call for an immediate investigation by some social service agency and would be condemned as inadequate for human habitation. Given the circumstances of the time, though, we were happy and better off than many others in post-war Germany. It was sad to occasionally see formerly prosperous East Germans scavenging through our dumps for extra scraps of food. The Bavarians did not like the Prussians and blamed them for the wars in which they were dragged. The locals wanted to enjoy their lifestyle—*Gemütlichkeit*—and drink beer at the inn.

Even though one main reason for our move to Kleinkötz was for us to find a school, when we arrived, there was none. Most of the Latvians who escaped to Germany represented the intellectual elite, which included many qualified teachers. They tried to start a school, which was difficult considering the circumstances—there were no textbooks, no library, and no laboratories for chemistry or physics. At first, there was not even enough paper for student notebooks. One of the more enterprising teachers collected German aircraft repair manuals with blank pages, which we used as our first notebooks. It took several months to get the school going, but it eventually started up. The camp authorities allocated part of a barrack to serve as the school, and carpenters erected partitions and built primitive school benches. The next obstacle was figuring out in which grade each student belonged—everyone had missed close to two years of education. Eventually, the allocation was made based on age and prior school record, when available.

School and studying did not require much of my time, so I looked for another activity during the winter months. One could not play sports outdoors. Another barrack was set aside for recreation, and there were two ping-pong (table tennis) tables. I took up the sport with a vengeance and played at least two hours a day, almost every day. After more than a year of playing, at age fourteen, I won the camp championship. Most likely, there was not very serious competition. Still, to keep this in perspective, one must remember that table tennis in post-World War II Europe was quite popular because there was no tennis, nor facilities for any indoor sports.

One day, I went with a friend to a nearby German town, Ichenhausen, and heard the clicking sound of table tennis. I walked into the building and found that it housed the local table tennis club. I was invited to play and easily defeated my first two opponents. Then, a pleasant-looking man in his late twenties introduced himself as Halla and asked me whether I would like to play with him. It turned out that he was the best player I had ever seen, and I lost.

I asked Halla where he learned to play such a superb game. Halla replied, "I was a gunner on a German bomber shot down over England and spent several years as a POW. The guards noticed that I was a good table tennis player and asked me to train them. So, I spent all the war years playing ping-pong in England!" Halla invited me back and became my friend and mentor. Even though I was young, I was invited to join the town table tennis team, which played in Division 3 of the local league. We had matches against teams from other towns every week. In the wintertime, I had a fun activity to do with my new German friends.

I learned from Halla not only how to improve my game but, even more importantly, its psychology. Halla told me,

If you reach a certain level of proficiency, table tennis becomes a brain game. If you are winning, continue to do the same, but do not get overconfident. You're on the road to victory—you do not need any advice! If you are behind, you must use your brain power. Never, ever believe that you have lost a match until the final score. There is always a chance for you to win! The best way to accomplish this is to put yourself in your opponent's frame of mind and try to anticipate his next move.

A year later, I had the opportunity to put this advice into practice. We were playing a decisive match to advance to the next division. Our opponents knew that no one could beat Halla, so they moved their best player to a lower slot, which meant he would play me. My opponent was excellent—at least ten years older and supremely self-confident. I barely managed to keep up with him, but at the end of the fifth set, I was down fifteen to twenty. My opponent only needed one point to win the match. I did have the serve, a slight advantage.

I mustered all my energy and remembered the advice given to me earlier: "Put yourself in your opponent's frame of mind and anticipate his next move!" It was clear that my opponent thought he had won and wanted to finish the game with a flourish to impress his friends in the audience. He was playing a gangly, relatively inexperienced teenager, who at this point probably did not know what to do. My opponent's best shot was a forehand slam, and as I expected, he used it right away—but missed. Then he thought, "Well, one error doesn't make much difference. I still have four chances." He unsuccessfully repeated the same slam! Now my opponent was slightly concerned and decided to try something different—a backhand slam, which also went awry. It was clear that he became nervous, and eventually I won the match!

After this experience, I always remembered Halla's advice: "Never give up. You can always win until the game is officially over. Your focus and determination combined with brain power will carry you toward success!" How true, even in life!

In the summer, after school was over, I looked for a new activity. In the center of the camp was a basketball court. The game intrigued me, even though I had never played it. I was fortunate, however, because one of Mother's relatives was married to a successful Latvian lawyer who, more than a dozen years earlier, had been a member of the Latvian Olympic Basketball Team. We became fast friends, and he taught me many of the moves.

As with table tennis, I started to practice daily, and a year later, I was invited to become a member of the camp's adult basketball team. I was still in my mid-teens. No doubt it helped that, at six feet two inches in height, I was one of the tallest members of the team; due to poor nutrition during the wartime years, others had not grown as rapidly. For my height, I had Mother's efforts to thank—she always ensured that we did not lack food.

I was so flattered by the invitation to join the team that I overlooked the fact that the basketball talent pool at the camp was rather limited. After a while, I even thought about a future career in basketball. "Who knows, maybe it could even lead to a U.S. college basketball scholarship!" Our team did reasonably well against other similar camps. Eventually, we were invited to regional tournaments and competed with other teams with players who were not only more experienced but taller. I then realized that my dreams of a basketball career had limited potential and decided that I should look for an another career path to bring me future success. Nevertheless, I continued to enjoy the game.

With other boys, I also explored an abandoned German ammunition depot in the nearby woods. We snuck into this guarded area and saw many blown-up bunkers with the remnants of scattered ammunition. When I saw this, I realized I had had enough of war and decided to focus on other activities.

In Latvia, my stepfather Christian was a successful landowner, serving on the boards of several local organizations. Now, over fifty years old, he had very little to do. Christian had always had an appreciation for art, and with the help of one of his friends, a well-recognized graphic artist, he began to make embossed leather albums. This undertaking required a great deal of skill and patience. Christian was fortunate to have original drawings made by his artist friend, which he then transposed onto the cover of the leather albums. He became quite good, and his works were displayed at the arts and crafts shows organized for American troops searching for quality souvenirs. These items sold well. Christian discovered another profession, which he not only enjoyed but also proved to be financially rewarding.

While the currency in Germany was still the Reichsmark, it had little purchasing power. The real currency was American cigarettes. At one time, the price of a pack of American cigarettes reached eighty Reichsmarks. For this amount, one could purchase a railroad ticket for travel close to one hundred miles. A carton of cigarettes was worth a small fortune.

I was intrigued by these opportunities and wondered how to take advantage of them. Soon I had a chance. My stepfather's artist friend—who later had a successful career at Disney Studios—was also an expert in wood inlays. He did not do the woodwork but prepared the original drawings. Other craftsmen, based on his designs, made wood inlay covers for jewelry boxes or decorative items. These items also sold well at the arts and craft shows.

With the help of my stepfather's artist friend, I started to make wood inlays too. This was a lengthy, complicated process that required a lot of patience and focus. I found it a new challenge. The process started with taking the artist's drawings and transferring them onto special parchment. Then, one had to trace each piece of the sketch to a different veneer that provided various colors. Then, each piece had to be precisely cut from the veneer and glued onto the piece of paper until the whole design could be put together like a jigsaw puzzle. This process required a lot of attention so each piece would fit perfectly to the next one.

To bring the design to life, one had to select different veneers to represent various colors. For instance, mahogany was red, birch was white, and there were many gradations of walnut and other exotic woods. One always had to have a supply of different veneers on hand—I had about thirty. After assembling the design, I glued it by applying pressure to the top of the jewelry box or decorative plate. Once the glue hardened, I sanded it with different grades of sandpaper to achieve a smooth surface. Then, later, I used linseed oil with pumice stone and other ingredients to finish the surface and ready it for polishing. Finally, when everything was ready, the object was polished with shellac and wood alcohol to give it a gloss. After several false starts, I was finally able to assemble attractive products that sold at the arts and craft shows. Now, I had a source of income, but I only took a part, with the rest going to the family.

While earlier I had only hoped to visit my sister Silvia, who lived in Berchtesgaden, now I could go on my own. After celebrating Christmas Eve with the family, on Christmas Day, I took a train to Berchtesgaden. Even though I was only in my mid-teens, I felt safe traveling alone on German trains.

The trip to Berchtesgaden on Christmas Day was lengthy—about five hours—and required several train changes. But I was excited and looked forward to seeing my sister and her family, which now included a baby daughter. At first, the train went through the typical Bavarian countryside, but later in the evening, as we approached the Alps, the scenery became breathtaking. To thoroughly enjoy the view, I stepped out into the cold on the platform between the cars. The sky was crystal clear, full of bright stars with a reflection that was multiplied by the adjoining mountains covered with snow. The homes near the train, with their Christmas lights, sparkled as if someone had thrown a handful of jewels into the snow.

As I looked at the sky, I felt I was an insignificant part of an immense universe governed by a beauty beyond human comprehension. But I did not feel alone—after all, without the unwavering support and love of my family, I never would have been there to enjoy the beauty that surrounded me. I felt a guiding hand above helping me along.

After a walk from the train station, I reached my sister's apartment and received a warm welcome. The Christmas celebrations continued!

During the next years, I made several other visits to Berchtesgaden. Once, I was invited to travel there as a youth delegate to a conference sponsored by the World Council of Churches. On other occasions, I simply visited my sister and her family.

On these trips, we hiked the Alps and admired the crystal-clear beauty of the lake below, Königssee. We also climbed The Eagle's Nest, or *Kehlsteinhaus*, where Hitler and many of the leading Nazis had their summer homes. The buildings were destroyed by Allied bombing raids, but the views toward Austria remained magnificent. Locals said that Hitler remained an Austrian at heart because it was the place where he was born.

One of my goals was to take a boat trip on Königssee. As a child, I had heard from my parents that a crew member of the boat would play a stanza on a trumpet. The echo would reverberate from mountain to mountain many times over. Whether the trumpeter was good or bad, it did not matter—the echoes continued.

It's the same way in life—when we act, the echoes continue whether we want them to or not. That's why it's best to always start out on the right note!

We adjusted to life in Kleinkötz, and it was starting to become more interesting. Now there were traveling theater groups, concerts, athletic events, and other activities. School was easy for me, so I had free time besides sports and inlay work, and I was looking for other challenges. Because I now had some financial resources of my own, I joined many bus tours. These tours visited notable churches, monasteries, and other historic sites, plus all of Mad King Ludwig's castles. Quite an experience for a teenager!

Another one of my goals was to attend one of the Passion Plays staged in the Bavarian village of Oberammergau. The beginning of these performances dates back almost four hundred years, to 1634. At that time, the bubonic plague raged throughout the region, and most of the population perished. The residents of Oberammergau believed that God had saved them, and as a tribute, they decided to stage a play based on Jesus' life. Almost all the villagers participated, and the performance took place once every ten years. The play lasted close to five hours, with an intermission for lunch. Initially, the Passion Play began as a religious tribute, but by that time, the performances had become a popular cultural event that attracted large audiences.

No one was interested in joining me, so one day, with my ticket in hand, I took an early train from Kleinkötz to Munich and then on to Oberammergau. I wanted to make sure I would arrive before 10 AM, when the play started. It was a spectacular setting. The stage was in a shell outdoors, with the audience in a large hall reminiscent of an aircraft hangar. From the seats, we could see the performance and the Alps beyond. A wonderful sight!

By 1950, our memories of World War II faded, and we looked for a location where we could restart our lives. Some friends and family had gone to Australia to be as far as possible from any communist threat. We chose to immigrate to the United States—it stood for freedom and allowed people to achieve their personal goals with minimal government interference. It also offered the best educational opportunities. In the United States, we also felt safe from the Soviet threat. A distant relative (my basketball mentor) had settled in Boston and helped us obtain the necessary documents. So, Boston was our next destination.

John H. Livens
to the U.S.A. 1950

The immigration process was painstakingly slow and involved background checks, physicals, and other bureaucratic red tape. To complete it, we had to move to Augsburg, another city in Germany. After several months, everything was finally in order, and we took the train to Bremerhaven to board a ship bound for the United States of America.

CHAPTER 7

NEW LIFE IN THE USA

To the USA

After almost five years in Germany, in October of 1950, we boarded the USS *General Harry Taylor*, a converted troop transport ship bound for the United States.

Before departing from Bremerhaven, the ship's crew served a huge dinner of spaghetti topped with meatballs in a rich tomato sauce, followed by an unlimited supply of vanilla ice cream. After this feast, the ship sailed into the stormy North Sea.

I stood on the deck and watched the shores of Europe disappear into the distance, wondering what lay ahead. It was a different feeling from when we left Latvia because, at that time, our hope was to return and resume our normal life. Now, we were leaving Europe for good, and we did not know what the future held for us in the New World.

My thoughts were interrupted when I saw passengers running to the edge of the ship due to seasickness. Many of them did not make it, and there was spaghetti all over the deck. I did not get seasick myself, but after this experience, I have never eaten spaghetti again.

After the ship passed through the English Channel, the seas became calmer and the voyage more relaxing. We learned that the trip was going to be longer than expected—our first stop was New Orleans (where we were not allowed to disembark), and from there, we would proceed to New York. The captain requested that all able-bodied men help the crew for a few hours a day. My assignment was in the food storage area, where we moved frozen supplies from large storage freezers, reapportion them, and deliver them to the central kitchen. I worked a few hours every other day. It broke up the routine of the monotonous journey and added a new experience.

I worked with three to four merchant sailors. They were in their early twenties and enjoyed practical jokes—one day, they locked one of the fellows into a walk-in freezer and pretended that all of us had gone away. The poor guy banged on the door, freezing. We let him out, and everybody had a good laugh afterward. The work also gave me an opportunity to practice my English. The crew also occasionally treated me to Coca-Cola—a delicacy, as it was not available in Germany, except in military installations.

Before the ship reached New York, I was given a commendation certificate for the fine work that I had done. This was the first time in my life that I had had to work. Even as a child, everything had been done for me. This experience gave me a feeling of confidence, a belief that I could handle anything that came along. It was a good omen for our new life in the United States.

We docked in New York and were met by Latvian friends from Kleinkötz who preceded us. They lived in a fourth-floor walk-up apartment on the Upper East Side, in a neighborhood that showed signs of deterioration. This did not matter to us because we were only there for a short time. The next day, with our friends, we went to Times Square. It was a true spectacle, full of flashing bright neon lights that I had never seen nor even imagined. At that time in Europe, there were hardly any neon lights that approached this magnitude. The next afternoon, with our friends, we visited a coffee house on 86th Street where everyone spoke German. It felt like we had never left Europe, except the pastries were superior. Continuously, I was impressed with the diversity and freedom in the United States. People here did not even have passports, nor any identifying papers. A different land and culture indeed!

My parents went to Boston to find a place where we could live. Mother, who spoke English, was able to rent us the first floor of a house just off Beacon Street in Brookline, Massachusetts. The requirements were that all of us had to work because we had limited financial resources.

I started my job a few days later. It was near the South Station, and I received minimum wage. The company cut and distributed various papers for wrapping gifts. My responsibility was to make sure the right product was packaged into the correct box and addressed properly. It was not a demanding job. During my free time, I read magazines or newspapers and underlined words I did not understand. Later in the evening, I would look them up in the dictionary.

My parents' goal was to find themselves positions that would allow my sister and me to continue our education. A few months later, through friends and a church connection, Mother found work that met these requirements. My parents accepted positions that were below their capability levels, but they did so to enable our school attendance. Mother had never worked in her life, except for supervising her country estate, but she never complained about her job.

My parents' willingness to sacrifice so that we could have a better education was a powerful expression of love and devotion. I have always been grateful and admire their commitment to assuring the future success of the family. Without my parents' support, I would not be here. Later in life, this made it more difficult for me to understand the somewhat distant relationships that many American families have among their members. I only hope we have not lost sight of the fundamental values that provide so many opportunities to those who seek them.

Framingham

After my parents accepted their new positions, we moved to Framingham Center, Massachusetts. We settled into a cottage on the estate of Henry S. Dennison, whose father founded one of the largest manufacturing companies in the area. His plant took up several blocks of Framingham and employed thousands of people. There were other plants in nearby towns.

The Dennisons purchased an entire hill and built a mansion at the top. On a clear day, one could see the outline of Boston almost twenty miles away. My stepfather's responsibility was to take care of the grounds of the estate, and he could hire outside contractors if required. Because he enjoyed the outdoors, it was a good fit for him. Mother cared for the younger Dennison family and their daughters.

The Dennisons were a very considerate family and made us feel welcome. The "old" Mrs. Dennison volunteered to give me lessons in English—while this helped, it was even more significant to see their genuine concern that I would succeed on my own. Where else could one find such an effort but in the United States.

As we settled into our new home, Mother invited several friends over for tea. I heard one of the ladies say, "Irma [Mother] seems to be repeating the same pattern as her mother, who after having completed a Teacher's Institute, served for a few years as a governess to a noble Russian family." The other lady replied, "On her husband's side [my father's], the same is true. His distant relative, the widowed Baroness von Lieven, became governess to the Czar's family. Her ward unexpectedly became Czar Nicholas I and rewarded her with more titles and a fortune." Personally, I did not care about the past and was only interested in finishing Framingham High School.

In January of 1951, Mother, with my sister and me, headed to Framingham High School. The principal looked at my transcripts and shook his head. He saw that the both of us had missed about two years of school, and the current year was already half over. The principal did not know what to do with us. After thinking it over, he decided to put me into the last term with the senior class so that I could improve my English and then repeat the same grade next year. Then, I would be ready for college. It was an opportunity, but I did not like the idea of repeating a year!

I started high school the following week. It was a strange feeling. The social sciences and humanities were not difficult, but because my English was poor, I could not fully understand the lessons. The headmaster anticipated this and thought that language would not be a problem in the sciences, so he put me in a physics class. He overlooked the fact that I had never taken physics before, nor had I ever been in a physics or chemistry laboratory. The sciences turned out to be the most difficult courses for me.

Because I had played basketball, I was asked to join one of the practice sessions. The quality of basketball was much higher than in Europe, and to be a proficient player, I needed considerable additional practice. Improving in basketball would take time, which I did not have.

After returning home, I made a major decision. I decided to give up everything, including socializing and sports, to concentrate on studying. From the past, I knew that I could memorize volumes of information, even if I did not fully understand the content. This was the time to take full advantage of my talent. The next few months were not much fun, but I made progress and received support from Mother, whose English was fluent.

I have never forgotten one occasion, at Easter, when, with the Dennisons, Mother attended a performance of Handel's *Messiah* and left at intermission to come home and help me with an English essay. Mother was always there when I needed help. Perhaps, even today, she is looking over my shoulder. I was never afraid of falling short of my goals, no matter how high they were. If I failed, I knew my family support was unwavering. The worst, in my opinion, is to be passive and not strive for your goals. To me, that is failure that can never be corrected.

As the school year unfolded, I made good progress. I also had free time for extra work. One of my neighbors asked me to help expand his lawn and remove brush. The next day, the neighbor called, concerned because he contracted extensive ivy poisoning and worried that I had the same problem. I told him that I was hardly affected, and from that point on, he and other neighbors paid me extra to remove poison ivy from their property.

By this point, there was no doubt that I would not have to repeat the school year, and in fact, it seemed I would graduate with honors. In this regard, I recall an incident which brought more teachers' attention.

History has always been one of my favorite subjects. In high school, I was intrigued by American history, even though I had no prior knowledge. On a final history test, I missed a question. The question was "Did General Frémont participate in the establishment of the state of California after the Mexican-American War?" My answer was "No"—I felt it was a trick question. The teacher's response was that this was a standard test, and

I was wrong. Because I could recall a lot of information, I pointed out that the question was right in one sense—as it related to the beginning of California in 1846—but at that time, Frémont was only a major in the U.S. Army, not a general. Frémont received his general's commission from President Abraham Lincoln in 1862 after the start of the Civil War. By speaking up for accuracy, I must have scored points because the school changed the test question, and I got a favorable recommendation from the teacher.

Because I was going to graduate with honors, I talked to a placement counselor about colleges. While I wanted the best (Harvard), the counselor said that would be a high hurdle because my secondary school educational record was incomplete, and my English was not good enough. The counselor suggested Boston University instead, as it had a large contingent of foreign students and would be a good steppingstone to graduate school. I completed the applications and was ready to go to Boston for an interview. Mr. Dennison heard about my plan and said, "Do not bother to take the bus to Boston. I will drive you there and wait for you until the interview is over!" So, I was driven to Boston by the Chairman of the Board of Dennison Manufacturing Company, who sat in the parking lot and waited for me while I completed my college interview. Mr. Dennison and other individuals like him, who showed confidence in my potential and were willing to reach out, were an inspiration. Their commitment gave me extra incentive to succeed—I did not want to let them down. My interview and school record were good, and I received a scholarship to Boston University.

To College

I graduated from Framingham High School in June 1951. High school was over, and I had to look for a summer job to finance my first year of college. Mr. Dennison suggested that I work in his manufacturing company and assigned me to a department that made tags and labels. I started work right after school.

Being in a manufacturing plant was a new experience for me, and it was entirely different from what I expected. The employees were mostly older women who used wooden mallets to punch metal dies, which then produced various forms of tags and labels. I had thought jobs like that were automated a long time ago, but traditions worked well at Dennison Manufacturing. It was my job to consolidate the finished product and turn it over to the shipping department for distribution. What I found surprising was that the old ladies on the factory floor were content and had high praise for the management of the harmonious labor relations— there were no unions. The employees considered the plant to be their second home, and they could not have been more pleasant to me. It contradicted what I had been led to believe manufacturing was all about.

In the summer, I had more free time, so I could swim and enjoy other social activities. Most of my friends were Latvian-Americans who knew my parents. I interacted with very few fellow students from the high school because they struck me as immature and seemed years younger than me. We had little in common.

My first year at BU passed quickly. The required freshman courses were routine, but my selected courses were far more challenging. I studied hard, and as part of the scholarship, I worked several hours a week in the school cafeteria. All these responsibilities limited my social life, but I considered myself most fortunate to be there.

At the end of the school year, I was surprised to receive the prestigious Professor Augustus H. Buck Scholarship, which, according to BU, is "The highest academic honor bestowed on undergraduates… for good character and exceptional future potential." The scholarship covered not only all my undergraduate expenses but also two years of graduate study. I felt honored, and my financial problems were over. Nevertheless, I eagerly looked for more challenges.

I looked at my life as a ladder with many steps. First, to start the climb, I had to be proactive and select the right ladder from many choices. I relied on individual intuition, prior research, and good advice—but the ultimate decision was mine alone. I would bear all the consequences of failure or success. I knew my goal was far away, and I could only see its outline ahead, not all the details. To move forward, I focused all my attention on the next step.

In my case, the next step was to learn English, go to college, and maybe then to Harvard. I may have missed part of my life along the way, but I knew that once I reached my goal, the reward would be even sweeter. I never looked back—the higher you are up the ladder, the dizzier you become when looking down. While it was not always easy to make the next step, the challenge made life exciting, and with each step of progress, I gained more confidence.

I knew that in life major opportunities, such as getting an excellent education, did not come along frequently, and they disappeared if not pursued. This was recognized almost a thousand years ago by the Persian poet Omar Khayyam, who in the *Rubaiyat* wrote:

"The moving finger writes and having writ—nor all your piety or wit *Shall lure it back, to cancel half a line.*"

Why not seize opportunity when it presents itself and do your very best to reach your goal? To not rise to the occasion is perhaps the greatest failure of all! One could gain more satisfaction by having tried and failed than remaining a passive bystander.

With these thoughts in mind, I contacted the Harvard College Admissions Office about a transfer, even though I risked losing my excellent scholarship at Boston University. I received the application, but it came with little encouragement—Harvard considered very few transfer students. After completing the application, I was granted an interview with the Harvard College Dean of Admissions, Wilbur Bender. This appointment was comparable to an ordinary mortal being invited to meet with St. Peter, guardian of the Pearly Gates. The primary difference in my eyes was that heaven was far away and inaccessible, while Dean Bender was just a short distance away in Cambridge.

On the day of my appointment, I arrived at University Hall in Harvard Yard. Note that there is no campus at Harvard—the grass area around the buildings is called the Yard (it was a pasture during colonial times for grazing cattle). As expected at an Ivy League college, University

Hall was covered with ivy. Unfortunately, succeeding generations of administrators removed all the ivy, thus destroying a tradition. College administrators like to leave their mark behind—whether that's by destroying old traditions or implementing their own policies (which usually do not enhance the reputation of the institution). At least it helps their egos because they left a mark behind.

After a short wait, I entered Dean Bender's office. He pointed to a chair, which of course had the Harvard emblem on its back. He gave me a penetrating glance, as if he wanted to see my inner soul. There was nothing for him to see there, except determination to succeed! He had a grave look, like he knew that he was very important—and he was. Like many others in those days, the dean wore a three-piece suit with a gold watch chain across his vest, to which all kinds of symbols were attached. One of them looked like a Phi Beta Kappa key. The others were probably more important, but I was not yet initiated into the ways of Harvard and thus could not fully understand their significance.

Dean Bender opened the interview with a standard question: "Why do you want to come to Harvard?" I responded with a well-rehearsed answer about seeking a challenge, excellence, experiencing the very best—qualities that only Harvard could offer. I am sure the dean had heard all those answers before. Then he went on to ask, "Why do you want to leave BU? You have a full scholarship there that covers all your expenses. You could come here for graduate school." My reply was that I wanted the best education possible—now.

The dean told me he could not be very encouraging because hundreds of students applied for transfers, but very few were admitted. While getting into Harvard College as a freshman is difficult, transferring in is exponentially harder. Incoming class sizes are limited, and once admitted, very few students leave—transfer students can fill only those open positions. Currently, about four percent of applicants are admitted in each incoming class. But for transfer applicants, less than one percent are accepted. Extraordinary luck, or some higher power, must be at work for those who are among the select few.

Also, there were hardly any scholarships available for transfer students—all had to prove their ability at Harvard, which had higher standards than other schools. The dean went on to say, "I know you earned all As at Boston University, but of course you understand that is barely equivalent to a B at Harvard!" I nodded in full agreement and said I would do my very best, no matter the challenge. Dean Bender added that preference was given to transfer students who had previously applied to Harvard but could not attend due to health or family reasons. I left the interview not exactly encouraged, but I had done my best, which satisfied me. If I had not tried, that would have been the real failure!

From Cambridge, I headed directly to downtown Boston to see a western cowboy movie. This kind of distraction, full of action, always cleared my mind. It put the past behind me and prepared to face the next challenge. Besides, in the western movies, the good guys with the white hats always win—so maybe there was a chance for me?

Harvard

In early spring, I was notified of my admission to Harvard College.

I received full credit for my studies at Boston University and was advised to contact the Financial Aid Office to work out the details of a small scholarship. At that time, scholarships were awarded based on academic merit, rather than financial need. Because I transferred from another institution, my past academic record was not of great significance. The arrangements also required that I maintain at least a B average, and besides, I had to work several hours a week. As I added up the figures, it still was not quite enough to cover one academic year's worth of expenses.

This financial arrangement was much worse than my prior scholarship situation at Boston University. I talked to Mother about my concerns, but she told me, "Don't worry, we will manage somehow!" Years later, I learned that Mother borrowed money from friends to make my first year at Harvard possible. Mother never told me this because she probably felt that it would put additional pressure on me and interfere with my studies. I already knew that I had to get good grades right away or my financial aid would be gone, and that would—at least temporarily—be the end of my college career.

My next step was to look for a well-paying summer job. Fortunately, with the help of a family friend, I found one—at the Perini Construction Company, as an assistant to a surveyor/engineer. The work was pleasant and interesting and paid well. After a week, a man introduced himself as a union representative. He told me I had taken a union job, and because

I was not a member and could not become one, I should leave. I told him, "No union man has been looking for this job, and I need to make enough to pay for college!" That apparently did not matter to him, and I was terminated. Unlimited union power was the first injustice I saw in the United States.

Thus, I had to find another job on short notice. The only one available was at Framingham Landscape Company—it paid minimum wage and required long hours without any overtime pay. I had no choice and took the job.

Initially, I dug ditches used as the foundation for stone walls. We traveled to different locations, which gave us occasional respite. Except for a few professionals, the work crew mainly consisted of people who would work for a few days and then use the funds to drink. They only returned sometimes. They were not great company, but it did not matter.

After a while, the manager saw that I was a dependable worker eager to earn more, so he assigned me to another job that no one else wanted— running a cultivator/plow from one end of the property to the other. It took a few weeks to finish the whole area, and when it was done, I had to start all over again. During the hot summer months, I stripped to the waist and walked behind the machine all day long with dust flying. There was so much dirt that the equipment occasionally broke down. I had to repair it, which gave me a small break. On some weekends, I had to clean the equipment without any overtime pay. After work, when I got home, I soaked in a bathtub for a long time to wash off the grime. It was not much fun, but it did not matter because I was working toward my goal of going to Harvard. The summer passed quickly, and before school, I finally took a week off to relax.

When I arrived at Harvard in the fall, I was assigned the smallest, and probably the cheapest, room at McKinlock Hall, Leverett House. The room had a bed, a desk, and not much else—it adjoined a larger room next door, but that door was locked. There was hardly even space to turn around. Years later, when I visited a monastery room in Palma Majorca (where Chopin composed), it looked palatial compared to my room at Harvard.

It was almost impossible to study in my room because the student in the room next door had placed his bed against the locked door and frequently thrashed around with his girlfriend. I only hope that subsequently the McKinlock Hall administration returned my room to its rightful use—a broom closet!

Fortunately, at Harvard, there were many other places I could study. One of them was the brand-new, state-of-the-art Lamont Library. The architects installed a supposedly environmentally correct fluorescent light, which generated a buzzing sound. I have never seen so many students asleep as I did in Lamont. Obviously, this option did not work for me.

Then I found the library at McKinlock Hall in my dormitory. It was a traditional setting—many bookshelves covered the walls, containing publications read by few, because most were not relevant to the current academic curriculum. At one end of the room was a beautiful, seventeenth-century Flemish tapestry depicting an imaginary rustic scene. As I sat studying at a long table in the center of the room, my eyes occasionally wandered to the tapestry—it reminded me that there was another world, one of beauty, outside the confines of academia. It was a pleasant distraction, and I returned to my work refreshed.

Years later, when I received my first significant partnership check, I purchased a similar Flemish tapestry that covered most of the wall of our Beacon Hill home. It reminded me that even if some struggles in life are demanding, the rewards, when they come later, are all the sweeter.

Before coming to Harvard, I studied its catalog carefully. I was amazed at the diversity of courses and quality of the teachers. Just their presence made Harvard a unique institution. It was an intellectual feast! I had always been interested in geopolitics, a field where most of the notable work had been done by Germans. There were very few outstanding American scholars, but one of them was Professor Whittlesey. I could not believe he was teaching a course at Harvard, which I could attend. There were only fifteen students in the class, and most of them were from the graduate school. At first, I was careful in selecting courses, but later, after talking to other students, I took the opportunity to further explore the rich academic feast that Harvard offered.

My scholarship required that I spend several hours a week working in a library. My assignment was Agassi's Library of Natural Resources. I filed obscure, dusty manuscripts about paleontology or fossils. Years later, I had a recurring nightmare on occasion—I worried that on some days, when I was tired and sleepy, I might misfile the publications. My fear was lessened by the fact that there was so little interest in these papers that, more than likely, no one would request them again for decades.

My social life was limited, but I still carried on. One weekend, I invited an attractive blonde for a movie and dinner. She was gorgeous, with long hair. The girl was extremely well endowed and wore a tight-fitting pink cashmere sweater with a pearl necklace, which further amplified her physical assets.

Because I was on a tight budget, I decided we would have dinner at my dormitory, the Leverett House dining room. On most weekends, there were not many students in the dining room. I timidly walked through the dining room serving line with my date and then looked for a quiet corner. Suddenly, the whole room exploded with applause. The lecherous eyes of my fellow students were focused on my date, who blushed. To minimize the embarrassment for both of us, I told her that this was Leverett House's way of expressing a warm welcome to visitors.

The next day, one of my classmates said, "No wonder I haven't seen you around much. I would do the same if I had a girlfriend like her!" I just smiled and did not say anything. He obviously had not looked in the McKinlock Hall library.

College Life

As the school year ended, my grades were good, so I knew that my scholarship was secure. For the first time, I could look for a fun summer job.

A private club in Centerville, Cape Cod, was looking for a student to work at the front desk. I interviewed with the club president. She appeared to be an intimidating lady, especially when she told me, "In the past, this job—as well as others—has been held by Dartmouth College ice hockey players. But now, since they are unavailable, I had to contact Harvard!" It was hard to believe she thought Dartmouth students better than Harvard, but I put up with it. I suggested to her that if she hired me, I could bring friends, and that would solve the staffing problem.

Mrs. Stuart turned out to be a fine person, and she understood college students quite well—her son was at Princeton. She told me that the club closed at 4 PM, and afterward we could host parties. Of course, the next morning, the entire area had to be in immaculate condition! This arrangement was great for a bunch of college students who just wanted to have fun—and we made sure to do so. During the summer, Cape Cod was full of college girls who liked to party, and now we had the place for it. For me, that summer was a welcome change from my many hours of dreary studying.

A hurricane came, and we all had to evacuate the premises. There was considerable water damage to the club, particularly to the wine and liquor cellar. It took us a few days to clean up the mess. During the hurricane, water flooded the basement, and many of the bottles lost their labels. The bartender asked Mrs. Stuart what to do. She replied, "We do not want to serve our guests unknown liquor or wine…discard the bottles!" Of course, that did not happen, and we had plenty of liquor for the rest of the summer. Most of the time, we did not know what we were drinking, but we knew it was high-quality stuff. Altogether, it was a happy summer and a sign of more fun to come.

After returning to Harvard, I attended several classes before making my final course selections. I discussed various options with my fellow students. One of them said that tenured Harvard professors are like cardinals in the Catholic Church—they rule their domain. I said that could not be entirely accurate because a cardinal still receives guidance from the Pope, but no one could give directions to a tenured Harvard professor—they were the bearers of ultimate truth! Many certainly acted that way.

Some skeptics, like Bill Buckley, doubted that. He wrote that if a person selected ten names at random from the Boston telephone book, these people would have more common sense than Harvard professors. It is up to you whether you want to believe a Yale graduate on this issue! To update these observations, one may look at recent Yale graduates, particularly those from its Law School, who have held prominent positions in the U.S. government. These individuals have shown even less common sense. In fact, ten people selected at random from the New Haven telephone directory would probably have done better (keep in mind that the New Haven telephone directory is less than one-third the size of Boston's).

Anyway, as I selected my main courses, I looked for easy options that would allow me to devote more time to my thesis. I found one—Canadian History, given by Professor Cherrington, who was known for his sharp wit and humor. The professor liked to tell the story that early Canadian missionaries, who were Catholics, were primarily interested in shacking up with the local Indian maidens, not bringing religion to the heathens. After hearing these remarks, several of the Radcliffe girls (female Harvard students) walked out of the lecture—mission accomplished! It looked like this class was going to be fun, would not require much work, and would lighten up the academic year.

Unfortunately, my expectations did not turn out. A month into the course, when one could no longer drop it, Professor Cherrington said that the dean learned that he was too easy on grading and sent a teaching assistant to do it. With this, he introduced a serious and nerdy-looking young man. The new teaching assistant skeptically glanced at the class through thick eyeglasses that resembled the bottoms of Coca-Cola bottles, as if he were selecting his victims. I knew right away that this was not going to be easy anymore! Even though I had little interest in Canadian history, I ended up getting an overdose. The lesson I learned here is that in life, when you become overconfident and expect that the past will repeat itself, do not count on it—you must be prepared for the unexpected!

Regardless, I not only enjoyed my selection of courses, but my living conditions improved as well. I now shared a small suite on a top floor with five other students. We had a living room with three adjoining bedrooms. It was a fun group of new friends. The most enterprising of them, Jack, somehow secured a player piano—though I never could figure out how he got it up to the fourth floor. One of our other suitemates managed to get a vacuum cleaner and rigged it up with the player piano. All we had to do was throw a switch and the space flooded with terrible piano music.

My grades at Harvard were good, and I no longer worried about scholarships. One of my favorite courses was International Affairs, given by Dean George McGregor Bundy—a very important man indeed! There were more than one hundred students in the class, and I was surprised to be invited for a thesis interview with the dean himself. Perhaps this was *noblesse oblige*, but whatever it was, it was an honor. It was like being invited to a preliminary visit with the Good Lord Himself. Dean Bundy was not only a brilliant scholar but also a capable administrator—a rare combination. Despite the "handicap" of being a Yale graduate, McGregor Bundy—while still in his thirties—was made the Dean of Harvard Faculty.

On the day of my interview, I timidly entered the dean's office. Like all other important Harvard professors, he wore a three-piece suit and liked to stick his right hand into his vest, resembling a portrait of Napoleon. The dean inquired about my thesis, and when I told him it was about the German occupation policy in Eastern Europe, he said, "You know, Eastern Europe is not my bag. I will call the Russian Research Center and get you someone with whom you will enjoy working."

The Dean added that his interest and experience lay in American foreign policy. All of us knew he had written a highly acclaimed scholarly work on the former Secretary of War, Henry Lewis Stimson. The Stimson documents were not available to others, but because Dean Bundy was a relative, he had access. His work on the Stimson papers gained academic accolades. Dean Bundy's rapid advancement at Harvard was not hurt by the fact that he was related to another Boston family that was influential at Harvard. Regardless of the circumstances, Dean Bundy was a brilliant academician and administrator. He later served admirably as the National Security Advisor to President Kennedy and was partially responsible for resolving the Cuban missile crisis.

After leaving the dean's office, I immediately headed to the Harvard Russian Research Center, which was farther away. I walked into the Center and looked around. It had none of the trappings of Dean Bundy's office. A young man who looked like a graduate student came up and asked if he could help. I told him that I was sent by Dean Bundy to meet my senior thesis advisor. This man said, "The dean called and told me you would come!" He then introduced himself as Zbig Brezinski. After we got acquainted, he told me that his family escaped from Poland before its collapse, so he understood my interest in the area. We set up future meetings, and I knew this was the beginning of a valuable and intellectually stimulating relationship.

One of my first tasks was to prepare an outline and possible sources of original material. Because I did not know how to type, the wife of a Harvard instructor typed for me. The typist, with her husband and small baby, lived in a dingy half-basement apartment. Frequently, I could hear a baby crying in the background while we worked.

The young typist, who a few years before had been an attractive Wellesley student, now lived in these miserable conditions and worked to help supplement her family's income. I asked her, "How long are you going to be here, and where are you going next?" Her husband answered that he had a two-year contract as a teaching assistant and did not know where his next assignment would take them. His wife chimed in, "I just hope it's not some remote, godforsaken Midwest college!"

Through this experience, I saw firsthand that it was difficult to obtain academic appointments at Harvard or any of the other Ivy League colleges. Most young academicians started at some backwater institution and hoped for future advancement—only very few could do as well as Zbig had done. He not only had a brilliant mind but also a charismatic personality. I already looked at him as a role model, but now I understood that he was truly exceptional.

Zbig urged me to consider a career in academia, but I was becoming less sure that this was the right path to follow. After all, my goal was to be able to attain a comparable lifestyle to what my family and I enjoyed before. Thus, my seemingly inconsequential encounter with the typist turned out to be a life-changing event and influenced my career decisions down the line. One never knows when major turning points will come along or how to tackle them. Knowledge does not reside only in books—it also comes from people, particularly those with relevant experience. It is up to us to recognize opportunity when it comes and apply it to our lives.

With Zbig's recommendation, my acceptance into Harvard Graduate School was easy, but I also applied to Harvard Law School, Harvard Business School, and the business school at Massachusetts Institute of Technology (MIT Sloan School of Management). I decided to make my final decision later.

After reviewing my thesis outline with Zbig, he suggested that the best research material for me would be at the Congressional Library in Washington. It contained publications issued by the German governing bodies, as well as the local authorities. Because I spoke two other languages besides English, I could access and understand the original material.

Mother arranged for me to stay with a friend in Washington. She also contacted a family friend, Professor Spekke, who was the Latvian Ambassador to the United States. Even though Latvia had remained under Soviet occupation for the previous fifteen years, the U.S. government did not recognize this, so the embassy was still functioning. The ambassador was a former history professor and could be of help on my thesis.

I also contacted our family friend, Mr. Zagers, who had come to the United States and now taught economics at Gettysburg College. I returned with a wealth of information. Zbig was favorably impressed and told me that I was a solid candidate for a *magna cum laude* honors degree.

It did not turn out that way because my academic work hit a bump in the road to success—the obstacle came in the form of an attractive Wellesley student, who I met through my sister, also a student there. The young lady was cheerful and friendly and invited me for frequent weekend visits. I enjoyed being at Wellesley College during the spring season, and it also gave me a chance to see my sister Peggy.

I always adored my younger sister, even though in many ways she was perfect—always well behaved and grades never less than A or A+. In Welleslu College my sister encountered a major crisis when she received the first B in her life. Peggy continued to do well, and at age twenty-three, from the University of Wisconsin she received a Ph.D. in biochemistry. She also met her future husband in a very romantic place—the chemistry laboratory. I never knew that love could sprout in a chemistry lab, but it sure worked in their case. They had a long and happy marriage. Both became recognized scientists and, in their thirties, delivered incomprehensible scientific papers all over the world.

My weekends at Wellesley continued to be a fun diversion for me. One day, one of my roommates asked, "What did you do at Wellesley?" I told him about my walks and about attending concerts and other events. He asked, "Where did you walk?" I replied, "Around the lake." He went on to ask, "How many times around the lake?" I replied, "Two, and we are planning another next weekend." My suitemate asked whether I knew the Wellesley tradition—after you walk with a girlfriend around the lake three times, if you do not ask her to marry you, she has the right to push you into the water. I did not want to take a swim, nor was I ready to make any permanent commitments; the relationship soon ended, and I went back to work. I graduated with a *cum laude* degree, which was still good considering that there was no grade inflation—and I had a lot of fun.

I was satisfied and thoroughly enjoyed my last year at Harvard College. I missed the company of Zbig but was glad to learn that shortly afterward, he became the head of the Russian Research Center at Columbia University. Eventually, he served with distinction as a National Security Advisor to President Carter.

In the spring, I learned that I was admitted to almost all the schools to which I applied, but I had not yet heard from the Harvard Business School. Only about fifteen percent of applicants were admitted. This intrigued me. I telephoned the Admissions Office and was told that my application was still under consideration. The problem was that I was only twenty-one years old, and the average age of the incoming class members was twenty-nine. Almost all the other applicants had work or military experience.

I told the admissions official that I too had varied work experience. The official politely agreed but noted that I worked on a factory floor, dug ditches for a landscape company, served as a lifeguard, and worked at private clubs. He went on to say that at the business school, they were looking for managerial experience. He recommended that I come back in two years. I responded, "I have decided to go directly from college to graduate school. If you do not take me, I am going to Harvard Law School, where I have already been admitted." That was the end of the conversation, and I did not know what to expect next.

Harvard Law School now appeared to be a viable option. I was not overwhelmed because most students there looked to me to be sanctimonious. They seemed to have an attitude of superiority and felt that, with their knowledge of the law, they knew what was best for the average person. They believed that elected representatives did not know what was good for the public, and they, as judges, would legislate from the bench.

Many students aspired to become a clerk of a famous judge. To me, this assignment seemed to be a passive support position with no decision-making power. The truly anointed ones focused on the U.S. Supreme Court, where there was a disproportionate number of seats reserved for Harvard Law School graduates. Lawyers in the business world did better, but the most successful were the "rainmakers"—those who brought in new business. Unfortunately, this was an area in which I did not have much interest.

I liked the Harvard Graduate School Ph.D. program, but this career path had lost its appeal for me. The MIT Business School was a good option, but it was mathematically oriented. (Years later, my son got an MBA from MIT.) I decided to wait until I heard back from the Harvard Business School to make my decision.

Two weeks after my call to the Admissions Office, I was admitted.

Sometimes, friends ask me if there is anything I would have done differently. My answer is that if I had had the resources and the time, I would have gotten a joint degree from the Harvard Business School and the Harvard Law School. While law was intellectually intriguing to me, the more tangible benefit would have been to never pay the frequently unjustified and overpriced bills for legal services.

CHAPTER 8

LIFE AFTER COLLEGE

The Harvard Business School

After graduating from college in 1955, I did not have to search for a summer job again—I already had one lined up thanks to my enterprising suitemate, Jack. He was the assistant manager of Club Casablanca, an upscale, well-known bar frequented by the academic elite and their hangers-on.

The club was located below the Brattle Theatre in Cambridge, where a Shakespearean festival was staged that summer. The producer and the actors were former Harvard graduates who achieved fame in the theatrical world. The tips were good—no group of people is more sympathetic to striving students than artists who have attained success. Furthermore, the festival attracted many female summer school students. I rented an apartment from a professor and experienced a fun-filled summer. It was a pleasant interlude before heading to business school in the fall.

At the beginning of summer, I would work past midnight and then attend parties with my work mates. I soon realized, however, that after hours of work, parties were not much fun. My routine became sleeping late in the morning and then taking some books with me to spend the rest of the day on the beach. I'd return in the late afternoon for work. I purchased books on business and finance to read, but frankly, they were no beach reading.

It was a pleasant summer. Sometimes I'd sail on the Charles River. I also visited my parents, who moved to a new home in Natick, Massachusetts, next to a small pond. It was a delight to be with them then—there was no stress about scholarships anymore, and we again had a home of our own. Mother missed her relationship with the Dennisons, particularly their children, of whom she was quite fond. She kept in touch with the Dennison family for many years and saw them at the Boston Symphony Orchestra, where she had season tickets.

The summer ended quickly, and I headed to Harvard Business School (HBS) later in 1955. It was a different environment from my undergraduate experience—everyone focused on practical problems, instead of ideas and concepts. In the first year, we had a pre-set curriculum that offered few options. In the beginning, HBS threw an inordinate amount of information at students, knowing full well that not all of it could be absorbed. The lesson was that one should learn early on how to set priorities and, by doing so, exercise judgment.

The average age of the incoming class was more than seven years older than me. They all had prior management experience, but for many years, they had been away from any sort of rigorous academic work. Because many of them were married, it was a significant change from their former lifestyle. As a result, the attrition rate for the first year at HBS was close to ten percent, while for the Harvard Law School, it was only two percent.

In the evenings, to have a short break from studying, I often walked on the John W. Weeks Footbridge, which crossed the Charles River and ended near my former college dormitory. I remember one night standing on the bridge, admiring the shimmering lights of Boston in the distance, and I thought how lucky I was to be in that place. At Harvard College, with its emphasis on ideas and concepts taught by an exceptional faculty, my horizons greatly expanded. At that moment, I felt as if I were standing on top of a mountain and could see farther and more clearly where the various paths were leading.

On the other side of the river was the HBS, which provided its students with the best tools to succeed in the practical world. It trained us to assess situations quickly and to understand the various options available. One of the characteristics of the modern world is rapid change, which makes the ability to respond promptly essential. I may not have fully understood the value of my HBS education at that time, because I had limited business experience, but gazing at that scene, I knew that I was most fortunate to receive the best education possible on both sides of the Charles River—Harvard College and Harvard Business School. They both made a significant difference in my life.

After my thoughts that night, I headed back to my studies with the reassurance that I was on the right path, and the future was likely to bring me pleasant surprises.

The volume of work at HBS did not bother me because I was used to long hours of studying. I could memorize data, so my grades were good. Even so, I did not fully understand some of the material. All the students participated in discussion groups, during which pending cases were reviewed. Though part of a study group, I was not an active participant—I did not have any significant managerial experience to share. I continued to attend my discussion group but preferred to study on my own.

One day, I talked to a fellow student about this problem. He told me, "I did not have any business experience before HBS either, but I know something about human nature and motivation. Since this is my strong point, I can contribute something to the study group." I asked him how he gained this knowledge without being in the business world. My new friend introduced himself as Steve Covey and said that after college, he served as a Mormon missionary abroad. He went on to tell me that one had to understand human nature to be able to portray religious ideas.

Steve was one of the most positive people I met at school, and we became friends. Steve invited me, as a guest, to his study group. I went but still preferred to study on my own. I was not surprised years later when Steve Covey became a celebrated management guru. His book, *The 7 Habits of Highly Effective People*, sold more than twenty million copies.

The school year passed quickly. Toward the end of the spring semester, I received a notification that the local military draft board classified me as

1A. I did not take this seriously—the Harvard hubris rubbed off on me. I thought, "How dare they draft anybody from Harvard!" Unfortunately, the draft board did not share my opinion, and the draft was set to call me up in July or August.

Two years as a private in the Army certainly sounded bad to me. I went to my academic advisor, and he said there was a program through which I could obtain a direct officer's commission in the Army Quartermaster Corps. This assignment sounded boring! I remembered that my friend Richard encountered a similar problem and signed onto the Naval Officer Candidate School in Newport, Rhode Island. The OCS sounded like a good solution, so I went to the Navy recruiting office and thought my problem was solved. Unfortunately, that was not the case—all the classes were full until the middle of September, and the draft would get me before then.

I now faced a real dilemma. As I was leaving the Navy recruiting office, a visiting officer in a khaki uniform with gold wings above his left breast asked me what had happened. I told him the story. He said there was another Navy OCS program in Pensacola, Florida, but their requirements were very tough. If I was accepted, I would receive a deferment right away. He went on to tell me that candidates had to be in excellent health and very physically fit with perfect eyesight. Marine drill instructors ran the program, and they were tough. If you failed to finish, you became a Navy sailor and "probably for the next four and a half years would be swabbing decks on a destroyer in some godforsaken place."

On the other hand, if you completed the four and a half months, you received an officer's commission and entered the Navy flight training program. He turned to me and asked, "Have you ever thought of flying?" All I could say was no because I had never been in an airplane. The officer said, "Think it over and come back to me with your answer." I immediately told him, "I've made up my mind. I accept this deal!" He turned to me and said, "You already passed the first test. We like decisive people!" Then he turned to a Navy clerk and told him, "Get this man's papers ready and make sure he gets a deferment." Considering the circumstances, I made the right choice. I passed the tests and started my Navy service, which proved to be one of the most exciting periods of my life.

As the school year ended, I looked for a summer job. Unlike my classmates, who headed for the business world, I wanted a job where I could relax and get in good physical shape before the Navy. I found one at a private club in Connecticut. It was located on the Long Island Sound, so I could swim and take long runs. It was also easy to travel back to Boston or New York. As soon as the school year ended, I started work and helped ready the club for opening. The other workers were mostly college students who wanted a fun summer.

On my first day, I met one of the most attractive and interesting girls I had ever encountered. Ann was vivacious, bright, and charming—I would run out of adjectives if I attempted to describe my vision of her. To me, she was perfection. Even better, it appeared that she was also interested in me.

I spent as much time as I could with Ann. It was an intoxicating experience. My perception of her was probably amplified by the summer sunshine on Long Island Sound, which looked so much brighter after my many dreary hours of studying at business school. This relationship appeared to be the beginning of a summer romance! While at this time I probably viewed the world through rose-colored glasses, my perception of Ann was not far off. Years later, one of her Smith College classmates told me that Ann was one of the most attractive girls in her class. At least my judgment was still sound!

After work, Ann and I took a stroll on the beach or sat on a rock, sometimes holding hands and admiring the beauty around us. As was appropriate for thoughtful collegians in those days, we talked about how this setting, with its flickering lights on the sea, inspired F. Scott Fitzgerald to write *The Great Gatsby*.

I thought that time and distance would not affect my relationship with Ann and expected it to continue. Our relationship did not progress much beyond kisses and warm embraces—Ann was a strict Catholic, and those were traditional times. Nevertheless, it was the beginning of a wonderful romantic relationship with great future promise. It was a flawless start—but as I had already learned, even when things seem to be going well, life can be full of surprises.

After a few weeks on the job, the club manager told me that the son of one of the members wanted my desk job. I would now work part-time as a *maître d'*, or head waiter. I felt that was unacceptable, as it was contrary to our original agreement, so I quit, even though I wanted to be with Ann. It was a difficult choice and a sad parting.

Even though my relationship with Ann proved to be brief, it continued to expand in my dreams. Ann remained a bright star upon whom I could always turn, no matter where I was. Our relationship was a warm comfort to my heart as I faced the uncertainty of military service. Later, when I dated other girls, I always measured them against Ann, who had become an unsurpassable standard in my mind. Perhaps in a brief "summer fling," you simply do not have time to see the faults of the other person. In this case, it did not matter because both of us were happy and hoped to be together again.

During my summer job search, I received another offer from an inn in East Hampton, Long Island, so I immediately headed there. My job behind the desk was pleasant, but most of the other employees were professionals so there was little social life for me. I had plenty of time in the mornings to take long runs on the beach, swim, and do push-ups (there were no gyms in those days). Ann and I frequently wrote to each other and hoped to spend more time together in the future. She still had one year left at Smith College.

Before the summer was over, the Navy required me to sign the final documents in person. From Long Island, I needed to take the train to New York, then on to Boston, and afterward, return to Long Island. The owner of the inn, Mr. Bradley, with whom I got along well, offered to fly me to Boston instead. He said, "John, as you know, I own a private plane [a Navion]. I will fly you directly to Boston, and that will save you a great deal of time." A most generous offer, which I immediately accepted.

On the appointed day, we drove to East Hampton Airport and boarded Mr. Bradley's plane. He also invited his girlfriend to come along for the ride. It was my first flight in an airplane, and the scenery below Long Island and the shores of Connecticut was spectacular—until, a little later, we found ourselves above a thick, overcast sky. Mr. Bradley contacted the Boston approach control and heard that the weather there was even worse—we had no choice but to turn back. Mr. Bradley said, "John, we'll try again tomorrow morning. I will get you to Boston!"

While I could have explained the delay to the Navy, for some unknown reason, I felt as if an inner voice was telling me that I needed to stick to the original plan and travel to Boston that day. Never before had I taken a firm stand against a supervisor who had been so kind to me, but I felt I had to say something. I said, "Mr. Bradley, I have to get to Boston today. Maybe you can land somewhere!" At that time, I did not know that Mr. Bradley did not have his instrument rating. He replied that we were above the clouds, and no local airfields were visible.

Then, as if a miracle, I saw a hole in the clouds and a small airport below. I pointed this out to Mr. Bradley, and he landed and dropped me off. I climbed out of the front right seat, thanked Mr. Bradley, and helped his girlfriend take the seat that I previously occupied. He took off for East Hampton, and I made it to Boston.

The next day, after my meeting with the Navy officials, I called Mr. Bradley to ask about his offer to fly me back to East Hampton. I could not reach him. Finally, one of the employees at the inn told me that on his flight back, Mr. Bradley had crashed his airplane short of the runway and sustained serious injuries.

I took the train back to Long Island Sound and, after a few days, was able to visit Mr. Bradley in the hospital. He was slowly recovering from multiple serious injuries and could only see me for a few minutes. I thanked him for his efforts and the enjoyable summer in East Hampton.

As I left, I asked the hospital attendant about his girlfriend, who had moved up to occupy my original seat. I learned that she was still in serious condition with a broken back, fractured skull, and badly damaged face. During the accident, her head smashed into the instrument panel. No visitors were allowed. I went back to the inn to finish my work and returned to Boston a week later.

It was an unsettling start to my Navy flying career, but I was not worried. Somehow I avoided a major disaster; I felt there had to be some guiding hand above me steering me in the right direction. That happened before in my life, and I hoped it would continue in the future.

On my last day in Boston, I made plans to meet with Ann, who finished her summer job in Connecticut. We only had a late afternoon together, and we walked along the Charles River holding hands and telling each other how much we cared for each other. We kissed under the bridge and then said goodbye. Ann was off to finish her final year at Smith College, and I was flying the next day to Pensacola to start my Navy service.

U.S. Navy Officer Candidate School: Pensacola

When I headed for the Navy OCS in Pensacola in 1956, I did not know what to expect, except that it would be physically challenging.

I arrived in late August in proper Harvard attire—a tweed jacket, flannel pants, and a necktie. When I entered the base, I immediately sensed that my appearance was inappropriate. On short notice, my civilian clothes, as well as most of my hair, were gone. With new gear in hand, we proceeded to our barrack quarters. Each of the bunk rooms had two double-decker beds with metal furniture and no air conditioning. We put on our uniforms, and with a friend, I left the barracks to explore the neighborhood.

Outside, we encountered Marine Sergeant Sterling, who introduced himself as our drill instructor. He looked at us said, "This time, they have sent me a truly sorry bunch of kids, who I have to make into military men!" The sergeant shouted at my companion, "You already have dirt on your uniform!" We had the uniforms on for less than an hour. My friend replied, "Sir, I do not see any dirt on the uniform. It's brand new!" Sergeant Sterling responded, "Are you questioning your superior's judgment? Who do you think you are?! I see a hair on your uniform, and that is dirt! Twenty-five push-ups, and make sure your uniform does not touch the floor!" Then, the Sergeant looked at me and said, "You do not seem to know what is going on. Fifteen push-ups for you!" After we completed the exercise, Sergeant Sterling inspected us, and we did not know what to expect. Fortunately, two other cadets came along, so he had new victims. We continued to explore the base, but frankly, there was not much to see.

Most of our time was occupied by PT (physical training), which included swimming, obstacle courses, rifle drills, and other forms of exercise. When we did not measure up to Sergeant Sterling's standards, we had to spend extra time drilling with a rifle and marching in front of the barracks, usually on Saturdays. None of us were perfect, and all of us received demerits for real or imagined offenses. We never questioned them. If you reached twenty-five demerits, you were called before a board and were in serious trouble. I did not know of anyone who did not have demerits. With fifteen to my name, I was in the middle of the pack.

The purpose of the training was not only to get you in excellent physical shape but to tear down your ego and then rebuild superior confidence. Even though I did not care for some of the methods, it was one of the most meaningful lessons in leadership I ever encountered. If today, Sergeant Sterling came down from heaven and told me to jump in a lake, I would not hesitate to do it right away. I knew he would only require us to do tasks that would help us in the future—and whatever Sergeant Sterling asked, he would do himself. Intuitively, I knew Sergeant Sterling always had our best interests at heart, and that heightened my self-confidence—what a great lesson in leadership!

We spent many hours in the swimming pool. Even in northern Florida, during the winter, the water gets cold—particularly if you spend hours there! The Navy gave us extra flu shots; no one dared get sick. After completing this phase of training, we had to pass multiple tests, which included swimming with our legs tied together, in flight suits, wearing boots, and other difficult scenarios. I remember a test that required us to swim underwater the entire length of the pool. When my turn came, I swam for a long time and was running out of breath by the time I reached the other end. The instructor was there waiting for me. He said, "You swam across diagonally with your eyes closed! Now you will have to do it again the right way." I was still out of breath. To this day, I cannot say how he knew I could do it for a second consecutive time. The human body, when driven by determination (or in this case, probably fear), can perform miracles!

One of the required tests to finish the officer candidate program was the "Dilbert Dunker." On first sight, it appeared to be quite intimidating. To start, you were strapped into an aircraft cockpit and pulled up in a tower. Then you were shot at high speed into the pool below. This simulated an aircraft crash at sea. We hit the water with a big splash, and then the cockpit turned upside down and sank to the bottom. You had to wait until the bubbles cleared, then open your eyes, and start undoing the various straps that held you firmly in place. When free, you swam to the surface. If you had problems, there were divers to help.

This exercise was an awesome sight, particularly for those who did not like the water. Some anticipated the underwater dive and undid the straps early. They were thrown against the instrument panel and banged up. Fortunately, we were required to wear helmets, and there were not many serious head injuries.

The purpose of the exercise was to instill confidence, no matter the conditions. At the same time, you learned that by following instructions, you would be safe. A good life lesson! For me, this test was not a problem; I compared it to a bad roller coaster ride.

There were frequent inspections of our quarters. Sergeant Sterling liked to open our laundry drawers and, with a tape, measure the squares into which our t-shirts and undershirts had to be folded. If the measurements were off even by one-eighth of an inch, we were ordered to do push-ups. Plus, our beds had to be so tightly made that one could bounce a coin on them. The result was that none of us ever slept under our blankets because it was too time-consuming to make a perfect bed in the morning. We never used our folded laundry—it was only in the drawers as a display to please Sergeant Sterling. We kept extra laundry in our dirty laundry bags, which were never inspected.

There was little free time, but during most of it, we spit-polished our shoes, did push-ups, and made sure our quarters were immaculate. I, however, managed to squeeze in time to write letters to Ann, and she responded. Several years ago, a Hollywood movie called *An Officer and a Gentleman* was made about the training of Navy officer candidates. While many of the scenes were accurate, there were no attractive women to cheer you up in Pensacola, and there was no time for romance. We were busy practically all the time.

Travel was restricted to a certain radius from the main base. One time, we decided to take a chance and drove to Mobile, Alabama. We wanted to live it up and went to a rather unsavory bar. While there, we heard a shout: "Shore Patrol!" We jumped out of the rear window, landed in bushes, and got all scratched up. After this little misadventure, I decided it was not worth taking any more chances until I completed the program.

On Sundays, we were mustered and marched to a church service. The Protestant chaplain was an elderly Navy officer who preached about the sins of the flesh and how to avoid a sinful life—a subject of limited interest to young men in our situation, who might even welcome an opportunity to sin! The next Sunday, a Catholic friend invited me to join him for their service. The priest was younger and could better relate to the audience.

Time passed quickly, and the Navy flew us home for Christmas. I managed to spend several days skiing with Ann—a very pleasant change from military life!

Before completing the officer candidate program, we still had to pass tests. The swimming program was completed, but the rest of the PT remained. For me, the most challenging test was climbing a rope to the ceiling of a hangar within a specified period. When my turn came, I took a deep breath and scampered up the rope and back down again within the prescribed time. The instructor looked at me and said, "I did not like the way you did it. Do it again!" To this day, I do not know how I did it a second time. I suppose I knew that if I did not pass this test, I would be "a sailor swabbing a destroyer deck" for four years! The academic tests, on the other hand, were a snap.

A new officer

After completing the tests, we graduated and each received an officer's commission. What a change of lifestyle! We headed back to the barracks to collect our belongings and moved into junior officer quarters. The first person to greet us was Sergeant Sterling. He snapped a salute, called us "sir," and congratulated us on our commissions. The military tradition is that your drill sergeant is the first to salute you as a newly commissioned officer, and in return, you give him $5. Life in our new junior officer quarters was pleasant. We felt different now that we were saluted by enlisted men and addressed as "sir." Plus, we now had access to the Officers Club, which offered good food and drinks at reasonable prices.

The Navy Aviation Officer Candidate School was an entirely different experience from academic school. Now I understood that I could perform well in any environment, no matter the physical demands. Even though the conditions were unpleasant, I knew I could cope with the stress. Training at the OCS gave me a much higher level of confidence than I had ever had before. I was impressed by the quality of leadership exemplified by Sergeant Sterling and understood that this characteristic was not necessarily derived from intelligence but was a God-given gift, provided to few. We were fortunate to have had Marine Sergeant Sterling as our instructor. Altogether, OCS in Pensacola was one of the most valuable experiences of my life.

We started the primary flight training program, which was fun. After a few weeks, we soloed and practiced landings during various short strips. The weather was good, and during the weekends, we spent a lot of time at the beach. We also occasionally traveled to New Orleans and other nearby towns, but there was still not much of a social life for us.

One of my lasting memories from Pensacola was a night landing practice. After dark, we took off and circled the airfield to practice touch-and-go landings. I was on top of the stack of airplanes, with more time to enjoy and reflect. I listened to the steady drone of the engine and could not help but be impressed by my spectacular surroundings. Below, the ground was covered with a tapestry of sparkling lights coming from the city and passing cars. People were enjoying their evening. In the distance, the Gulf of Mexico glimmered with lights from passing ships. Above me was a bright, starlit sky unobscured by pollution or haze. It felt like I was floating in space, the stars unencumbered by the earth below. In a sense, it made me feel like an insignificant part of the endless universe, and yet I felt privileged to enjoy it.

As I admired the splendor, I could not help but recall that many years before, I looked at the same sky with trepidation as we escaped by ship from Latvia. The heavens and stars were the same, but there were no lights on the ground there—only fear in people's hearts. I was lucky to have survived! I wondered to whom I owed my good fortune and how I could ever repay. My thoughts were interrupted by instructions to commence landing.

Afterward, one of my buddies suggested, "Let's go to the Officers Club and celebrate." I was happy to join. While there is a time to reflect, one cannot dwell on the past, only learn from it. To enjoy the full measure of life, one must engage in the present and build new memories.

I continued to think of and write frequently to Ann. She always responded, and in February, she invited me to her prom. It was a fun experience, being away from military service. I was also asked to attend her graduation, but I could not make it because of flight school. Ann wrote that her parents provided her enough funds for a summer in Europe. After that, she would come to Boston so we could spend more time together.

The Navy budget changed, and I was assigned to an electronic warfare school in Brunswick, Georgia, before joining an operational squadron.

Brunswick and Quonset Point

My limited knowledge of Georgia came from an unreliable source at Harvard. All I knew was that Georgia was in the Deep South, inhabited mostly by rednecks who grew cotton, attended religious revival meetings, and guzzled moonshine. They supposedly practiced racial discrimination and believed that the South should have won the Civil War.

When I got to the Naval Air Station in Brunswick, Georgia, located near Sea Island, I encountered a place entirely different from what I had expected—the local people were friendly, gracious, and entertained us in their homes. We were invited to tea to meet single ladies (mostly schoolteachers), and I met a semi-retired gentleman who asked me to play tennis every weekend at The Cloister at Sea Island. I also became a great fan of a washboard band that performed regularly at the King and Prince Hotel. I thought Sea Island was one of the most attractive places I had ever seen.

Just before Christmas, I went to a performance of Handel's *Messiah*, one of my favorite choral works. According to my hosts, the best chorus was at a Black church, and it was excellent. After the concert, there was a reception, and I did not witness any racial discrimination. Even though I enjoyed my stay in Georgia, I thought frequently of Ann and hoped we would see each other again soon. The local ladies were pleasant, but Ann was still the greatest!

After completing the training course, I was assigned to Navy aircraft squadron VAW-12, based in Quonset (outside Providence, Rhode Island). This location had been my first choice because of its proximity to Boston. My stay in Georgia only lasted a few months, but I became fond of the state and its people. Still, I was also happy to return to New England, where I had spent such a significant portion of my life.

At Quonset Point, my squadron was equipped with AD-5W propeller-driven aircraft used for electronic warfare; it was a time before jets or turboprops. The Quonset Point Naval Air Station was of modest size, and served as the base for one of the oldest Navy aircraft carriers, the USS *Leyte*. My fellow officers were good company, and duty was pleasant enough—the base had a library, where I read almost all fifteen volumes of *The History of United States Naval Operations in World War II* by Admiral

Samuel Eliot Morison. Our flight schedule was light, and most of the time, we flew around the east coast. We also had a lot of free time and could take leave. As soon as I settled in with a fellow officer, we took off and skied for a week in Canada.

Occasionally, we attended lectures at the Naval War College across the bay in Newport, but otherwise there was not much to do. Our proximity to Boston, however, gave me a chance to visit my family in Natick. It was good to see them enjoying retirement after all the turmoil of the past.

Of course, life at the base was not always pleasurable. In early March, I participated in escape and evasion training, which taught us what to do if our plane was shot down behind enemy lines. I had undergone similar training in Florida, but that was not very difficult—a few days in the tropical wilderness was almost an adventure. This time, though, was different.

On a wet and snowy day, we were dropped off in the Great Swamp in Rhode Island. This location was the last American Indian stand against the encroaching colonials. The conditions were miserable. Wet snow covered the ground, and there was intermittent rain. We had our parachutes and revolvers, which were useless. Fishhooks and material for snares mattered more, but none of this made sense because we first wanted to be dry. It was impossible to sleep on the ground; we tried the parachutes as hammocks, but it rained on top of us. Finally, we found shelter under a pine tree. No one bothered to fish in the muddy waters, and the rabbits were smart enough to hide in their burrows. As a result, save for a few power bars, we had nothing to eat, and we were wet and cold. Plus, it was impossible to leave the swamp because the roads were patrolled by Navy sailors who would be delighted to catch an escaping officer. We heard that if they caught one, they made him sit on top of a manure pile and bury his wristwatch, which he then had to dig up with bare hands. After two days in the wet swamp, we finally found an abandoned barn, so at least we were dry.

The exercise lasted three days, and then we returned to the base. I took a long shower to wash off the grime and then went to the Officer's Club and ordered two large steak dinners. I ate everything and washed it down with several beers. Life was back to normal! The experience taught me that even with youthful confidence and excellent physical condition, a lack of food, sleep, and miserable conditions have the power to lower one's resistance level. My sympathies go out to POWs. I also decided I would never get in that position. Fortunately, I never had to make that choice.

When I was stationed on the base, in the summer, after flying for an hour or so, I would go sailing on Narragansett Bay. One day, while I was sailing, an enlisted man caught up with me and shouted, "This is an alert! Report to your squadron!" There had been a crisis in the Middle East.

On short notice, we flew to Norfolk and then onto the USS *Forrestal*, the largest and most modern U.S. aircraft carrier. The ship could accommodate more than eighty aircraft and housed a crew of over four thousand. It was basically a floating city, with all the modern conveniences.

I was assigned to a junior officer bunk room, which was quite comfortable by my standards. I told a steward that I did not bring many uniforms because we left in a hurry. He replied, "Sir, do not worry. We have one-day laundry and dry-cleaning services!" Quite a convenience!

Flight operations continued as we sailed toward the Mediterranean. Before we reached Africa, however, the crisis was over, and we turned back. My stay on a modern aircraft carrier was a remarkable experience. Most of the sailors were barely twenty years old. They worked long hours in dangerous conditions, but morale was high. At sunset, which is spectacular in the South Atlantic, if there were no flight operations, sailors gathered on the flight deck and were mesmerized by the beautiful scenery.

We returned to Quonset Point. Our daily routine had not changed. I received fewer and fewer letters from Ann, who extended her stay in Europe. I was concerned—even though I occasionally dated others, Ann remained the star in my firmament. Finally, I received the welcome news that Ann was returning to America and would live in Boston.

Even though I had not seen Ann for almost a year, she looked as ravishing as ever when we finally saw each other again. Intuitively, I sensed that our relationship had changed, but I did not understand why. In my naïve mind, I attributed this primarily to our long separation. Despite these misgivings, we made plans to spend the week of New Year's together on a ski trip. The time together looked to me like it would be a much-needed opportunity to renew our relationship and think about the future.

It was not easy to get free time at New Year's. To make this work during the Christmas holidays, I had to volunteer for the worst duty possible—which required spending close to a month, including Christmas Day, on the old aircraft carrier, the USS *Leyte*. The ship was going to take part in an exercise with a new nuclear submarine. It would take place in the North Atlantic between Newfoundland and Greenland. Weather conditions at that time of year were poor: high winds, snow, and bitter cold. I had served briefly on the USS *Leyte* during the summer, but this stint was different. In the winter, we had to wear a rubberized immersion suit on top of quilted underwear, which was at least an inch thick. This outfit was very uncomfortable, especially if you had to sit tight in an airplane for hours. If the plane ditched in the northern Atlantic Ocean, the gear gave you about fifteen minutes before hypothermia set in.

From prior experience, we knew this was a serious matter. The previous winter, a flight crew from our sister squadron ditched in the rather calm Narragansett Bay. Before the plane hit the water, the pilot declared "mayday," and a rescue helicopter was on the way. Both pilots were picked up and delivered to the base. The one who had worn the rubberized immersion suit with the prescribed underwear was fine and spent the evening over drinks at the Officers' Club; the other, who had worn long johns instead of the required underwear, died of hypothermia.

To complicate matters, the engines of our planes had recently been overhauled by Pratt & Whitney. It turned out to have been a faulty procedure—metal particles accumulated in the sump of the engine, which could stop functioning. The solution was to install a cockpit light that would glow red before engine failure—not very comforting when you are flying over the freezing North Atlantic. Even though the red light sometimes came on, we never experienced an engine failure. In the Mediterranean, the possibility of engine failure did not bother us too much because the water was much warmer.

The USS *Leyte* was also the only Navy aircraft carrier that had a straight deck. When an aircraft landed, if its hook did not catch a cable, it was impossible to go around for another landing. At a high speed, the plane would head straight for a wire net strung at the end of the flight deck, which was there to protect aircraft. Still, getting caught in the wire mesh damaged the aircraft. Fortunately, I never had that experience.

The USS *Leyte* also had the last hydraulic catapults for launching aircraft. A hydraulic catapult launch was like being shot out of a cannon, and usually you blacked out for a few seconds. The hydraulic catapult was different from the steam catapults used on all other aircraft carriers—a steam catapult provided gradual acceleration to the same terminal speed. Plus, on old ships like the USS *Leyte*, you always had to wear gloves and hold onto the handles; otherwise, your knuckles would be bruised raw.

My deployment went on as expected. The weather was terrible, and on many days, flight operations were suspended; sometimes waves broke over the carrier deck, which is more than fifty feet above sea level.

Still, none of this mattered to me because I counted down the days until skiing with Ann. On Christmas Eve, we were allowed one telephone call; to me, hearing Ann's voice was the best Christmas gift.

I placed the call to Ann in Boston. One of her roommates answered, and I could hear a party in the background. Ann picked up the phone and said, "My Spanish boyfriend flew in and asked me to marry him. I said yes!" I was devastated. The image of Ann I had created in my mind shattered—it turned out this image did not correspond to reality. I should have realized something had changed when Ann extended her stay in Spain and her letters became less frequent. Perhaps it is sometimes better to temporarily dwell in a world of dreams, as long as the contrast is not too harsh when the real world breaks in. I was sad to have my hopes shattered in the middle of the dreary and stormy North Atlantic—an assignment for which I had volunteered only to make the New Year's trip with Ann possible. However, as in the past, I was able to put my disappointments behind me and look with even greater optimism toward the future, which always seemed to bring unexpected and pleasant surprises.

I was also lucky to have good friends. My Navy buddy Ed told me, "Do not worry—you will find another girlfriend. I will go skiing with you in New Hampshire. Plus, before, you did not want to deploy to the Mediterranean because you were waiting for Ann, and now you are free to go! One of my friends is the personnel officer, and I will help you get there."

Ed was a true friend and lived up to his word. A week later, after skiing in New Hampshire, I was sailing on the USS *Intrepid* to the Mediterranean.

The beginning of a new adventure!

USS *Intrepid* (CVS-11)

The Mediterranean cruise started in Norfolk, where we loaded four AD-5W single-engine propeller-driven aircraft and a detachment of pilots,

Approaching the
USS Intrepid CVS - 11

accompanying flight crew, and support people board the USS *Intrepid*. The ship had seen service in World War II and now had all the advanced features. Its size was little more than half of the USS *Forrestal*, yet it carried more than fifty aircraft, with a crew of more than three thousand. The junior officer's quarters were adequate and located directly underneath the catapults. When aircraft launched, there was a loud noise, but after a while, we got used to that. I shared the bunk room with five other junior officers, all of whom were from our detachment. Most of the time, when not flying, we were in the squadron's ready room. We ate in the officer's wardroom, where coffee and sandwiches were available at almost any time. The ship had a library but no gym—for exercise, we did calisthenics.

The farther we got away from U.S. shores, the better I felt. After Ann, my life was like an old, grainy black-and-white movie with scratchy sounds. The surprising disappointment from Ann was still coloring my perception of life. But the closer we got to the Mediterranean, the quicker everything changed. Now I saw the world in three-dimensional technicolor with stereo sound. The future was only going to be better and brighter.

After crossing the Atlantic, our aircraft carrier briefly stopped in Gibraltar, a location that had a fascinating historical background. I remembered from history class that Gibraltar was where an Arab general, Jabal al Tariq, crossed the straits from Africa. Later, after 711 AD, the Arab domination of Spain began and lasted for the next seven hundred years. For the past three hundred years, Gibraltar has been a British possession. Even though the local population was primarily Spanish, they publicized the approved association with Britain with a ninety-plus percent plurality.

After a brief stay in Gibraltar, the USS *Intrepid* participated in naval exercises and relieved another aircraft carrier. The ship spent three weeks at sea and then anchored just outside Cannes, on the French Riviera. Whether due to Navy planning or coincidence, we arrived during the International Movie Festival, now known as the Cannes Film Festival. The town was full of glamorous people, and one could feel the excitement in the air.

Ready to go!

We were not invited to any of the festival events, but we still wanted to be part of the action. My Navy friend Ed and I headed for the very elegant Cannes Casino, where the movie crowd gathered late in the evening. The staff added to the atmosphere, with their powdered wigs and eighteenth-century costumes. We tipped one generously, and he told us to come back later. In the evening, when we re-entered the casino, he greeted us warmly, "*Monsieurs*, we are glad to have you back. Your presence has been greatly missed!" The tip had done its job. Others looked at us as if we were important.

The gaming room was crowded with elegant people. Most of the men wore black tie attire, and the ladies were elegantly attired as well. It was a mixed group, with swarthy-looking Middle Easterners, a few Asians, and plenty of socialites and habitual gamblers. We passed the roulette tables, a game that I knew from childhood—after returning from Monte Carlo, my parents gave me a miniature roulette set. I was about six years old at the time. For years, I played roulette with my buddies and learned that the only winner was the bank—the casino. From then on, gambling never appealed to me because I knew the odds were against me.

Eventually, we encountered a group of the most glamorous women I had ever seen. Their bodies were gorgeously shaped, and they wore low-cut, revealing gowns. They had a lot to reveal! Their laughter sparkled like the light from the crystal chandeliers. The jewelry that adorned them was luminescent (and probably fake). It was a festive atmosphere! The scenery looked to us like a dream come true. I remembered that the Muslim religion rewards the righteous in heaven with the company of twelve virgins. We were not Muslims, nor that particular—any female company was welcome—after three weeks at sea, it looked to us like heaven had descended to earth. Ed and I pondered how we could approach these beautiful creatures. We figured we would start with cocktails at the casino, follow that with an intimate dinner in a romantic place, and who knew what afterward? We knew from the magazines the fast lifestyle of the Hollywood crowd!

But despite our valiant efforts, none of the ladies paid us any attention. They politely nodded and then continued to rivet their attention on a few elderly, greasy-looking men. We thought that at least these ladies would feel compassion for us sailors who spent weeks at sea defending their freedom and liberty, but even that did not work. All our efforts were in vain. We realized that the ladies were more interested in the movie producers and directors; the young actresses wanted to be recognized and discovered to further their careers. They were more ambitious and focused on their careers than today's business school graduates. We could do nothing but admit failure and leave. Ed wistfully remarked, "We will have another chance when we get rich and old!" I thought that would take too long.

Our deployment continued with two to three weeks at sea, followed by an additional two weeks in port. While at anchor, we had every other day off and sometimes could take a longer leave. One night, while the USS *Intrepid* was in Barcelona, I had shore duty, which meant that I supervised sailors returning from liberty to make sure they behaved and boarded the tender in an orderly manner. While on deployment, aircraft carriers never docked—we always had to be ready to leave on short notice. As I stood on shore in full white dress uniform, a gentleman came up to me and said, "Not long ago, I was a proud German officer. We lost the war, and now I barely exist in Spain. Enjoy it while you can, and make sure the Russkies don't get us!" I understood what he was saying—that one's status in life is transitory. Instead of worrying about the future, we might as well enjoy the full measure of life now. It did not take much to convince me to follow this advice.

Later, we had a few days leave and flew to Madrid. It was a pleasant change to be in a beautiful city untouched by tourists. Before visiting a new location, I always studied travel guides. Because Spain was a conservative Catholic country, there was no chance that we would meet any worthwhile local ladies, so we focused our attention instead on local attractions, like flamenco shows and the Prado Museum.

One night, I made dinner reservations at Horcher, one of the best-known restaurants in Madrid. The original restaurant was in Berlin, but during the war, it relocated to Madrid. Many years prior, my parents dined at the original Horcher—now I wanted to do the same in Madrid. The restaurant also attracted the well-known, former German commando, Colonel Otto Skorzeny, described as the most dangerous man in Europe. It was only later that we learned that the colonel, after the war, also worked for the Israeli intelligence agency. Ed and I had an excellent dinner served by waiters who probably had been German soldiers. When one of them found out we were Navy officers, he called over the manager, who greeted us as fellow military men, invited us to the wine cellar, and handed each of us a bottle of champagne. One never knows where an adventure may take you! It was an unusual experience, and to this day, Horcher remains among my favorite restaurants.

After two more weeks at sea, we anchored outside Palma de Mallorca, probably one of the most romantic places in the Mediterranean. The next day, we decided to tour the island, and three of us rented motor scooters. The shop owner did not speak English, so he explained in Spanish how to operate the scooter. That was not a problem for my friends, who owned motorcycles. But I had never been on a scooter or motorcycle before and did not know how to run one.

I let the others get on their bikes and watched what they did. While the motorbike was on its stand in the garage, they gave full power to test the engine and then lowered the bike and slowly drove out of the garage. When my turn came, I gave full throttle to check the engine and planned to drive slowly out of the garage like they had. Unfortunately, it turned out that my bike was not on the stand. When I gave full power, the bike—with me on it—shot out at full speed through the garage, across the sidewalk, and then into the street. I almost hit the opposing wall. I barely regained control of the bike before doing so, and the garage owner shouted at me in Spanish. It did not take long to learn how to operate the scooter after that, and we had a spectacular tour of the island.

It had been a day full of fun, but there was more to come. In the evening, we met several vacationing Swedish girls. I thought one of them, Viveca, was exceptional. She was a beautiful blonde—bright and great company. It was fun to have her at dinner and then dance on the outdoor terrace that overlooked the shimmering harbor below. It was a spectacular view. One could see in the distance the USS *Intrepid* lit up like a Christmas tree. The music was romantic—a famous song in those days was *Ciao, Ciao Bambina*. We were full of youthful exuberance and enjoyed every moment we were there. We had no worries about the future and felt life could only get better. Sadly, late in the evening, we had to return to the aircraft carrier, but Viveca and I made plans to see each other again in the following days.

For us Navy officers, Majorca was an incredible place with attractive young people, excellent restaurants, and romantic places. After the USS *Intrepid* sailed, as a farewell, we flew around the shores of Majorca at low altitude to say goodbye. I was sad to leave Majorca, but I continued to correspond with Viveca. She invited me to Sweden, but by that time, I was back in school.

After a few weeks at sea, the ship anchored in Naples, Italy. Ed and I had a few days of leave and went to Rome. The tourist season was in full swing, and we met touring college girls. They were there, as we were, to see the city. The company of fellow young, exuberant people always makes a visit so much more enjoyable. We told the girls that, sadly, we had to head back to our ship in Naples, but it turned out they were heading to Pompeii nearby. We were able to invite them for dinner aboard the ship because we were on duty.

When our dates arrived at the pier, we made sure they were escorted to us, and then we met them aboard the USS *Intrepid*. As most first-time guests did, they wanted a tour of the ship. We were able to guide them because we had almost unlimited access. On the flight deck, there were always four aircraft on the catapults, ready to be launched. The bombs underneath them were covered with a canvas awning and guarded by armed Marines. One girl asked, "What kind of bombs are those?" All we could say was that they were serious weapons—and a reminder that there was still the possibility of war.

The food aboard the ship was traditional American, usually a steak with French fries. White-coated stewards served us in the officer's wardroom. In the port, when visitors came, the table was set with silver candelabras. Our guests were more impressed by this setting than that of the restaurants ashore. Because these lady guests so enjoyed their visit, we later invited others. When we met the same girls in the United States years later, they still talked about their dinner aboard the USS *Intrepid* and reciprocated many times over.

The ship's next stop was Palermo, Sicily—not exactly a favorite Navy town. Ashore, there was relatively little to do. On our day off, Ed and I went out to explore ancient ruins, which abounded in Sicily. I do not know of any other part of the world that has been exposed to so many different cultures. It started with the Phoenicians, then the Greeks, Vandals, Byzantine Empire, Normans, Bourbons, and even an Arab caliphate. From a historical point of view, Sicily is fascinating, but when you are young, history is not a viable substitute for good dates (of which there were none).

However, at one of the archaeological sites, Ed and I met an English professor who offered to guide us. Afterward, he invited us to the local yacht club. The commodore's wife was an American, and she was pleased to meet Navy officers. This lady and her husband generously invited us to be their guests while stationed in Palermo. Ed and I spent the rest of the day on the beach and were served unknown exotic drinks by white-coated waiters. We had a terrific day in Palermo.

When we returned to the ship, our squadron mates complained about the city. Some were recovering from food poisoning and blamed it on the local restaurants. One of them asked Ed about his day. Noncommittally, he mentioned historical sites. Our squadron mates said they did not plan to leave the ship again because there was nothing to do in Palermo. I asked, "Would you mind taking our duty, then?" They replied, "If you want to go spend the day in this miserable town, sure!" The next day, Ed and I were back at the yacht club and continued to enjoy the owners' hospitality. I learned from this that one never knows where opportunities lie, but if you are alert, you are more likely to find them. If you are passive, you will remain where you are.

After a few weeks at sea, our next port was Livorno, Italy. Ed took leave and went to Florence to meet a girlfriend who flew in from Boston. A few days later, I joined them for dinner. Because I had no social plans, it was an opportunity for me to explore Florence. I went through the Uffizi Gallery, the Florence Cathedral, Ponte Vecchio, and other tourist attractions. One could only admire the rich cultural heritage of Florence. I felt at the time that it would be more fun to share the experience with someone I loved—and my wishes were fulfilled half a century later, when my wife and I toured the city together. We topped my first trip by spending over a week flying hot air balloons over Tuscany. Life has its rewards, deserved or undeserved!

Aircraft carrier operations represent one of the most dangerous environments, so it was no surprise that accidents occurred. One night, a squadron commander disappeared while making a night landing. No one could find any trace of the pilot or his plane, so we concluded that he must have become disoriented and flown into the water when approaching the aircraft carrier. Another day, we were the third plane to launch. The first that took off was an F-8 Crusader fighter, the fastest Navy fighter. Suddenly, the launch stopped. We heard that the plane had a "cold cat shot," which meant that there was not enough acceleration, and the plane went straight into the drink. There was always a rescue helicopter and an escort destroyer standing by to help in such cases, but all they could find was a map that floated to the surface. We were the second plane to take off and were confident that the mechanical problem had been repaired. While it was sad to lose a fellow flyer, we continued to perform our duty. We were all young, full of zest, and felt almost immortal. Our future and its adventures seemed more important than any past problems.

Late in the summer of 1959, the USS *Intrepid* moved to the eastern Mediterranean. We flew among the Greek islands, which looked like a string of pearls scattered throughout the azure sea. It was a spectacular scene; being there, one could understand why the ancient Greeks

AD-5W

appreciated beauty so much. Because our AD-5W aircraft were propeller-driven and originally designed for close air support, we could fly low easily, just a few hundred feet above sea level—or "above deck," as we called it in the Navy. We flew along the shores of the islands, near yachts with people having fun. As we banked and turned around, some of the girls took off their bikini tops and cheerfully waved at us. No wonder the ancient Greeks wrote about mysterious mermaids who lured wayward sailors to their demise! We were willing to try but did not have the opportunity. We anchored outside Piraeus and then went to Athens to admire the ruins of the Parthenon. At night, we listened to the melancholic *bouzouki* music, but otherwise, there was not much to do.

On our return to the western Mediterranean, the USS *Intrepid* assumed its station at the boot of Italy. The carrier did not enter the Adriatic because it was too landlocked. Our detachment explored the Albanian coast. Albania was a communist country, and there were indications that the Soviets were constructing a naval facility. We flew at night because we knew the Albanian Air Force did not have all-weather night fighters. One night, near the Albanian coast, our radar suddenly picked up fighter activity. We immediately dove into the cloud layer below, knowing that jets avoided low-altitude intercepts. While in the clouds, our single engine stopped—a deadly silence! It was difficult to ditch at night, and while there was still enough altitude, I told Ed, "If this persists, I am bailing out!" Ed shouted, "Hang on!" It turned out that in our excitement, we had not switched over to the reserve fuel tank. Once corrected, the engine quickly restarted. For years, Ed kidded me that he saved me from bailing out over the Adriatic. Whatever the reason, we remained close friends for life and laughed about our past experiences together.

My deployment was nearing its end, and I began to make plans to return to graduate school. I had nearly one year of service left, but because the Navy budget was cut, an early release was possible. As much as I enjoyed my time in the Navy, I knew that sooner or later I would have to face the reality of life—another year and I might succumb to the pleasurable lifestyle the Navy afforded me, but I knew it was not permanent. With these thoughts in mind, I looked for an opportune time to ask the commander of my detachment, Lieutenant Commander Cory, for an early release. Soon, such an opportunity arose.

Late one evening, when the USS *Intrepid* was off the coast of the French Riviera, Lt. Cdr. Cory returned to the ship wearing a *beret*— and not in a sober state. Because I was on duty, I helped him up the gangplank and said that I would like to talk to him in the morning. He said, "Let's talk now!" I told him, "Lt. Cdr. Cory, I would like you to approve my early release from the Navy so that I can finish my last year at Harvard Business School." He put his arm around my shoulders and led me to the edge of the deck so that we could see the coast of the Riviera. We saw the lights in Cannes and the shimmering tree-lined boulevards, and we looked out at the places we visited. Music drifted from passing party boats, which left a phosphorescent trail in their wake. The festive atmosphere was made more vibrant by the sailors' laughter as they returned from shore. It was a magical Mediterranean evening—the kind we experienced before, and we knew that more were to come. In that moment, I felt that life was endless and filled with continuous joy.

As these thoughts passed through my mind, he turned to me and said, "Livens, when looking at this beautiful coast, do you think you've seen all the fun places and girls? There are more than you can imagine! Do you want to get out of the Navy now? Come with us next summer, and we will have even more fun! On the other hand, if you are that stupid, and you want to go back to school instead, I will approve the early release."

To this day, I sometimes wonder whether Lt. Cdr. Cory was right—whether I was stupid for wanting to return to school instead of enjoying life in the Navy for another year or more. Nevertheless, it was a turning point in my life. I learned that while there is a time and a place to have fun, eventually it will come to an end. While it might be difficult to do, one must face reality and confront the next stage of life.

In late August 1959, the USS *Intrepid* left the Mediterranean and sailed for Norfolk, Virginia. Before we arrived, Lt. Cdr. Cory said to me, "We are flying to the home base and you will stay behind to take care of the gear and the sailors. Make sure that everything is properly unloaded and returned to the base. Take particular care of my Carrara marble tabletops!" Then my fellow officers flew off, and I stayed behind.

After the ship docked in Norfolk, the lengthy unloading process began. The sailors were eager to go home and unhappy about the delay. Though I oversaw the details, all the work in the Navy was done by senior chiefs, and I was lucky to have a good one. I simply watched and made sure that there were no problems. Unfortunately, a problem arose—one disgruntled sailor dropped Lt. Cdr. Cory's Carrara marble crate. I heard a cracking sound. Now I had a real problem! The chief came up to me and said, "Sir, do not worry, I will take care of this matter. I will tell the commander that the ship's company did it!" What the chief did, I do not know, but there was never a complaint to me.

After returning to Quonset, I was ready to leave for HBS. I came to say goodbye and thank Lt. Cdr. Cory. He told me, "I know that graduate schools are expensive, and you have worked hard. I am assigning you on temporary duty so that you can complete the paperwork, contact the Boston Naval Annex, and join the reserve squadron in South Weymouth. You will remain on duty and pay!" A generous proposition indeed! For several weeks, after I registered at HBS, I was still in the U.S. Navy.

The USS *Intrepid* will always have a special place in my heart. Today, it serves as a museum in New York, and I like to visit it. When the museum first opened, the aircraft on display were the same as on our cruise. Now everything has changed, but the spirit remains the same. On my visits, when I close my eyes, I can hear again the careless laughter of my squadron mates, tales of their shore adventures, and hopes for more to come. To us, life was a never-ending adventure. We saw it in brighter colors than most. Perhaps our perception was sharpened by our youth, or the danger we occasionally experienced, but the latter did not bother us. When I am there, I also think of my Navy friends, many of whom are no longer with us. I hope that someday we will have a reunion in the great beyond. As I think about the past, sometimes tears come to my eyes. I feel privileged to have served, and I am thankful to the U.S. Navy, my friends, and the adventures we encountered. The experience gave me a solid foundation for a better future.

Graduation and Career Beginnings

In early September 1959, I registered at Harvard Business School to complete my last year and earn an MBA. I was still in Navy uniform, as I had to report to the South Boston Naval Annex and then to the Naval Air Station in South Weymouth to continue on active duty. I had been away from HBS for three years and did not know any of the students anymore. Fortunately, a familiar face from college, Latimer, invited me to be his roommate. In retrospect, this chance meeting had a significant impact on my life.

Even though I had been away for a while, I had no difficulty readjusting to the business school routine. As in the past, whenever necessary, I could put in endless hours of studying—but this time, I better understood management because I had supervised people in the Navy. Management and real-world business environments were no longer abstract subjects to me, as they had been in the past; thus, my second year at HBS was much more valuable. Also, I had more freedom to select courses of my choosing.

As the school year ended, I began to look for a permanent job. My academic advisor suggested that I consider staying for two more years to help write cases for the school's Swiss affiliate, IMD. The job would be beneficial for a future career, and I was suited for the position because of my familiarity with Europe and my knowledge of German. While the opportunity was intriguing and challenging, I felt that the time had come to look for a business career that would provide me more permanency and opportunity for future advancement.

Subconsciously, I was probably trying to avoid repeating my tumultuous and unpredictable past. Perhaps it was in my blood to seek a predictable life in a stable environment, as my ancestors had before me. This goal always seemed to elude me, though, and unexpected circumstances would develop, with which I had to cope. With a few interludes, this tendency continued to plague me for decades.

After several interviews, I accepted a job at Chase Manhattan Bank. At the time, this bank had the best training program. It had excellent management, grew rapidly, and offered diverse opportunities for advancement. So, with some business school friends, I rented a rather luxurious apartment in Manhattan and planned to start work after a brief vacation.

After graduating from HBS in 1960, my roommate Latimer and I decided to celebrate by traveling to Europe. Our trip began in London. It was interesting to travel with Latimer because his undergraduate degree at Harvard had been in fine arts so he knew the best historical sites, museums, and architectural masterpieces.

To start, we decided on a celebratory dinner at London's Simpson's in the Strand, one of the best traditional British restaurants in the city. After our meal, I looked at Latimer and said that I had to agree with the French—I could not understand how the British attained such a high level of civilization and culture with such unimaginative cuisine! Latimer conceded, and from then on, we ate in pubs, which we liked. While our visit to London was enjoyable, the city had mostly lost its dynamism, as it was still recovering from World War II.

Our next stop, Paris, was exciting, though, and had its own *joie de vivre*. To celebrate our arrival, we decided to splurge and have dinner at one of the best restaurants, La Tour d'Argent, which at the time had three coveted Michelin stars. What a difference in cuisine and ambiance, and with a spectacular view of Notre Dame! Later, the restaurant lost one of its Michelin stars, but it remains one of my favorites. Always a great experience to be had there!

In Paris, we rented a car and drove across France to Strasbourg and on to Germany and Austria. In Germany, we visited one of the places where I had gone after World War II, but everything had changed. Life seemed to move on, and the past had almost been erased. We had a good time in Austria because both of us knew German (Latimer served in the U.S. Army's Military Intelligence Corps). From there, we headed to the

Italian Lake District and spent a few days in Bellagio—a charming place. We had lunch at Villa d'Este and admired its beauty and the surrounding gardens. The trip was a pleasant change from our business school routine and gave me another, more intellectual, dimension for appreciating the beauty of Europe. Now I was ready to go to work!

As I headed back, it seemed that my life would become predictable now, and I would have more control over it than ever before. Unfortunately, excessive confidence and a belief that you are in charge of your own fate is misleading and will give you a false sense of security; we are never completely in control of our lives. I was quickly reminded of this after my return from Europe.

Soon after my return, my stepfather had a heart attack and was hospitalized. Because, in the past, my parents had been very supportive of me, I decided to stay on in Boston to be with them. I called Chase Manhattan Bank, and they kindly offered that I could join them later. However, in the meantime, while my stepfather recovered, I needed a job.

At HBS, I met the Vice President of Finance at Raytheon Company, a large electronics manufacturer outside Boston, who told me that if I ever wanted to remain in the area, I should call his office. I did so and was offered a position in a new management/audit program that required working about six months in different company operations before deciding on a permanent career. I thought this program would provide me excellent industrial experience.

I called my friend Latimer, who worked at the leading bank in Boston (where his father had been a vice chairman), and he invited me to be his roommate in a house he and two friends rented. The building was in the flat part of Beacon Hill, and we rented the second and third floors. Even though the accommodations were rudimentary, it was fun to be in an area with many other young people. In fact, I liked the ambiance of Beacon Hill so much that I lived there for the next fifty years.

CHAPTER 9

CHAPTER 9

CAREER AND MARRIAGE

Beacon Hill

In the 1960s, the Beacon Hill neighborhood of Boston was populated by young people just out of college. The rents were reasonable, the location convenient, and there was always various events taking place. It was the place to be!

Our two-floor apartment was comfortable and contained furniture discarded by our parents. The bedrooms on the second floor were not air conditioned and were very hot during the summer, so we kept the windows open and could hear street noises below. Sometimes, to get a good night's sleep, I visited my parents, who lived about twenty miles away. They had a much-deserved tranquil life after their tumultuous past; Mother, from childhood on, was trained to be a gracious hostess, so there were always visitors. I was pleased to see that they enjoyed their retirement.

In Boston, I was fortunate to have good suitemates. Latimer was a friend from school, and I also liked the other two suitemates, Bill and Dick. Later, Bill married Polly, one of my friends, and the two remained my best friends for the rest of their lives. Whenever I needed support or encouragement, I could always rely upon Polly and Bill. I only wish that I had expressed adequate appreciation to them, and hope there will be another chance to do so in the great beyond.

Because all of us worked, we took weekends seriously and made the most of our time. We were healthy, happy, and unconstrained by financial needs. For me, winter provided a great opportunity to ski, a sport I had enjoyed since childhood. I had friends who shared my enthusiasm and became a regular visitor at their ski house in Waitsfield, Vermont. It was a great group of people who enjoyed skiing and the socializing that went with it. Two to three of us left on Fridays after work and drive almost four hours to Vermont, regardless of road or snow conditions. On the way there, we met others for dinner. We skied all day Saturday and part of Sunday and then returned to Boston late at night.

The accommodations at the ski house were primitive—I slept in a sleeping bag in an unheated attic. Occasionally, it was so cold that in the middle of the night I put on my heavy-duty ski underwear before I could fall asleep. The skiing conditions were not always good at Mad River, where we skied, and there was no snowmaking equipment. We had fun anyway. Sometimes we brought dates, but that was not necessary because single girls also stayed at the ski house. The problem with bringing a date was if she happened to not be a good skier and somehow was injured, then you probably had to stay behind in Boston to be helpful. Most of us did not want to take that chance.

In the summer, I had another group of friends with whom I rented a house in Orleans, Cape Cod. The house had been a farm, and now we stayed there for the season. On Fridays, we drove to the Cape, and the first arrival to the house could select the best room. We could accommodate close to twelve (in rudimentary conditions, but who cared!). In the morning, we loaded everyone into a large four-wheel-drive vehicle and headed to a deserted beach for the rest of the afternoon. In the evening, we stopped by the fisherman's wharf, bought fish or lobster, and cooked it at our house. It was a great summer!

While I had a great personal life, I grew disappointed with my job, which I had only taken because of a family emergency. My first assignment at Raytheon was at the corporate headquarters, updating the financial manuals used by the company's divisions. We did this, though I doubt the divisions adhered to the corporate rules. Raytheon had excellent technology but poor business management. The chairman, Charles Francis Adams, had been an investment banker with no manufacturing experience. His father was a former Secretary of the Navy and a direct descendant of the second U.S. president. Through his Washington contacts, the chairman garnered missile contracts. They were all on a cost plus fixed-fee basis, and business management did not matter much.

My next assignment was at the Andover missile plant, which was downsized due to the loss of a contract. Several hundred people were going to be laid off, and our responsibility was to review finances and staffing. Andover had been economically depressed because the textile industry moved to the south—until Raytheon came to town. The new Raytheon plant hired many of the former mill workers, who had limited qualifications and experience. Now they were going to be out of a job. When this occurs in California, workers move to the next town to seek new opportunities. This kind of employee mobility was not available in the old textile towns of Massachusetts, where residents had deep ethnic roots. Many of the workers were of Greek, French-Canadian, Italian, or similar backgrounds with strong family ties and were not willing to relocate. A layoff for them meant they would be unemployed for a long time. While I worked there, some of them came to me and told me their stories. I was a junior man on the team, merely collecting data to be forwarded to the corporate headquarters—I did not make any decisions. I felt sympathy for the workers and found the situation depressing and one that could have been avoided through better management.

My next assignment was to Lowell Missile Division, where I helped write business plans for government contract proposals. The business plan was only a formality because awards were made for technical competence. The Lowell plant was the only well-managed operation I saw during my three years at Raytheon. Later, the manager, Tom Phillips, became the president of Raytheon and turned the company around.

Life in Beacon Hill was fun—it was exciting to be young, attend many functions, and meet attractive girls with similar interests. I had no serious romantic involvements because of my active life of skiing, Cape Cod summers, and work. Latimer and I tended to gravitate to smarter girls who were also good cooks and good company. The star was Polly, who later married our good friend Bill. Latimer saw Margo, a very bright and competent woman who later became Assistant Secretary of Defense. Another one, Ruthie, became the U.S. Consulate General in Switzerland. I occasionally dated Ann, who at age twenty-seven was already an assistant editor at Little Brown Company. But because she was not a very good skier, the romance did not progress.

After enjoying the company of all these attractive, smart, and competent young women, I was surprised when, later in the year, Latimer told me he fell in love with a girl he met at his parents' home and planned to get engaged. I was happy for Latimer but surprised that his fiancée, Judy, had only gone to a junior college and was not at the same intellectual level as the others. When I met Judy, however, I understood why Latimer fell in love. Judy was a lovely young woman—gracious, socially adept, and willing to do anything to make Latimer happy, including long and uncomfortable sailing cruises. It was a match made in heaven because Judy's father was vice president at the same bank where Latimer's father had been the vice chairman of the board. Their families knew each other, and in anticipation of the wedding, friends organized social functions. Because I was in the wedding party, my attendance was almost mandatory. While I enjoyed the celebrations, they primarily took place in the winter and therefore interfered with my skiing—I usually counted down the hours until I could leave.

To one of these functions, Judy invited her college roommate, Mary Ann, who was escorted by one of my suitemates. We all met in our apartment for cocktails before heading out to the different parties. I arrived with my date, Ann, and left shortly afterward. That is how I met my future wife. Even though it was a brief, initial meeting, I could not forget Mary Ann's sweet smile. A week later, I was seated next to her at a party and realized that she was a warm, enthusiastic, and compassionate person. Even though Mary Ann came from a prominent social background, she truly cared for others and wanted to help those who were least comfortable in formal social settings. I had a few dates with Mary Ann, but then I was off on my previously scheduled ski trip to Europe.

My old friend from Harvard, Steve, and I had planned this ski trip a long time prior. We planned to meet two girls from Boston who earlier flew to Zermatt, Switzerland. Zermatt is one of the most picturesque and attractive alpine villages; no cars are allowed. The Matterhorn and surrounding snowfields overshadow the town, creating a unique atmosphere, and the skiing is fabulous. Shortly afterward, the two Boston girls left for St. Anton am Arlberg, Austria. We felt relieved because they were poor skiers.

Steve and I were scheduled to depart a few days later, but an avalanche covered the railroad tracks. The local train could only travel a short distance, and then we walked across the railroad tracks to change to the Geneva Express, which made a temporary stop. We had a few minutes, so I generously tipped the conductor and told him to carry my bag while I grabbed my skis and boots. Steve shouted to me, "Take care of your baggage! You may lose it!" After boarding the express train, when we were on our way to Geneva, Steve looked around and asked, "Where is your bag?" It turned out that we only had one bag—the one Steve was carrying. He said, "I told you to take care of your baggage!" But we had almost identical bags, and it turned out that Steve had carried mine— so he was the one who had lost his luggage. We stopped in Geneva so Steve could track down his lost bag. Fortunately, I remembered a girl from Boston who was a distant relation of Mary Ann and was now in Geneva. She asked me to call her if I ever was in town. I reached out, and she invited me to ski in Verbier. We planned to meet Steve after he retrieved his luggage.

Verbier was full of young people, and the only space available was in a youth hostel. About a dozen people slept in a large room, and that included men as well as women. I had no problem with the arrangement because I had slept in Navy bunk rooms, but it was a problem for my friend, who was a somewhat prudish Boston woman. It was quite the show, seeing her wrapped with sheets and blankets as she put on pajamas. The European students had a good laugh. It looked like a striptease in reverse.

We had a fabulous time skiing in Verbier, and I got a prize that was awarded at a local nightclub—a large bottle of Bolls liqueur. In the middle of the bottle was a figurine of a dancing ballerina, which was part of a music box. When wound up, music started, and the ballerina danced. I kept this prize for many years, and whenever I played it, it reminded me of our great ski adventures.

Steve joined us a few days later without his bag, but he purchased new equipment and was ready to ski St. Anton. We previously canceled reservations at the best hotel there, Hotel Zur Post, and now had nowhere to stay. Because the town was full of young people, we could barely find a room.

The next day, we were off skiing and breathed a sigh of relief because we would not have to be with the two Boston girls, who kept their original reservations at the hotel. Soon we met and skied with two gorgeous Swedish girls, who were a lot of fun, in addition to being good skiers. Normally, I would have thought this could be the beginning of a great relationship, but now I did not feel that way: Mary Ann was still very much on my mind. After skiing, the girls suggested we go tea dancing. This meant having drinks and tea, then dancing in your ski boots. Our new Swedish friends selected Hotel Zur Post for the occasion, where we had our initial reservations. As we sat down, the two Boston girls came up and said, "We have been looking for you everywhere!" Well, that was the end of that. A few days later, we flew back to Boston.

After returning to Boston, I resumed my routine. I completed the job at the Lowell plant, and I was assigned to a small semiconductor operation recently acquired by Raytheon. It manufactured passive electronic components. In my opinion, this product line did not fit in the company's portfolio. The operation was likely not very important to the company because I was sent there alone. This project required that I spend a great deal of time in Connecticut, which gave me an opportunity to see more of Mary Ann, who was in Long Island. I had grown very fond of her. I knew our relationship was getting serious because I thought more about Mary Ann than skiing. I hoped that someday we could ski together in Switzerland.

One weekend, I invited Mary Ann to join my ski group in Vermont. In the morning, we headed for our favorite spot, Mad River, but it was a challenging mountain with poor ski conditions because there was no snow-making equipment. I skied at a slower pace to enjoy Mary Ann's company. Unfortunately, the next day, she fell and later complained of a mild headache. We left promptly because Mary Ann had to fly back to New York.

The next morning, I called her family home in Long Island to ask how Mary Ann was doing. She had just returned from the doctor, who diagnosed a mild concussion. I told her, "I'm glad you're with your parents—in a few days, I will fly to see you." Mary Ann replied, "Yes, I'm at my parents' house, but they do not have time for me and will be leaving shortly for their Florida home in Hobe Sound. I will fly to St. Croix in the Bahamas to be with my sister while I recuperate." This plan surprised me, as I could not understand why any parents would leave when their child, no matter what age, needed their attention. Both of Mary Ann's parents were very proper and nice, and it was difficult for me to understand their actions. From the past, I knew that strong family ties were key to a happy life. While this incident was bothersome, I dismissed it because I was falling in love with Mary Ann and valued my relationship with her parents.

Because I was in Connecticut most of the week, I could spend weekends and time with Mary Ann in New York or Long Island. The more I saw of her, the more I liked her. Mary Ann's presence always lifted my spirits. I completed the Connecticut assignment and, in the final report, suggested that not only would this semiconductor operation likely remain unprofitable, it did not fit into the Raytheon strategy. At the time, I planned to look for a new job in Boston that offered better career opportunities. I also hoped it would allow for more time with Mary Ann. I did not want to consider marriage until I had a job with sound future potential.

Someone in the corporate office must have liked my report, for I was offered a prime assignment in London to review the finances of two recent Raytheon acquisitions. This also would look good on a future resume. The problem was my relationship with Mary Ann—I did not want to leave her for several months. We discussed this, and I said I would occasionally fly back to be with her and perhaps she could visit me in London. I also implied that I did not want to make any decisions about our future until my business career was on more solid ground. I wanted to avoid the uncertainty that plagued my past life. Mary Ann said she did not care what I did or what happened to my career—she was happy to be with me no matter what. Even though she did not know much about business, she was convinced I would do well in life and we would be happy together. To me, these comments demonstrated confidence and love. Being with Mary Ann was like experiencing a wonderful spring day that brings forth vivid colors and promises of more happiness ahead. Her cheerful personality and spirited laughter brightened the darkest winter days and delivered sunshine. I knew that Mary Ann was a special person whom I loved and asked her to marry me.

Married Life

The wedding was in August 1963—a huge Long Island affair with more than four hundred guests. The Harrises, my new in-laws, already married two daughters off, so everything was well organized, as if on autopilot. There were many parties in Boston and Long Island, but it was all a blur to me—I just wanted to be with Mary Ann. After the wedding, we had a two-week honeymoon and then started the new assignment in London.

Immediately after the wedding, we flew to Lisbon, a place we had not visited before. We wandered around Estoril, Portugal, and admired the scenic beauty. Estoril was one of the few places in Europe untouched by World War II. At night, we listened to the romantic *fado* music.

From Lisbon, we flew to Palma de Mallorca, Spain, one of my favorite places. It was as beautiful as I remembered it from my Navy days, but now I had a lovely wife to accompany me, which multiplied my happiness. We rented a Vespa motor scooter, as I did before, but this time, I was an experienced driver. It was not easy since I was six feet two inches tall and Mary Ann just three inches shorter, but we made it work.

For lunch, we drove to a restaurant in a castle on top of a high hill. It was quite an effort to get the scooter up the mountain with two large adults, but we finally made it. There, we turned the Vespa over to the valets, and they parked it next to a Rolls-Royce and a Mercedes. An acquaintance, whom we saw at the wedding, owned the restaurant and invited us to be his guests. He was not there, but we had a delightful lunch.

Afterward, we drove to the studio of a well-known British artist. In recent years, he had become quite famous. When we arrived, all the artist's works were sold, and he was working on a silhouette portrait of his Spanish wife. When he heard that we were newlyweds, the artist offered to sell us the painting after finishing it. It was a unique rendering of a young woman on a gold background, based on an ancient Byzantine technique. We purchased the painting and had it shipped to Boston. Now the children have it, and I hope it will remind them of the happy times I shared with their mother.

From Majorca, we flew to Marseille, picked up a car, and drove through France. It was a delightful trip—Mary Ann spoke French, which she learned in Paris while studying voice. On our way to the English Channel, we stopped at a small restaurant, La Pyramide, in Vienne. It recently received its third Michelin star. This was an opportunity to celebrate. We ordered the special chef's dinner that included ten courses. With great delight, I consumed all of them and helped Mary Ann with the last two, which she could not finish.

We continued the trip through France, crossed the English Channel, and settled down in London, where we rented a furnished apartment. My job was to review a recent Raytheon acquisition, AC Cossor Ltd, which was in Redding, outside London. My superior had relatively little formal education and worked his way up through the corporate hierarchy. He told me that the acquisition was made by the chairman, Charles Francis Adams, after dinner with a friend at a London club. The corporate staff had seen the audited financial statements but not much beyond that; they had a cursory understanding of the company's technology and had to rely on the chairman's judgment. My superior went on to say that while we could point out some shortcomings if we found any, we should not question the soundness of the acquisition because it was the chairman's decision.

With this agenda in mind, my first task was to review AC Cossor's inventory. I soon found several significant discrepancies—one of them being that the company's fully valued military electronics equipment inventory was delivered to the Indian Air Force years before. From my Navy years and experience with military electronics, I knew that most of it was obsolete and should have been written off. Furthermore, the company's middle management was weak and their labor relations poor, with some unions still espousing Marxist ideas. Also, the financial controls were lax. When I mentioned these findings to my superior, he said, "I don't want to hear about problems like that. You better go work on the other acquisition, Sterling Cable." My new assignment was different and more interesting. Sterling Cable was a smaller company managed by a crusty, old Englishman with little formal education, though he was a good executive. The company was profitable, but it did not quite fit into the Raytheon portfolio, in my opinion. Even so, that was not for me to decide.

While work was not exactly uplifting, the rest of our life was superb. We enjoyed London and traveled weekends through the beautiful English countryside. When I could get an extra day off, we went to Paris or Belgium. My father-in-law visited while he was attending the Texaco Board of Directors meeting held in London. At the reception, we met other young Americans and developed another circle of friends. London was a great place for theatre, museums, and ballet. Both of us shared an interest in the arts.

My job assignment ended just before Christmas. The supervisor showed me the draft of our report and asked for comments. I said, "We cannot state that AC Cossor was a good acquisition without mentioning the serious problems that we found." The supervisor looked at me and said, "You do not understand corporate life. Your signature on the final report will not be necessary." I knew right away that my days at Raytheon were numbered. I had already planned to leave the company and look for another job, but after that, I immediately contacted two executive search firms so I could set up interviews as soon as I returned to Boston.

In 1964, a day before Christmas, we arrived in Boston from London. Because I gave up my bachelor apartment, Mary Ann's grandmother, Mrs. Webster, graciously invited us to stay with her. Accommodating us was not a problem because Mrs. Webster had the largest private residence in Boston. It was located on the corner of Commonwealth Avenue and Dartmouth Street. Both of us were very fond of Mrs. Webster, and Mary Ann was one of her favorite granddaughters. She also had several other homes. One was only a few miles away in the suburbs, surrounded by greenhouses and gardens that provided fresh flowers. During Christmastime, Mrs. Webster's house on Commonwealth Avenue looked spectacular, decorated with dozens of poinsettias and other flowers. Many passersby took photographs of the beautifully decorated windows. It was a great feeling to be back in Boston among friends and family.

Immediately after the holiday, I went to Raytheon to pick up my mail and tell them I was going to take accumulated leave, so that I would not have to show up at the office. There was good reason to do so—when I picked up my mail, I saw that my letters from the executive search firm were opened. It was clear that I was on my way out.

Fortunately, business in Boston was booming, and the combination of my Harvard Business School degree, Navy experience, and work in an industrial enterprise opened many doors. After a round of interviews, I found two great opportunities. It was difficult for me to decide which one to pursue—the openings represented two entirely different approaches to investment management.

The first firm was Fidelity Investments. Its president, Mr. Johnson Sr., was a visionary lawyer which was unusual. He had rapidly grown a small company by hiring talented people with diverse backgrounds and giving them early responsibility combined with generous compensation.

Mr. Johnson did not mind if some of these young, aggressive people received a lot of publicity because that generated business. He also understood that the future of a successful investment management firm was based not only on an investment record but also on marketing and a strong, supporting corporate structure. Later, this concept was brilliantly implemented by his son, Ned, who made Fidelity into one of the most successful investment organizations in the United States.

The other organization, State Street Research and Management Company, had a different approach. It had a core of exceptional professionals with degrees from the best universities, mostly Harvard. The company had hardly any individual clients because its minimums were very high—it primarily served large corporate and institutional clients (one of them was the Harvard University endowment). It had no marketing organization and did not need one—the firm could be very selective about whom they took on as clients. It was a low-key partnership that abhorred publicity.

Before making a final decision on which option to pursue, I had lunch with a family friend who was head of a Boston brokerage firm. This man intimately knew both firms and gave me the best advice I ever received. He said, "When you make a choice, do not look where the company now stands or its plans. The real world is always full of unanticipated changes, and the pace of change is accelerating. Do not consider the starting salary, nor the position offered, but look instead at which employs the highest caliber and the brightest people. Do not believe that a single individual can bring the company long-term success—it requires a team of highly motivated team."

He went on to say,

If you get an offer from State Street Research and Management, take it. The founder, Paul Cabot, was one of the pioneers of investment management and is an outstanding investor. At an early age, he was made the treasurer of Harvard University and manages its endowment. Cabot laid the foundation that made the Harvard University endowment the largest and most successful of all educational institutions. He also serves on the boards of many leading companies: J.P. Morgan, Ford Motors, etc. The other founder, Richard Saltonstall, is one of the finest gentlemen I know. He managed successful political campaigns for his brother, Leverett Saltonstall, who was the U.S. Senator for Massachusetts and its former governor. The founders are not only outstanding investors, but real gentlemen and pillars of the Boston establishment. State Street Research has the brightest group of investment people in Boston and has no turnover because it is a partnership. While almost all have MBAs and excellent academic records, Paul Cabot thinks this only provides the basic tools, and it is up to each to come up with creative investment ideas." My friend concluded by saying that the problem was this organization hired only one professional every other year. He insisted, "If you get an offer, take it—you will never regret it!

I was impressed with his analysis and glowing recommendation. Silently, I told myself: *Here again the odds are stacked against me, like they were on many occasions before, but I succeeded. Perhaps this time everything will also work out well.* I ended up getting an offer from State Street Research and Management and accepted it. It was a privilege to work there, and later, I became one of the partners of Cabot and Saltonstall. I admired both men, and this was an incredible opportunity that changed my life.

While I struggled to decide between the various career options, our domestic life was great. We were guests of Mrs. Webster, Mary Ann's grandmother, and planned to rent an apartment later. Mrs. Webster was very fond of Mary Ann and invited her to many functions. Mary Ann made many new friends, though some of them probably used their relationship with her to advance socially.

I talked with Mary Ann about my work, but she did not understand the business world. However, she was always most supportive. She told me, "I do not care what you do as long as we are together. It would even be fun if we were to be poor!" I realized Mary Ann did not understand the practicalities of life and could be of limited help in business, but I was glad to have her moral support.

Most evenings, we dined with Mrs. Webster. She had a superb French chef and an English butler. Afterward, we had coffee in an elegant salon, followed by discussions. Mary Ann went to bed early but encouraged me to stay behind to talk to her grandmother.

While I appreciated Mrs. Webster's hospitality, which was enhanced by the opulent surroundings, I did not want to become dependent on it. Other relatives had done so and accepted positions in organizations that were influenced or controlled by the family. For me, it would have been a simple solution, because I was searching for a job, but this was not the course I wanted to follow in my life. I knew I could forge my own way, unencumbered by obligations and gratitude. Secretly, I hoped to soon find a suitable apartment, but a surprise came along the way.

One night, Mrs. Webster asked about my work, and when I told her, she quickly grasped where I stood. Then she added, "John, I know what you are trying to accomplish, but my daughter [my mother-in-law] and your wife [Mary Ann] do not!" Now I understood—for several generations, my in-laws were removed from the practicalities of life, and that included my wife. Subconsciously, I wanted to protect Mary Ann from the harsh realities of life, which gave me extra incentive to work hard and succeed.

One evening, Mrs. Webster told me the story of her family. I found it fascinating because it reflected a part of American history. Mrs. Webster's future husband, Mr. Edwin S. Webster, was a graduate of MIT in 1897. His father was a successful Boston investment banker and, as a managing partner of Kidder & Peabody, made an early fortune. The young Mr. Webster had an interest in science so instead of Harvard, he went to MIT. Before graduation, Mr. Webster and his friend Mr. Stone told their MIT professor they wanted to go into the electricity business. The professor told them, "That is a risky undertaking—I doubt the two of you will make a living!"

However, the two young men did not take their professor's advice. They started the engineering firm Stone & Webster. Initially, it was rough going. On occasion, Mrs. Webster had to pretend she was a secretary and pound on the keyboard (even though she did not know how to type). Once the business took off, Stone & Webster became the world's leading designers and constructors of electric utility power stations. Some of the clients did not have much cash and offered to pay in stock instead. Because both founders came from well-to-do families, they could accept equities. Eventually, the electrical utilities and pipelines became successful, and Stone & Webster made a fortune. The family used their wealth thoughtfully and generously supported many charities.

The Websters also amassed one of the largest art collections in New England. The four houses that Mr. and Mrs. Webster owned were full of paintings, including several Monets, Titians, and other Renaissance and Hudson River artists. They were close to Winslow Homer and had many of his works—there were also portraits of Mrs. Webster by Sargent and Benson. Today, when I am at the Boston Museum of Fine Arts, I usually wander to its impressionist exhibit. The most prominent Monet painting there is *Madame Monet and Child,* donated by the family. This painting conveys tranquility, motherly love, and happiness. It was Mrs. Webster's favorite painting and was donated to the museum. We had many lengthy conversations below it that influenced my life. When I close my eyes, I see myself in her elegant Commonwealth Avenue house, sitting beneath that painting and dreaming of what the future might hold. My fate turned out better than expected, and the warmth conveyed by the painting has not changed. It will enrich the lives of all who view it, but it will always have a special meaning to me.

One evening, Mary Ann mentioned that her grandmother was going to ask me a favor. I said I would be glad to do anything Mrs. Webster wanted. After dinner, Mrs. Webster mentioned that in a few weeks, she planned to visit her friends in the south. She would take a private railroad car with a personal maid and chauffeur, but the rest of her staff of seven would remain in Boston. Mrs. Webster asked Mary Ann and me to keep an eye on the house and make sure everything was in order. She went on to say that she would like us to keep her staff busy, meaning the French chef, the butler, and the others. So, after Mrs. Webster left, Mary Ann decided to have a dinner party. She informed the butler, who took care of all the arrangements. One evening, I asked the butler what the main course would be. He responded, "Mrs. Webster has a deer park outside Boston in Chestnut Hill, so we will have fresh venison!" What could I say?

On the evening of the party, the house looked spectacular, with fresh flowers and candles everywhere. Mary Ann graciously welcomed the guests and made sure they were at ease in the somewhat ostentatious surroundings. She wanted everyone to have a wonderful time. During the cocktail hour, a guest asked Mary Ann about a painting in the style of the Impressionists. Mary Ann replied, "It's a Monet—and there are four more!" Then she proceeded to give a guided tour of Mrs. Webster's art collection. Afterward, we ate a gourmet dinner. During the dessert course, the young lady next to me picked up a spoon and remarked that it was very unusual. The stuffy English butler behind her said, "Madame, it's pure gold!" I am glad she did not turn around and ask about the painting behind her (it was a Rembrandt).

After the dinner, Mary Ann was happy that she could share her lifestyle with friends, who all enjoyed a lovely evening. She wanted to bring happiness and pleasure—feelings of envy were unfamiliar to her. Mary Ann felt that because everyone had a good time, we should host another. But I did not want to start my business career in this manner, so that was the only party we hosted.

While we enjoyed being guests of Mrs. Webster, we started looking for a place of our own. Shortly afterward, we rented an apartment in Boston. It was convenient for me because I only had to walk across Boston Garden and the Common to commute to work. No matter the season, it was a refreshing, beautiful walk and even gave me some exercise. My job and the work environment at State Street Research and Management (SSR&M) was fantastic—better than I expected.

I started as a technology analyst covering aerospace and emerging technology companies—at that time, there were not many. I reported to a senior partner, Alan, who was the Director of Research, but I worked independently. Alan was very bright, and he was one of the most thoughtful people with which I ever worked. As a starter, Alan showed me the detail files on our investments in the industry. He suggested that I review the material and then reach out to investment bankers to hear their opinion. Then, if I wanted, I could visit the companies and meet their executives. I asked about travel procedures. Alan replied, "There are none. You can travel anywhere you want. We travel first class!" He also went on to say, "All of us will review your reports. This is how the firm evaluates performance. We like strong opinions, and you should not be afraid to make mistakes. A committee reviews all recommendations, and they too can be fallible!"

I enjoyed meeting my counterparts in New York. All of them were very welcoming because I represented a large and important client. Similarly, I did not have trouble making appointments with the senior executives of the companies I covered.

While I was preoccupied with my new job, Mary Ann was busy decorating our new apartment and helping her grandmother with various social activities. It was a busy and happy time. Many of our old Boston friends were glad to see us, and we had many other friends who were newly married.

Not long after moving into our Boston apartment, Mary Ann auditioned for a role in a charity musical sponsored by the Vincent Club, which supported the Massachusetts General Hospital. On her first try, Mary Ann landed one of the lead roles—she studied voice in Paris and was a talented actress. I was so proud that I attended at least five of the performances with friends.

Because my work involved a considerable amount of travel, I invited
Mary Ann to join me on some of the trips. Most of the meetings were
in California. Our favorite places were San Francisco and Carmel. In
the company of corporate executives, Mary Ann could not relate; she
did not understand that some people had to work for a living. While
this remained an unresolved issue between us, we enjoyed several fun
business trips to California and France.

While we carried on a busy social life, I also worked hard. I rarely
stayed late in the office but often brought work back home. With Mary
Ann (and later the children) in bed, I stayed up late at night so I could be
ready for the next day. Every other week, I spent a day in New York, but I
tried to be back at night so I could be with the family. Almost every other
month, I spent the better part of a week on the west coast. During the
day, I had three to four appointments with corporate executives. Then I
returned to the hotel and dictated reports late into the night. The next
morning, I sent them by express mail to my secretary. When I returned
to the office, the drafts were ready. One time, the Director of Research
compiled a list of reports and pages written by the different analysts.
The volume of my output was far ahead of others (though I am not
necessarily vouching for its quality). I was assigned a full-time secretary,
which made my life much more efficient.

We continued to see Mrs. Webster, and I also visited my parents,
who lived outside Boston. Their retired life was happy. My stepfather
resumed his hobby of making delicately embossed leather albums, and

surprisingly, there was considerable demand. Mother was raised to be a hostess and enjoyed entertaining her friends again. Her great pleasure was going to the Boston Symphony, where she sometimes met the Dennisons.

Occasionally, we saw Mary Ann's parents, but she had a tenuous relationship with her mother, which I could not comprehend. Her parents were nice people and always pleasant to me. Still, for several generations, they were brought up in a sheltered environment, removed from the realities of life. Perhaps one of the reasons I got along with them so well was that I was the only family member whose career was not dependent on their help. The other family members worked for organizations that had family ties or ownership. Mary Ann's father was the chairman of a large family brokerage firm, Harris & Upham. The second name on the firm was his wife's last name. It seemed as if they wanted to have identity and control. The firm had more than seventy offices worldwide. According to his nephew (a good friend of mine), the founder of the firm (my father-in-law's father) had been such an overpowering individual that the subsequent managers had not dared make any changes. In a sense, the company operated in the past. This family background must have influenced my father-in-law's character, but I liked him. Even though my father-in-law was the director of half a dozen significant U.S. corporations, his fondest memories went back to Harvard, where he had been the assistant manager of the football team.

My mother-in-law was Mrs. Webster's daughter and had a similar background, but she never finished secondary school. She was low-key, always correct, and devoted to her family. Despite these positive qualities, her relationship with Mary Ann was not harmonious. None of the family members knew, nor cared about, my background. At one time, the issue came up, but they did not understand, nor could they relate to it. Frankly, I did not care—I preferred to look toward the future, rather than the past anyway. Mary Ann felt the same.

Because my work was going well, we were now able to purchase a small house on Beacon Hill. Because of my position, it was easy to obtain a mortgage. We were thrilled to have a house on the flat part of Beacon Hill, a block from the Boston Public Garden. The home was on one of the few private streets that allowed us to park two cars in front of the house. This was important because we used cars for weekends. It was a unique carriage house that had been completely reconstructed by a developer who engaged a young and creative architect. To bring in daylight, the architect designed a glass-enclosed atrium in the center of the house. One could sit in the dining room, look across the atrium, and see the fireplace in the living room. The atrium also had a small garden with a fountain. One could hear the peaceful rhythm of tinkling water throughout the house.

To celebrate our first Christmas there, my ski buddies from Vermont delivered a huge fifteen-foot Christmas tree, which we placed in the atrium. For several months, we had a Christmas tree with lights, sometimes covered with real snow. It added Christmas spirit to our lives. The house was an architectural success, even featured in *Better Homes and*

Gardens. We were very proud of our new home and loved it very much.

Mary Ann attended Boston University to get a B.A. degree because she only graduated from a junior college. While she liked the lectures, she did not have the self-discipline to meet the other requirements. Mary Ann, however, attended an interior decorating course given by a society lady. Also, she continued to help her grandmother with her many social functions.

In the winter, we occasionally skied in Vermont with my old friends. On summer weekends, we visited my old Cape Cod place, but because we were now married, it was less convenient. On the way home, we occasionally stopped by to see Mary Ann's grandmother. She had a beautiful house in Quissett near Woods Hole—a stunning replica of a French château. Around the house, there was a large multi-tier rose garden. So many people wanted to see the gardens that Mrs. Webster purchased the land across the road for visitors' parking.

On one of our visits, Mary Ann told me that my responsibility was to entertain Mrs. Webster's brother, Chandler Hovey. This assignment presented a challenge because Chandler was very old—eighty—and wore a hearing aid in his shirt pocket. Being a real Yankee, he did not like to talk much.

I did my very best to meet this challenge. All of us took a stroll through the rose garden. While the ladies chatted amiably, Chandler and I dragged behind in silence. Afterward, when we sat down for tea, the ladies continued to talk. To get the conversation going with Chandler,

I asked about his twelve-meter yacht, the *Eastern*, which he had entered in the America's Cup trials. No response. A hard nudge from Mary Ann followed. As a last resort, I asked Chandler about the weather. I did not know of any sailor who was unwilling to talk about the weather, but this attempt was also unsuccessful. I was in desperate straits, headed for social failure. Just as I was giving up hope, Chandler suddenly turned to me and exclaimed, "I knew they could do it! The Red Sox beat the Yankees!" It turned out that Chandler replaced his hearing aid with a portable radio and had been listening to the baseball game all along. This incident heightened my respect for Chandler, and I figured that with advanced age also came unanticipated wisdom!

As we drove back to Boston, Mary Ann said that I did an excellent job with Chandler. I started to voice my reservations, but she interrupted and said, "I know it was difficult, but you did great!" I tried to explain that I had not done anything, but Mary Ann went on to say how proud she was of my accomplishments. What could I do but remain quiet and accept her praise? Now, many decades later, it is time to confess what really happened that day.

Altogether I could not have asked for a more perfect life than the one we enjoyed. I hoped it would continue forever, and it lasted for five more years. We were happily married with no obligations and the flexibility to do almost anything because we did not have any children yet. Mary Ann was happy with her life in Boston, and I thought my job was great.

Both of us liked to travel, and during winter vacations, we skied in Switzerland—Zermatt, Klosters, and Davos. Then we took a few days in

Vienna, one of my favorite cities. In the winter, with all the snow-covered palaces, I thought it was one of the most romantic places in Europe. We usually attended one of the Vienna Boys' Choir concerts, saw the Lipizzaner horses, and at night attended the Vienna Volksoper. Operettas were my favorite form of light Germanic music. After a few days, we boarded the Alpenrose Express and continued our ski vacation in Zürs Lech and St. Anton am Arlberg. It could not have been a better vacation anywhere in the world!

During summer vacations, we traveled to some offbeat places, like Scandinavia, where we toured the whole length of Norway. Afterward, we liked to return to familiar places, like Italy and France.

In the winter, we occasionally visited Mary Ann's parents in Florida. The warm climate was a pleasant change for Mary Ann because she did not like cold weather. I was glad to note that Mary Ann's relationship with her mother was better, but I still could not comprehend the family dynamics. My personal experience only demonstrated how essential a family was for mutual happiness and success. Here, my in-laws had all the material means the world could offer, but there was still an undercurrent of uncertainty. While I liked my in-laws, I did not spend much time in Florida—I thought it was for old people.

As I look back at these years, they represent a period in which we could hardly do anything wrong. It was like a golfer who sees all his shots land on the green, and his first putt goes into the hole. Or a tennis player whose shots used to go past the baseline but now land just inside.

In sports, such moments are typically brief, but in my case, that stroke of "luck" continued for a number of years.

After having worked at SSR&M for four and a half years, the managing partner called me in for a review. He said, "Normally, our firm considers associates for partnership after seven to eight years tenure, but you have done so well that we would like to make you partner now. This is the shortest amount of time that anyone has made partner." I was amazed and considered this an honor. It was clear that my happy home life and great work environment made this possible.

We talked about starting a family and began looking for a house in the country. Both of us liked Squam Lake, New Hampshire, where Mary Ann's family had a long history. There, Mrs. Webster owned a large house overlooking the lake, which she rarely used. She often offered us the house and its facilities—including tennis courts, stables with horses, boats, etc.—on the weekends. Years before, the property also had a private nine-hole golf course. Most of all, we enjoyed the unspoiled, natural beauty of the lake.

One of my wife's relatives, Frank, was an avid conservationist who bought up land to keep it out of the hands of greedy developers. (Later, Frank, we sold the land to the "right people.") He showed us several properties, and we considered a purchase. A few days later, Mrs. Webster called and told us, "You are the only ones of my numerous relatives who have not asked me for land. Since the family owns close to twenty thousand acres, including half a dozen islands on the lake, you will have a good choice!" I replied that I was an independent person and did not want to impose on others. Mrs. Webster said, "Both of you look around and select a favorite spot, and I will sell it to you as I have done for other relatives." Later, I learned that the land price was set decades earlier. Mary Ann and I wandered around the property and finally selected a home site at the tip of a peninsula, with a panoramic view across the lake. It was not far away from the main road, which meant we could use the house for skiing. Both of us were excited about our new country house and the thought of starting a family. When making plans, we decided to take advantage of Mrs. Webster's offer to use her Squam Lake house for a weekend.

When the weekend came, we invited a dozen friends. We rode horses in the morning—the property had a stable of horses with grooms to help. Riding the mountain trails was great fun, and the scenery was spectacular! For lunch, we were picked up by a boat and delivered to an island in the middle of the lake. In the afternoon, we played tennis, and when evening came, we prepared dinner, usually grilled steaks. It was a fun weekend, and we repeated it several times. I remember that one of the guests counted the beds and came back with a number over forty. Mary Ann was in her element as a gracious hostess—she made everyone feel welcome.

On Sunday evening, after everyone departed, Mary Ann and I went out on the terrace overlooking Squam Lake. The sun was setting—you could hear the loons calling, and the view was magnificent. The scene inspired me to ponder how lucky we were and how perfect life was—a happy marriage, great friends, and plans to build a house and start a family.

I turned to Mary Ann and expected a similar response. To my surprise, she looked at me wistfully and said, "Who am I? Did my parents love me more than my governess did? What is my validity and purpose in life?" I was surprised that, amidst this beauty, her thoughts were somewhere else, and that after so many years, Mary Ann was still bothered by her mother firing her beloved governess while she was away. The incident left a lasting impression on her. I viewed it more like a small, dark cloud floating across a sunny sky that, shortly afterward, fades over the horizon. It was difficult for me to understand her feelings because I grew up in an environment where family relationships like hers did not exist.

Even so, life continued to be happy for us, with shared interests and friends, helped by my business career. I was glad when Mary Ann's relationship with her mother improved—she began to enjoy spending time with her parents, particularly in Florida. Mary Ann was brought up on a large thirty-five-acre Long Island estate but preferred to visit her parents in Hobe Sound, Florida. The Harrises also had a place in the Adirondack Mountains, along with a New York City apartment, but we were seldom there.

In the winter, we visited Mary Ann's parents in Florida. On one of these occasions, my father-in-law said, "Both of you should go see my mother, who is not well. She lives in the family house in Palm Beach."

In the past, he talked very little about his family—I had only met my father-in-law's younger brother, an Episcopal minister, whose son was a good friend. I was friendly with the minister, and he told me more about the family background. This was helpful because I wanted to better understand Mary Ann and make our marriage even happier.

The minister told me that my father-in-law's family had five children. The head of the family was the founder of a successful investment firm and apparently did not have much time for the family. His wife, my father-in-law's mother, had her own social commitments in New York and Palm Beach. At an early age, the children were shipped off to boarding schools. The eldest son was the mother's favorite—he became a socialite and was only peripherally involved in the family business. My father-in-law, while growing up, had done everything right but never received any well-deserved parental recognition. Another brother, after Harvard, became a devout communist—he gave away his inheritance and lived in the Soviet Union during the 1930s. Quite a family background, but it still did not explain why Mary Ann once said, "The sins of your fathers shall revisit you."

I was intrigued by our forthcoming Palm Beach visit, even though it was only twenty miles away. My in-laws implied that Palm Beach was a "sin city," but I wanted to see for myself. Sin— from the puritanical perspective of my in-laws—was probably just ostentatious living, mainly by those with new wealth.

Before Mary Ann and I left for Palm Beach, my father-in-law told me more about the family. He said,

My father spent part of the winter in Palm Beach, and I occasionally visited. One day my father's good friend, a well-known Wall Street investor and speculator named 'Bet-a-Million' Gates, came and said, 'Harris, I'm tired of making money on Wall Street. I want to build a real company. I am asking you and a few friends to participate.' My father knew that 'Bet-a-Million' Gates was a talented businessman and immediately agreed. As Gates was leaving, my father casually asked him, 'What will your business be?' Gates replied, 'Oil looks good—I will take over a small startup and grow it. It's in Texas, so I'll name it Texaco.'

Not surprisingly, Gates and Texaco were very successful, and the Harrises served on its Board of Directors for three generations.

My father-in-law was unusually talkative that night. He continued, In the late 1920s, my father bought two adjoining plots of land on South Ocean Boulevard, a premier location. He hired Mizner, the best-known architect in Palm Beach, to build a mansion [El Castillo at 4 El Bravo Way]. Since my father was an avid golfer, he had the home built one block from the ocean, and the plot in front was a chipping and putting green [now another mega-mansion]. My father and some of his friends, including Ed Shearson, felt that the golf course at the Everglades Club did not offer enough of a challenge, so they bought land and started the nearby Gulf Stream Golf Club in Delray Beach. To make it special, they hired Mizner to design the clubhouse.

This was a lot of history before I had even set foot in Palm Beach. We subsequently made several visits to see my wife's grandmother and aunt. Mary Ann's grandmother was in her late nineties and hardly talked, and the Moorish-designed El Castillo mansion was dreary, filled with musty, dark furniture, and looked like it came from a bad Hollywood movie set. My tastes were still influenced by plain Boston living, so I just tagged along (and sometimes wished I was skiing).

While this might disappoint some, I saw no sin in Palm Beach. The town abounded with elegantly dressed ladies who wore a lot of makeup— some, according to Mary Ann, enhanced their looks with plastic surgery. Also, many of the wives were much younger than their husbands. In general, though, people were gracious and friendly. They hugged and kissed each other all the time, as if they had been apart for months, though they had probably been together at a cocktail party the night before. It sure was different from Yankee Boston, where hardly anyone talked to strangers unless they were checked out beforehand. With few exceptions, there was limited graciousness and hospitality. I spent the better part of my life living or attending schools in Boston and felt quite comfortable in that environment, but the sunshine and friendliness of Florida began to grow on me.

While visits to Florida were a pleasant change, our life in Boston also became more exciting. With the help of an architect, we designed our new country house in New Hampshire. It was a spectacular location. We owned most of the peninsula that extended well into the lake—from any direction, one could see the sparkling water and the mountains beyond. There was ample privacy; no other houses were nearby. We designed the house so that one could have a different view of the lake from each room. There was also a floating dock that extended more than fifty feet into the lake, which could be used for swimming and to dock a boat.

We were expecting a family and were ecstatic when our daughter, Lisa, was born in 1968. Our son, Jay, followed two years later. To have a family was a fulfillment of my dreams. I wanted to do everything possible to make my children's life a happy one and avoid the turmoil that I experienced in my childhood. I was convinced that Mary Ann shared the same values, and I knew that together we could achieve this goal.

Our growing family and a new country home made our life almost perfect—or so I thought. In the summer, I commuted on alternate days from Boston and took off Wednesdays to spend the maximum amount of time with my family. There was no need to take a vacation anywhere else—we had the perfect place. Mary Ann was a devoted mother, and we always had babysitters, au pairs, or live-in help to make life easier.

Days in New Hampshire were always beautiful, whether in the summer with swimming and picnicking on one of the islands or in the fall with its spectacular display of colors. One only had to look out of the window to see a rich tapestry of reds, yellows, and all the different shades in between. This display was multiplied by the reflection in the lake. The mountains in the distance added even more color, and one had the feeling of being amid an immense flower garden. In the winter, there was skiing nearby, or one could just sit in front of the large fireplace and watch ice storms moving across the lake. Regardless of the season or circumstances, being in New Hampshire gave me a feeling of peace and tranquility. All other problems seemed to dissolve into the past.

My most lasting memory is when, after a swim, I rested on the float that extended into the lake and savored the sweet smell of water on the wooden planks. I could hear the lapping of waves from passing boats, interrupted by the occasional loon call. As I closed my eyes, I heard the patter of little feet running on the dock and a shout, "Dad, play with us!" What more could I ask for? This memory left such an indelible impression that, years later, whenever I could not sleep on a plane or elsewhere, I thought of it. This scene vividly appeared in the air in front of me. I was transported back to a time that gave me a feeling of peace and tranquility. With these pleasant thoughts, I could doze off no matter where I was.

One day, in Boston, I received a notice to serve on a jury. When I left in the morning, I told Mary Ann that this would require a brief stop at the courthouse, but I would most likely be dismissed. That was not the case. I was selected to serve on the jury for a murder trial. All the individuals involved were African Americans and the jury was not sequestered. The trial lasted almost a week, and throughout it, we tracked the daily lives of the individuals involved. The trial required several field trips to the location of the crime, their homes and hangouts, as well as other activities.

This experience opened my eyes to a segment of society I had not been aware of before. While I focused my time and energy on education, work, and family, I realized that there were others less fortunate than me, who either did not recognize or did not pursue opportunities for advancement. I considered the United States a land of opportunity, where one could forge his own destiny, but there were also those who missed the chance—held back by lack of education or family, social, or economic conditions. I wished I could help focus their energies in the right direction. This experience also made me aware that, despite my war experiences, I led a somewhat sheltered life.

Shortly afterward, I was invited to become a trustee of the Boston Children's Hospital, one of the most prestigious and recognized institutions in its field. In the past, I declined such offers in order to focus on work and family, but this time I decided to accept. As a trustee, I served on several different committees, dealing not only with finance but also with planning and evaluation of the various programs. It was a satisfying feeling to help others because I had benefited so much in my life.

I served the Boston Children's Hospital as a trustee for several terms. To attend the meetings, I was occasionally offered a ride by a fellow trustee, who was the president of the largest bank in Boston. He had a car, a driver, and a bodyguard—an important individual indeed! Most of the other trustees were leading Boston businessmen or heads of large organizations. They were able to do much more for the institution than I could.

When my term as a trustee ended, I accepted a position to serve as the treasurer and a member of the Executive Committee of The Parents and Children's Services, a relatively small but well-regarded social services organization founded after the Civil War. At that time, the practice was for families with serious problems was to give children for adoption. The Parents and Children's Services pioneered the idea that with social counseling, families could stay together, which ultimately benefited the children. As a board member, I had frequent contact with social workers and occasionally with the families who were counseled. This gave me the feeling of more involvement in the community.

Unlike other social-service organizations, The Parents and Children's Services had a substantial endowment. One of my first acts as treasurer was to find the best investment manager in Boston and ask him to oversee the management of the endowment. That was easy because I knew most of the best investment professionals. The organization's policy was to withdraw around five percent annually from the endowment and supplement the rest of the operating budget with grants. The latter, however, were unpredictable, so sometimes we had to make more substantial withdrawals. I am gratified to report that after having served more than twenty-five years as The Parents and Children's Services treasurer, our assets at the end of my term were higher than at the beginning.

Unfortunately, after I retired from the board, the endowment, in a way, led to the demise of this exceptional organization. Many other social-service organizations were underfunded and wanted to merge with The Parents and Children's Services because of its assets. While serving as treasurer, I opposed this course of action, but after my retirement, the organization ceased to exist as an independent entity.

Changing World

When I first met Mary Ann, she was one of the loveliest, most considerate, and compassionate individuals I had ever encountered—she was gracious and never said a harsh word to anyone. I never saw her angry. I loved her very much. She made my life worthwhile and in a sense inspired my business success. Mary Ann's positive characteristics continued throughout our early years of marriage, but after the children were born, her personality began to change. My initial reaction was that as a new parent, she was simply adjusting to a different lifestyle. While our responsibilities changed, Mary Ann's daily routine was not demanding or significantly different. We always had domestic help, so there was plenty of time for Mary Ann to pursue her interests.

Also, our friends started to change—most of our old friends were replaced by Mary Ann's new acquaintances, primarily divorced women whose economic conditions deteriorated and who complained about the lack of support from their "male chauvinist" husbands. Initially, I attributed the change to Mary Ann's compassionate nature and willingness to help those less fortunate. This was probably also her first exposure to the harsh realities of life. Mary Ann was brought up in a sheltered environment and never had to work a day in her life. It occurred to me that her new women friends might have undue influence because Mary Ann was impressionable—there was an element of jealousy on their part because our life was going well and theirs were not. Perhaps combining a junior college education with her upbringing inhibited

Mary Ann's ability to see clearly where the new ideas of her friends could lead. Naively, I believed that Mary Ann would not fall into the trap of the women's liberation movement, which looked to me like a passing phenomenon. After all, Mary Ann came from a traditional background with solid family values.

Before this change, I was always greeted when returning home from work, and then both of us had an early dinner with the children. At this time, however, when I came home, Mary Ann was frequently away attending a women's meeting. When I asked about it, she replied, "I have to find my identity and self-validity. Most of my new friends have found theirs." Frankly, I did not understand—I was still hoping it would soon end.

On a few occasions, I attempted to talk to Mary Ann about the growing pressures I experienced in the office. While my business career continued to do well, my responsibilities also increased and demanded more attention. Mary Ann showed hardly any interest or understanding of my work—she was preoccupied with her own life. It was disappointing to me, but I could cope because I had been on my own for most of my life.

For a change, I took Mary Ann on a business trip to California. In the past, she enjoyed social dinners with corporate executives. Now, she inquired how their corporations treated women employees—not an appropriate subject at a social function, especially when brought up by someone who had never worked. The trip was not a success, and she left early for Boston. One change that always brought happiness to Mary

Ann was our Florida visit. We planned to visit in a few months, and I looked forward to its positive influence.

As before, we spent part of Christmas with Mary Ann's family in Long Island. This year, however, was not as pleasant as normal—Mary Ann continued to be militant in her assertiveness and insisted she would do whatever she wanted, regardless of others. While there, I drove her father around on errands because the family chauffeur was away. I liked my father-in-law and admired his low-key gentlemanly manner. Unfortunately, he had early signs of Alzheimer's, and it was sad to see his cognitive functions deteriorating. I remembered the evenings when he invited me to join him for Metropolitan Opera performances. Because he was a director of Texaco, which sponsored Metropolitan Opera broadcasts, he had excellent season tickets. It was a pleasure to have dinner with him, attend a superb performance, and then be driven in a chauffeured limousine to their apartment.

I wondered how my mother-in-law was going to cope with her husband's health problems. She had been brought up in a sheltered environment and never finished boarding school—she had a narrow perspective of the world, but she was a caring grandmother. My mother-in-law's mother, Mrs. Webster, was different. She was an exceptional person—gracious, bright, and a philanthropic leader in Boston. I was a great admirer of Mrs. Webster and figured it had not been easy to be her daughter. Despite their comfort, it looked to me like the life of my in-laws had not always been easy, and the future turned out to be even more difficult.

After Christmas in Long Island, we returned to Boston, accompanied by Mary Ann's sister and her family. I arranged a special treat for all of us: to attend a performance of the Ice Capades. It was an upbeat event, and I felt this would put the stressful holiday experience behind us. When the evening was over, I looked forward to the next morning, when I could return to the peace and quiet of my office.

A happy family in New Hampshire 1971

End of Marriage

On January 2, 1977, after the New Year celebration, I went happily to my office, thinking that for the time being, all my problems were behind me. I not only enjoyed my work but liked the company of my partners and associates. The office and its environment had always been a sort of sanctuary. As I settled down for my daily routine, the receptionist

Visiting Florida

Family in 1990

telephoned and informed me, "There is someone in the lobby who insists on seeing you right away." I said that I had no appointment scheduled and figured the unexpected visitor was probably an insurance salesman.

A short while later, the receptionist called back and said, "The man is causing trouble and requesting that you see him immediately." Such a scene was unusual in our traditional office. To diffuse the situation, I went to the reception area. I saw a shabbily dressed man—he ran up to me and handed over a bunch of papers and said, "You have been served!" I did not know what to do, so I took the papers and went to my office. I discovered that the documents came from one of the most aggressive and unsavory divorce law firms—my wife wanted to separate. My joint checking account, as well as other accounts, were frozen and could not be used without permission from the lawyers. I was shocked—I had not had any prior conversations with my wife about separation or divorce. My understanding was that if one spouse desires divorce, the parties first contact a marriage counselor and seek reconciliation. If this did not work, then both parties together developed a plan that led to the least amount of stress on the children.

Subsequent events indicated that my assessment of our situation was naïve and wrong. Also, I probably bear some responsibility for not understanding the turmoil that took place in Mary Ann's life. I did not grasp how quickly her values changed.

This became the worst day of my life. Family has always been of paramount importance to me, and this feeling has only been reinforced by my experiences. Had it not been for my family and its unwavering support, my survival and eventual success would have been doubtful. It had always been my goal to pass these values onto my children, with the hope that this would make their lives easier; now, in a moment, all these dreams appeared to be shattered.

While I probably did not fully understand all of Mary Ann's concerns, I was aghast by her sudden and unexpected actions. I was devastated—if this had been her purpose, she succeeded! However, she underestimated my resiliency. I continued to believe that the future would eventually be better, and my "good luck" would continue.

All of us occasionally encounter problems that initially appear to be insoluble, but if we do not lose hope and try hard, we can overcome them. Our eventual success will be so much sweeter, our characters will be strengthened, and the future is likely to bring us happiness.

With these thoughts, I tried to contact Mary Ann and stop the proceedings before they got out of control. I set up a session with a marriage counselor, but Mary Ann never showed up. The legal hassle continued, and my wife's lawyers continued to request documents, financial statements, and other materials. Because I did not have an attorney, I did not know what to do. I called my old Navy friend, Ed, who practiced law in Boston. When I explained my predicament, he said,

I cannot help much because my senior partner, Monroe, is the one handling your wife's case. All I can say is that you are facing serious problems, so be ready for it. If you want more information about your wife's attorney, all I can do is refer you to a series of articles that appeared in the Boston press.

He went on to explain, "My senior partner, Monroe, is very successful and is regarded by men as one of the most vicious divorce lawyers in Boston. He has won important cases and collected huge fees." This was bad news. I asked Ed what to do. He said, "The same article goes on to say that Monroe's frequent opponent is Bob, his former partner. Even though they argue in the courtroom, both have the same objective— to make money for themselves." I asked, "What are the chances of reconciliation?" Ed replied, "Do you think they want to cut off cash flow from rich clients? They want the process to go on forever!"

After hearing this, I was disappointed and knew that if we continued this path, our marriage would end. I did not think that was Mary Ann's goal, and I doubted her parents understood what was going on after she hired the sleazy law firm. This was a different world for her family. The guidance must have come from her women's liberation group, who had plenty of prior experience. Subsequent developments proved even more disappointing, after I received an invoice from a firm that, several months earlier had made a detailed appraisal and inventory of our two houses. This proved that the divorce had been orchestrated months in advance. I was devastated that the woman who I loved and trusted had done this, but I probably deserve a share of the blame for not sensing what was wrong.

I did not want to involve lawyers, but there was no choice. The next morning, I went to see Bob, who greeted me with a smile like an old friend. One of the first questions he asked me was, "Has there been any physical violence or abuse in the family?" My answer was no. His next question was, "Were there any arguments about finances?" Again, my answer was no. I had a successful and financially rewarding career. Mary Ann never worked a day in her life, but she had some assets of her own and received an allowance of $150 a month from her parents. Bob went on to ask, "Were there any problems with alcohol or substance abuse?" I answered that both of us hardly drank, except for the occasional glass of wine. Then he asked, "Were there other relationships involved by either of the parties?" The answer again was no—both of us devoted most of our free time to our family.

I continued to be hassled by lawyers and made many court appearances for inconsequential matters like visitation hours, holiday travel, and allocation of furniture. I asked my attorney Bob why all this could not have been agreed upon earlier by the respective attorneys. Bob said,

We have agreed, but when Monroe [Mary Ann's attorney] goes to her for final approval, he is turned down. The message he gets is that a deal worked out between two male chauvinistic attorneys is unacceptable to her women's liberation friends. They urge Mary Ann to go to court because the judge is a woman.

This was true, but after a while, the female judge became quite sympathetic to my case. Mary Ann fired Monroe. With her new attorney, life seemed to settle down.

This period represented a dark page in my life, but help came unexpectedly at just the right time—in the form of my secretary/assistant, Barbara, who said to me, "Mr. Livens, I know how busy you are and how all this legal stuff has gotten you down. Let me handle the details with the lawyers. Also, I will find you apartments so you can spend more time with your children." Her kindness made a great difference. I asked, "How can I ever repay you?" She replied, "I do not expect a reward. I am doing this from the kindness of my heart." Several years later, Barbara was accepted into the special Ada Comstock Scholar program at Smith College, which included students that experienced interrupted education. It was an exceptional award—and an expensive proposition. Barbara did not have enough funds to cover all the associated expenses. At that time, I was able to help, so I said, "Barbara, do not worry. I will take care of all of your finances." It gave me a great deal of satisfaction to repay someone who had been so kind to me. Still, I felt that I was only able to repay a small part of her generous help. While life was not always pleasant, it gave me an opportunity to see the kindness and generosity in people's hearts that remains hidden under routine conditions.

Shortly afterward, I settled into my new condominium. The prior owner was an acquaintance of mine and told me that he purchased the unit after his own divorce. Now he was happily married and moving to the suburbs. He said, "John, from my experience, I'm sure you've had a miserable time and probably do not want to make any decisions right now about purchasing an apartment. You can buy it at any time, and I will credit your rental payments toward the sales price." Then he added, "The apartment comes with positive vibes and has brought me happiness. Years ago, it was occupied by the famous actress Sarah Bernhardt, so you have good company! I know it will bring you happiness, too." The condominium had a large living room with two bedrooms. The windows overlooked Commonwealth Avenue and the side streets, and it had been beautifully decorated by one of the leading designers in Boston.

While I missed my family, I had the children on alternate weekends and took them to New Hampshire. We also traveled to Bermuda, where I owned a house with my partners, available at almost any time. It was a pleasant place, not far from Hamilton, and overlooked the harbor. One could see cruise ships sailing by. The house had several bedrooms and staff, if needed. I was also a member of the Coral Beach Club, which had a spectacular location overlooking a beautiful pink beach. In the evening, one could dance and dine on the terrace, which rose sixty feet above the sea. It could not have been more pleasant. On other occasions, I brought friends who had entertained me in the past. Spring was one of the most beautiful seasons in Bermuda—the moment you arrived, you smelled the fragrance of the oleanders that cover a large part of the island. Quite a change of pace from dreary Boston!

During our marriage, Mary Ann organized our social life. Now, more than a decade later, I was again on my own. I did not know how to enter the new "singles" scene, but I was pleased when my Beacon Hill friends invited me for dinners, weekends, and social functions. They disapproved of Mary Ann's new friends and the way I was treated. I went to the gatherings without a date because I still hoped our marriage could be resurrected. As time went on, this proved to be more and more of an illusion.

Mary Ann started dating. I was disappointed and figured I should also participate in more social activities. Friends began to invite single ladies, most of whom were recently divorced and looking to start a new life. They welcomed me warmly, and new acquaintances treated me with respect and consideration. It was quite different from what I experienced in the preceding months. The new friends said I was charming, intelligent, generous, and lots of other nice adjectives. One of them even told me I had a scintillating personality—I had to look it up in the dictionary! Altogether, it seemed I discovered a charming, hidden personality that had previously been unknown even to me.

One day, I told my good friend Polly, the wife of my former suitemate Bill, about this experience. Polly said,

Bill and I think you are a great guy and a good father, but you have to look realistically at your status. Most of the ladies you have met are recently divorced and are facing deteriorating financial and social conditions. Some of them have started to look for jobs and have had to take their children out of private school. A relationship with you would put all their financial and social problems behind them, and they would enjoy a superior lifestyle.

I knew Polly was bright and socially aware, so my dream of my new, sparkling personality evaporated. From college, I remembered the Marxist theory that economic conditions shape human behavior. Even though I disliked Karl Marx's teachings, I had to admit that in this case, he might be right.

Still hoping our marriage could somehow be restored, I finally had to consider the people with whom Mary Ann associated. One of the leaders of the group was a woman with an unusual background; she came from a wealthy Midwest family and had been married to a pleasant Boston doctor, who I knew. After twenty years of marriage, the woman told her husband it was time for him to change his last name to her maiden name because she had been subservient long enough. The doctor did as asked. A few months later, the wife told her husband she lost respect for him and filed for divorce. Afterward, the woman went to seminary and became an ordained minister. Because it was difficult for her to fit into the church structure, she started a counseling service for recent divorcees and others seeking guidance. This woman also attempted to organize a demonstration against the Pope's visit to Boston because he was a male chauvinist. This woman became one of Mary Ann's spiritual advisors. Our prospects for reconciliation were slim.

One day, I called the children at the Boston house, and Mary Ann answered. I tried to be as brief and polite as possible and said, "Mary Ann, would you please get the children to the telephone?" She said, "My name is no longer Mary Ann but is now Melova, and I want to be called that way." I asked why. Mary Ann replied, "I underwent past life regression and found out that in my prior life, I was an African slave girl called Melova." I was distressed and realized that the lovely, charming person I married more than a dozen years ago was no more.

Mary Ann's appearance also changed. Gone was her long, beautiful light brown hair—it was now cut short. Mary Ann wore no makeup, and her skin looked pale and parched from excessive, prescribed (and non-prescribed) medication. Also, she gained a great deal of weight. Mary Ann no longer seemed to care about elegant dresses or her appearance. In the past, her presence and personality added cheer to any social gathering, but now she was a different person. I felt saddened and wished Mary Ann well, but understood her well-being was now beyond my control and responsibility. Despite the changes, Mary Ann remained a devoted mother and occasionally showed sparks of her old personality. I never could call Mary Ann "Melova" because I wanted to remember her how she was when I loved her.

During my free time, I played tennis, sometimes five days a week, with my son as a partner. We did quite well in doubles competitions. I could now also spend more time with Mother, who lived alone in a large house in the Boston suburbs. My stepfather had passed away after a battle with pancreatic cancer. To a large degree, Mother was responsible for our family's survival and success. No matter the conditions, whether privileged upbringing or mere survival during the war, my mother faced all circumstances with grace and dignity. She was also an excellent hostess, and people tended to gravitate to her house. On weekends, after tennis, I would visit and see Mother in the garden, playing cards with friends. It gave me pleasure to see that all of them enjoyed some peace after the hectic circumstances they experienced in the past. Additionally, Mother was always available to me to provide invaluable, unbiased advice. She never told me what to do because she believed each person is ultimately responsible for his or her own life. She gently prodded me at times— "Have you thought of this or that?"—but it was always non-judgmental and gave me perspective.

One day, while in the office, I received a telephone call from a friend. In an urgent tone, he said, "John, you are in deep shit!" I thought this was strong language for an investment banker. He said, "John, I'm getting divorced. Natalie, my wife, told me she prefers women over men!" This couple had been friends of ours, as well as houseguests. I expressed my sympathies. He went on, "There's more. Natalie is an attorney and will now be representing Mary Ann in your divorce case. She works for her father's law firm, which is not doing well, and Mary Ann is going to be a substantial client." I asked, "What are you going to do?" He replied, "I cannot stand Natalie's harassment and told my firm I want to get as far away as possible. I managed to be assigned to our Hong Kong office and will leave shortly. I just wanted to give you a warning, to prepare you for trouble ahead—Natalie hates men, and you will be her target." This sounded terrible!

My friend was right. A few weeks later, I received a barrage of subpoenas, requests for depositions, and other demands. I had enough of the legal processes and finally realized our marriage was not going to be salvaged. I told my lawyers to file for divorce and expedite the process. My action was unexpected and only served to generate more anger and animosity. The women's group with which Mary Ann was associated probably viewed me as a male chauvinist and wanted to teach me a lesson and modify my character. I think they picked the wrong target!

CHAPTER 10

A NEW BEGINNING

My new apartment was farther away from the Boston business district than my Beacon Hill home. I walked to work every morning—the distance was longer, but my walk was more picturesque. I started out along Commonwealth Avenue, considered one of the most attractive streets in Boston and then continued through the Boston Garden with its beautiful flowers, which were regularly and carefully tended. I crossed a bridge that adjoined a lagoon with swan boats, a spot frequented by tourists. Then I went across the Boston Common, where at one time, the early colonists grazed their cattle. At the end of this park, near a subway station, there were merchant stands frequented by homeless people looking for handouts.

Usually in deep thought, I walked past. I remember one street person, Mike, who always cheerfully greeted me with "Good morning and have a great day!" I nodded and moved along, thinking that with his kind of personality, Mike would do an excellent job as a host in a restaurant—yet his choice was to work the streets. Even though I did not give money to Mike, it did not seem to bother him—every morning, he continued to be as cheerful as ever.

My regular encounter with Mike, and his consistent cheerfulness, prompted me to reflect on my own life and consider my attitude toward others. Mike probably had many bad days. When it rained, hardly anyone stopped to give him money. I do not know where Mike lived—it could have been in a shelter or on the streets. None of this seemed to worry Mike or affect his positive attitude, which was almost contagious. I compared this to my life—I did not lack for material possessions, yet I did not exude the same cheerful, optimistic attitude as Mike. I knew I would be better off if I could put the past behind me and accept the present with hope that the future would be brighter. I also remembered that Mother once said, "Negative thoughts can dim and extinguish even the brightest future lights." By reflecting on the past, in a sense, I was being selfish—my attention was preoccupied with my own life, which left no space for others. It occurred to me: Why not be like Mike and start the day with a bright smile? If this day does not turn out to be the best, tomorrow for sure will be better! So, I tried to start each day with a smile and gave a generous tip to Mike—but still doubted I could ever achieve his level of cheerfulness.

Years later, I walked along the same path through the Boston Common, and there, still, was Mike. He was as happy as ever. I was glad to see him, but I think his subtle message to me was, "I hope you are not reverting to your old, negative thinking!" Most of us believe the proper place to learn is in school or from family, but life is full of surprises, and you can learn valuable lessons from unexpected sources. Just be alert and open-minded—knowledge can come from anywhere! I learned from Mike to start every day with a smile and a positive attitude and not to be discouraged if initial efforts failed. Persistence and a positive outlook will eventually pay off, but even if not, you have the satisfaction of having tried your best.

My friends continued to include me in their social activities, but I was a passive participant. At one gathering, I met a lovely and thoughtful young lady; Diana and I had crossed paths in the business world, where she held a supporting role, but we never developed a social relationship. She already knew a great deal about my life because we had some of the same friends, but Diana never pried or inquired into my past. She sensed it was unpleasant and painful for me. Even though Diana worked in the business world, she was a talented artist with a great deal of sensitivity and understanding. She had never been married—thus, she had no bitter memories. I felt that Diana was a breath of fresh air, and I continued to see her. I remember calling her one day, after being in the courthouse for a long time in a sad situation. She replied, "When you get through, come to my apartment and we'll have dinner!" Diana's place, to me, was like an oasis in the midst of a dismal desert. It turned out Diana was also a superb horsewoman, a good shot, and a skier. We rode horses on a western ranch and skied together in New Hampshire. Life looked better and better!

Through the summer, I had the children for a week in New Hampshire. After such visits, I was lonely and ready to return to Boston. It was always a sad moment, but fortunately, Diana called and said, "Why don't you come to Maine, where I am with my family?" It was a superb invitation and came at just the right time. Diana's mother had a large house on a rock promontory overlooking the breaking surf of the Atlantic. It was near the location of many of Winslow Homer's beautiful Maine scenes. At night, there was a family dinner with Diana, her two sisters, and her mother. To this day, I have to say that I have never been in the company of four more beautiful women.

As Christmas approached, I did not have the children. It was not a happy time for me, so Diana recommended we do something special. I knew what to do—I made ski reservations in Klosters, Switzerland, at Chesa Grischuna, one of the most charming and romantic alpine hotels. The skiing in Klosters and Davos was not challenging, but the scenery was superb—no wonder the area is frequented by artists and celebrities! I skied there before and thought the Küblis *piste* was fun. It started in the snowfields at the top of the mountain, passed a few inns, and eventually took you to a railroad station. The same trip by train took almost an hour.

We arrived in Klosters a day before Christmas, and the beauty of the village surpassed any postcard or travel poster. Snow covered the roofs of the houses, and even though the streets were plowed, there was enough snow for horse-drawn sleighs to occasionally glide by. In one of the sleighs was Santa Claus, who handed out candy to a crowd of happy village children. It was a winter dream come true, and it was doubly pleasant to be there with an adorable companion.

After a candlelight dinner at the inn, we wandered down the street, snow crunching under our feet, mesmerized by the alpine beauty that took a different form at night. There were streetlights, but the moon and stars also shone brightly, and their sparkle was multiplied by the snow covering everything with a white blanket. You could see the warm glow of lighted Christmas trees in the windows of the homes, in contrast to the dark sky. We passed a pathway to a church and heard organ music as parishioners hurried in. We followed them. The path to the church was bordered by snow several feet high. Embedded in the snowbank were candles that guided you to the church door. We entered, and the service was in full progress. The minister read a Christmas passage from Luke about the birth of Christ, and it went like this: "*Es begab sich aber zu Zeit, das ein Gebot von dem Kaiser Augustus ausging, da alle Welt geschatz wurde...*" We all know the English version: "In those days, Caesar Augustus issued a decree that a census should take place..."

It did not matter the language or how this message was delivered—it was a universal message of hope and rebirth, a promise of a better future. I closed my eyes and saw myself standing next to my father almost fifty years before as he read the same passage. *Where is he now—heaven?* I wondered. I also began to think of my children and family and caught myself not paying attention to the attractive and compassionate lady beside me.

We spent Christmas Day skiing but had to quit early because winter daylight in the Alps is short. Diana told me, "I have a special surprise for you after our early dinner." After we finished the meal, outside the inn, there stood a sleigh with a driver. We traveled along narrow mountain roads that wound through snowfields. There was no traffic nor people—it was quiet and peaceful. All you could hear was the jingle of the bells from the horse's harness. The scenery was breathtaking—you never knew where the snowfields ended and the heavens began, and it seemed as if we traveled in an immense, sparkling crystal bowl.

It was a true winter wonderland, and I sat next to a lovely lady who planned this magnificent event. She was supportive and tried to better my life. To a degree, she restored my confidence in good relationships. What more could I ask? We had known each other over a year, and this seemed like a more than appropriate setting to make a permanent commitment. The atmosphere could not have been more picture-perfect.

Upon further reflection, however, I did not feel this was the right time to start a new married life—my divorce process was not yet over and could drag on further. Also, I had not been able to completely put my old life behind me, and I did not want to start out with a shaky foundation. So, I let this magic moment pass.

After returning to Boston, my relationship with Diana ended. Each of us had different expectations for the future, and she began to pursue a different course in her social life. Diana had been a ray of sunshine, breaking through dark clouds to make my life more enjoyable again.

While I missed her, I knew it was best for both of us. I am glad Diana went on to fulfill her life's goals and had a happy marriage and family. She certainly brought happiness to my life, and I am pleased that hers worked out well, too.

A New Life

After returning from Europe, my social life changed because I was once again an unencumbered bachelor. Friends continued to invite me, but my focus was on work and the children, who were always paramount in my life.

My work required considerable travel, particularly in the early phases when I started out as an analyst. This gave me an opportunity to meet some of the electronic industry pioneers—many of them later became famous. Bob Noyce, the inventor of integrated circuits, was an acquaintance. I first met Bob before he started Intel. After the first few rounds of private financing, he asked me whether I would also like to invest. I carefully reviewed the offering prospectus and was dubious whether the company would succeed—there were large, well-financed competitors, like Motorola, Texas Instruments, and upcoming Asian companies, so I turned down the opportunity. That was probably one of the most significant business mistakes I ever made. Eventually, Intel achieved great success and became the world's leading manufacturer of semiconductors. I was also privileged to know Bill Hewlett and David Packard who, in my opinion, represented one of the best managements in the industry. We remained close to this organization, and later, my senior partner became a longtime director at Hewlett-Packard.

Not only was my work fascinating, but the environment could not have been better. My partners and associates represented a collection of the brightest investment minds in Boston. Almost all of us had MBAs, mostly from Harvard Business School, as well as undergraduate degrees from Ivy League colleges. This was not a requirement, but we felt that the admission offices of these schools had done a thorough preliminary screening for us. At one time, our firm's assets were as large as Fidelity's. Because, numerically, the organization was relatively small and very profitable, our compensation was generous.

Essentially, we worked on our own, set our own schedules, traveled whenever we wanted, and searched out the best investment ideas. Our performance was evaluated based on the investment ideas generated and our overall contribution to the organization—a perfect work environment for me! Though my work involved travel, I could set my own schedule. While I was married, I returned home every weekend. But as a single man, I could spend weekends away. I played tennis with friends in California, sailed to the Catalina Islands, and went shooting on the east coast.

While I continued to see the children, I also had time for other activities and began to look beyond tennis and skiing. When I was young, I hunted with my stepfather, who was an excellent shot. With fondness, I recalled the many beautiful fall days when we wandered through the open fields of our property in Latvia, following a hunting dog. It was exhilarating to be outdoors on a beautiful fall day. Now life was different, but I still shot skeet and hunted with my New Hampshire buddies in the hills that surrounded our house on Squam Lake. We usually headed out at 4:30 AM, trudged up the mountains, looked for a favorable spot, and waited in the freezing cold morning, sometimes with snow on the ground. I again found it exciting to be outdoors with friends surrounded by spectacular scenery. Most days, I was so overpowered by the beauty of the surroundings and the sunrise above Squam Lake that I hardly noticed the deer. No wonder that, even though I hunted deer with my local buddies for more than ten years, I never shot one. Many probably passed by while I was deep in thought. Anyway, the unsuspecting New Hampshire deer were quite safe when I was out hunting.

My Connecticut friends also invited me to join them in pheasant and duck hunts at their clubs. The setting and their company was fun, and the hunts were successful. Afterwards, we shot skeet and trap, but at this, I did rather poorly. Not wanting to be a slouch at anything I tried, I enrolled in the Orvis shooting school a few weeks later. After four days of intensive practice, I joined my friends and expected to see better results, but my improvement was only modest. That was not good enough for me, so I enrolled in the Orvis postgraduate shooting school. Again, my results were only slightly better.

My Connecticut friends were sympathetic and looked at my gun, which was an old Remington, and compared it to theirs, which were

Purdeys, Holland & Hollands, and custom-made Berettas. In their opinion, my shotgun was the problem. My good friend said, "I will find you a great gun." He selected a Winchester Grand Am 21. He assured me, "This is going to solve all your problems!" He even had it engraved by Ronald Reagan's gunsmith. The gun had a beautiful scroll of hunting scenes and my initials inlaid in gold (and cost a small fortune). Now I was ready to perform! Unfortunately, I did not score much better this time either because my new gun had more recoil. Only then did I learn that one of my friends had tried out for the U.S. Olympic Trap Team, and another had been a member of the U.S. Army Rifle Team—stiff competition. Despite the outcome, I enjoyed shooting and spending time in my friends' company. The lesson I learned from this experience is that even if you engage in friendly rivalry, learn beforehand the skill level of your friends before expecting success!

Occasionally, my Baltimore friends invited me to shoot on a small island they owned in the Chesapeake Bay. The Baltimore crowd could not have been more hospitable and fun. It was great to be with them for the weekend. Early one hunting morning, I saw a pair of ducks in the distance, flying at a high speed, and I reached for my gun. My friend told me, "They are too far away!" The other argued, "John has gone to the Orvis shooting school. I'm sure he can hit them!" I had no choice but to rise to the challenge. I took careful aim at the first duck, which was moving fast. As I fired, the second duck, which was following far behind, dropped dead—but that duck had not been my target. My friend said,

"What a great shot!" Of course, in true hunter's style, I did not say anything and only nodded. My advice: when you are complimented, do not question it! Let the positive comments ring—even if they're not entirely accurate, they will not harm anyone and could boost your ego.

I would not be a real hunter if I neglected to regale you with another tale (by now, you probably know that hunting and fishing are more about the stories they generate than the actual results). A few years later, my son and I were invited to hunt deer on a large Texas ranch. It was a spectacular setup with friends. Early in the morning, I was given the prime spot on top of a twenty-foot tower near a clearing. As the sun rose above the scrub brush, I saw a large buck about one hundred and fifty yards away. I took careful aim and was successful. It was a great trophy, but I could not climb down from the tower before other hunters arrived because this was against the rules. As I watched the deer from afar, I noticed a large vulture circling above it, getting ready to descend. I did not want to have my prize damaged, so I took very careful aim at the circling vulture with my rifle and, at one hundred and fifty yards, hit it—one of my better shots. Orvis finally paid off!

One day, before I left for New Hampshire with the children, I received an unusual telephone call. "Mr. Livens, I am calling from a Hollywood studio and would like to set up a meeting with you in New Hampshire." My immediate reaction was that the studio called the wrong telephone number. I had been intrigued with Hollywood ever since my brief (and somewhat unsuccessful) encounter with the movie producers at the

Cannes Movie Festival during my time in the Navy. My friends knew about this experience and had played jokes on me before. One time, while at the Beverly Hills Hotel, I was paged at the swimming pool over the loudspeaker: "Mr. Livens, call the studio!" I ran to the phone only to hear a friend laugh and say, "At the Beverly Hills Hotel, you should be recognized as a celebrity!" I returned to the pool, but an hour later, there was another page: "Mr. Livens, you are urgently required at the studio!" The same joke, but the people around the pool began to look at me as if I were a celebrity.

With these thoughts in mind, I continued our telephone conversation and set up a meeting for the following Saturday. As scheduled, two cars drove up, and several young, pleasant people emerged. I knew the local representative, who was a well-known architect, and he introduced me to the director of the movie, whose first name was Mark. They told me they were going to film a movie on Squam Lake called *On Golden Pond*. I showed them around the house, and one of them said, "We would like to rent this house to accommodate an elderly actress [Katherine Hepburn] who is starring in the movie. It will be easy for her to commute from your dock directly to the shooting site." They invited all of us to visit the island where the movie was going to be filmed. I knew the location and was impressed with the fine craftsmanship the Hollywood people had done by adding to a simple cottage a floor, porch, and gazebo. Everything was constructed as if it had been there for fifty years.

The Hollywood people were polite and said they would like to rent my house for two months while the movie was being filmed. The cost was not an obstacle, and they seemed to know that my daughter was interested in the performing arts, so they invited her to watch the filming whenever possible. Also, all of us would be their guests at the Hollywood premiere, which was scheduled for late 1981. Quite an invitation, and I almost felt I had made the grade to be accepted by Hollywood! It was then that my son piped up and said, "Dad, you told me you would spend two weeks with me at our New Hampshire house!" The Hollywood representative said, "Don't worry, we will rent you any other house, and you'll be able to use your own boats and everything else." My son responded, "Dad, you promised to be at *our* house!" He was right. I promised, so I kept my promise to my son and declined their offer. My hope for Hollywood friends evaporated once again.

A few weeks later, a local, who was the boat patrolman on Squam Lake, called and said,

John, I know you are interested in the movie that's being filmed on the lake. I am going to be patrolling the area, and two days from now, they are going to film a scene on the dock. They have a good-looking actress [Jane Fonda] in the scene. If you want to see, I will allow your boat to get as close as possible!

I invited my Boston friends, and we had a picnic in my boat and watched the dock scene being filmed. This is as close as I ever got to the movie industry. The film was released in December 1981 and was one of the most successful movies of 1982, with ten Academy Award nominations and three Oscars. It was the only movie for which Jane

Fonda won an Oscar, while Katharine Hepburn received her fourth. The scriptwriter also received an Oscar.

Besides occasional hunting adventures and skiing in the winter, my life in Boston fell into a pleasant routine. Work was going well, and the children attended boarding school. They were busy with their friends, and I had more free time on my own. One day, my good friend Polly said, "Bill and I are planning a trip to China, which only recently has been opened to outsiders. Would you like to join us?" I had no one special in my life and would have to travel on my own. Bill went on to assure me, "Don't worry—I will scout out some single ladies for you!" This is how one of the most fascinating trips I ever took began. It was 1982, and no American travel companies served China—wishful visitors had to make arrangements through Lindblad, a premier Swedish company. Up to this point, for the last few decades, China was visited by very few Westerners.

We arrived in Hong Kong and were met by an old acquaintance, the former husband of Natalie, my wife's lawyer. He had moved as far away from his former wife as possible and was now happily married to an attractive American lady. After a brief stay in Hong Kong, we moved on to China, which I found fascinating. Lindblad arranged for us to stay in the state guesthouses, which were quite comfortable (at that time, there were none of the modern western hotels that now abound). We were accompanied by a Mandarin-speaking Lindblad representative and had local guides, who were usually the children of government officials. They were there to meet Westerners and learn English. One of our fellow travelers asked, "What about the Mao Tse Tung era and its suppression of people?" The guide answered, "Mao represents only a blip in the thousands of years of Chinese history, which brought many innovations to the world. Unlike the Russians, we are proud of our past achievements and never treated people as badly as the Russians did, with their numerous gulags." He went on to say that he expected China to be great again because of the industrious nature of the people. Perhaps a little optimistic, but he turned out to be right.

We crisscrossed China for more than two weeks and visited areas where no Caucasians had been allowed to go for decades. I found the Chinese people kind, curious, and hospitable and quickly became a fan of the country and its people. While in Hangzhou, I walked along the lake to a mansion, which at one time belonged to the family of a good Chinese friend of mine. He had given me the location of his family manor and asked me to visit it. Here I was, in front of this magnificent building with a great view over the lake—but instead of a family living there, it was now a communist institution. I thought about my own past and wondered what had happened to the Biksti estate where I grew up, which was now in communist hands. It looked to me that the communists had done damage across the world, no matter the nationality or location—but everything, including evil, eventually comes to an end. After China, we spent a few days in Japan, but it is China that left an indelible impression on me and opened for me a new perspective on the world.

I continued in the tradition of my family—travel—and wanted to share it with my children. Shortly after returning to Boston, friends invited me to join them on a trip to Club Med, a place I never considered visiting. Because we had a group of people, including children who were my son's age, we all traveled together and had a lot of fun. I found the Caribbean to be enjoyable and became an avid scuba diver. Later, my son and I shared a love for this activity and continued to dive at other Club Med locations or on our own. We dove in Guadalupe, the Bahamas, Bermuda, Grand Cayman, the Turks and Caicos Islands, and even Phuket, Thailand—close to the island shown in the James Bond movie. Those were fun adventures with my son.

While in Boston, I continued to see Mother, who had married Eugene, another an old acquaintance. I became fond of him. A scholar himself, he collected old manuscripts, maps, and the like, and he had a small specialty shop in Beacon Hill that was open a few hours a week for other collectors to enjoy. When Eugene retired, he gave some of his collections to the Boston Public Library, and they named the room in his memory.

After Eugene passed away, I invited her one weekend to the Squam Lake house. She asked me about the divorce, which by now had gone on for more than five years. I admitted to her that it was a burden, particularly because the proceedings limited the scope of my activities—in a sense, I lost some of my freedom. I explained that there were two elements holding back the final settlement: first, the court gave me the Squam Lake house, and Mary Ann wanted it back, and second, Mary Ann's attorneys refused to disclose her trust funds, which put an additional financial burden on me. In the lower New York courts, my attorneys won to have these assets fully disclosed, but my wife's attorneys appealed this to the Supreme Court of the State of New York, which led to years of delay.

Mother advised,

Do not attach yourself to material possessions—they can be replaced. Perhaps you hope to restore past feelings, but that is unlikely. The New Hampshire house will always remind you of the past, which is gone forever. Start anew, as you have done before, and you will succeed again! Remember, when the family lost all its property during the war, we never looked back. Do not become a captive to the past!"

I asked, "What about my savings and the stuff that we accumulated in our two houses over the past ten years? If I do not have the information about my wife's assets disclosed, I will lose all of it!" Mother said, "Is not your freedom more important than material goods? You already had to rebuild your wealth once. You can do it again." I thought for a moment and said, "You are right. I should move on, no matter what it takes." The next week, I contacted my attorneys and said I wanted to expedite the divorce. I only wanted to add one condition, formal or informal— that the New Hampshire house would eventually go to the children. My lawyers were not happy—for more than six years, they received a very substantial compensation, which would now come to an end.

In early 1984, a five-day trial started before the court-appointed master. Everything in the past was rehashed, but frankly, it was all meaningless by now. Almost all physical assets went to Mary Ann, except for several items: my favorite Flemish tapestry, which I bought with my first partnership check; a Grandma Moses painting; and a few other minor items. I would also receive a portion of the Beacon Hill house after it was sold years later. In terms of material goods, I did not get much—I got my freedom, and I was happy. After seven years of separation, divorce proceedings, and numerous law firms, it was finally over in mid-1984.

The main benefit of the divorce was intangible—if I had been divorced early, I probably would have remarried the first nice lady I met, and the odds of that working out well were slim. Now, I had learned more and could make better decisions, and that was the real blessing.

The legal fees, adjusted for today's dollars, represented a small fortune (though mine were a little less because of the work we did). What a waste of energy, time, and financial resources, which could have been better devoted to some worthwhile cause! The lawyers are probably the only ones who would disagree with that sentiment—I resented one incident that took place on Christmas, when I briefly attended a party in my lawyer's office. The chief attorney, Bob, led me to the window and pointed to a beautiful Mercedes parked below. I said, "What a beautiful car. I sure would like to have one like that!" Bob said, "It's mine—and you paid for it!" As soon as the divorce proceedings ended, I let my attorneys go with pleasure.

Mary Ann also terminated Natalie, who supposedly told her that all the legal fees would be paid by me. That was not the case, and Mary

Ann's family received a substantial bill, but it probably did not make any difference to them. Shortly afterwards, Natalie quit the legal profession and enrolled in seminary. After graduation, she married and moved to a New Hampshire parish. Her second marriage quickly ended in divorce, but the last I heard, she remarried again. I reflected on this and knew that, deep down, all of us are sinners. We try to be better by doing good deeds and hope for redemption. Three years of seminary, three husbands, and life in the boondocks of New Hampshire—Natalie must have been quite a sinner! I am sure there is redemption for all, and only hope Natalie continued her straight path. I wish her well on her journey.

I was lucky in my life before, and my luck did not leave me now. Someone must have been looking over my shoulder every step of the way. Shortly afterwards, it was announced that my firm, State Street Research and Management, was going to be sold to a large insurance company, and the transaction would make me financially independent. I was not happy—I enjoyed my work and was not looking forward to working for an insurance company, which I knew would eventually destroy the existing culture. My life changed again, and I had to adjust and reset my goals. It was not easy to leave my firm right away because all the partners had to sign a two-year contract. I had a long discussion with the managing partner, and by leaving substantial money on the table, I could finally be free. As I left, the managing partner said, "Why don't you go to Bermuda and think it over? The new owners will sell our Bermuda house anyway, so you might as well enjoy it!" I accepted the offer because I had already made plans to be in Bermuda, though I added that I was unlikely to change my mind. I had visited this house on many occasions, and it brought back happy memories for me.

I went to the office for the last time and packed up my files. I was sad to leave, but life changes for everyone. I did not worry about the future because finances were not a problem, and several people talked to me about other employment opportunities.

I wanted to start my new life phase on a positive note and leave the divorce experience behind. I had no definite career plans—I just wanted to enjoy the present and then make my decision. I invited friends to join me on the Bermuda trip and stay at the house still owned by my partnership. I was invited to play in the Bermuda Open Invitational Tennis Tournament, but now I could stay at the house instead of the Coral Beach Club, where I was a member. The participants in the tournament were grouped by their respective ages, which gave me a better chance for success.

For the previous several years, in the summer, I played tennis at least four to five times a week at a private club in Brookline, Massachusetts, which had superbly maintained clay and grass courts. I could play regularly after work because it was easy to find a good game. On the weekends, it was even more comfortable. With so much tennis behind me, my game at least was consistent, and I was in better physical shape than many of my contemporaries. Now, on top of this, I felt great, with my past difficulties behind me. I was playing as well as I ever had and managed to reach the semifinals. This called for a celebration at my favorite restaurant in Bermuda, the Four Ways. The piano player, Xavier, was one of the very best, and I dined there many times. It was one of the most beautiful and romantic settings, and it brought back many pleasant memories.

The next morning, when I readied for my afternoon match, I received a call from my Boston attorneys, who told me that my ex-wife's lawyers issued a twenty-four-hour notice to remove my personal belongings from the New Hampshire house. I had no choice but to immediately fly back to Boston, drive to New Hampshire, and move my belongings to a nearby ski condominium, which I had purchased several years earlier. This was not a traumatic event, but it stopped my tennis career short. I doubt I would have won the next match anyway because my opponent was an excellent player.

After settling back in Boston, my good friend, Polly, telephoned and said, "Bill and I know that your life is changing, so why not celebrate with us and join us with your children for an African safari? We are going to travel with two other families and their children, and all of you know each other." My response: "When do we leave?" There was still no one special in my life, but I was delighted to have another chance to travel with my children.

We started the trip in Boston and flew to Athens, where we were entertained by friends. Because I had not seen my daughter as much as my son, I flew with Lisa in first class while all the others were in the back of the plane—a special treat. From Athens, we flew to Nairobi and started our trip through Kenya. Polly had a friend in Nairobi who arranged a private tour with the best guides available. We had four guides, four jeeps, and two trucks with support personnel. While on the safari, we stayed at some very elegant and well-known lodges, but on other occasions, we camped out on our own because we had all the necessary equipment and help. The wildlife in the environment was spectacular, and the safari turned out to be one of the grandest adventures for my family. Years later, the children still talked about the safari experience.

After several weeks in Africa, Lisa and I flew to Rome, where one of my ski friends, Contessa Maria, promised to show us around. My son, Jay, flew to London with our friends, where I would join them later. Rome in 1984 was one of the most exciting cities in Europe, with glamorous movie stars surrounded by paparazzi. Plus, there were always the historical sites to be visited. Contessa Maria was an excellent host. Together with her Italian friend, who was a member of the Senate, she invited us to an opera performance at the Baths of Caracalla—a grandiose event! One day, as we walked down the street, Lisa asked, "What is that beautiful building across the street?" Maria told her it was the Borghese Palace. The next afternoon, we had tea with Princess Borghese.

Lisa left a few days later. I called another ski friend, Sarah, who was staying with Maria, and asked her for the best florist in Rome. I wanted to send a magnificent flower arrangement to Maria as a gesture of appreciation for her hospitality. Sarah informed me, "Maria has already thought about this and contacted her jeweler. She has made a selection, and you can call him directly." Not wanting to be an ungrateful slouch from the provinces, I called the jeweler and purchased the gift. An expensive but fun visit to Rome!

I flew to London and caught up with Jay and my friends. Jay and his buddy, Andrew, were miserable. Andrew's mother, Polly, made them go to museums and many antique shops; before departing, Bill and Polly purchased a large home in the finest location of Beacon Hill, and now they were buying a full container of antique furniture for it. They invited me to join them on one of their antique searches. Polly saw a beautiful grandfather clock and said, "I know you've missed the grandfather clock you had in your house, which always reminded you of the passing time. Why don't you buy one here? This is a beautiful one!" I reflected on my already rather expensive sojourn in Rome and politely declined the suggestion. Also, I could tell the boys were unhappy and wanted to rectify the situation.

I hired a large Daimler limousine and, with the boys, went to the "really important" sites, such as the Imperial War Museum, Henley, and more. A few days later, the two boys (aged twelve) flew back to Boston. I was concerned about them traveling alone and took them to the airport. I asked the driver to wait until I could deliver them to the departure gate. (at that time, there were no security checks). As we entered the airport terminal, Andrew said, "Mr. Livens, thank you and goodbye!" I asked, "Don't you want me to bring you to the gate?" Andrew replied, "When two young boys travel alone, the airline people always treat us well by giving us candy. If you come with us, you will spoil it!" All I could do was tell them goodbye. I knew then that with their enterprising nature, the boys would go far in life.

A few days later, I flew from London to Boston and was ready to embark on my new lifestyle—the divorce and the sale of my old firm was now behind me, and I looked forward to what lay ahead. A friend asked me to join his firm, which he started a few years before. I contributed some of the initial capital and was now invited to become a partner. I checked the firm's investment performance, and it was good, but I did not make further investigations and relied primarily on my friend's advice. After contributing more capital, I was now an equal partner. Before starting, I told my new colleagues I would only work on a limited-time basis because I wanted to spend more time with my children and traveling. That was fine with them, and now I had a new job with a great deal of flexibility. Initially, I was concerned about how I would maintain my past business relationships because I was now with a small organization instead of a leading Boston financial institution. That did not seem to be a problem, however, because most of my business contacts reported that they viewed me as a personal friend. That really lifted my spirits!

As I settled down to my new daily routine, I unexpectedly received a subpoena issued by the Superior Court of Massachusetts at the urging of my former wife. I was furious—I thought the divorce was over after seven years and both parties terminated their attorneys. The lawsuit related to real estate taxes on my Beacon Hill house, where I had not lived for the past seven years. The amounts involved were not significant, but the principle bothered me—that outsiders could still interfere with my newly established life. I decided to take matters into my own hands and appeared in court on my own, without a defense attorney. Before doing so, I contacted my old Navy buddy, Ed, who practiced law in Boston.

On the day of the trial, I showed up in court, confronted by two attorneys representing my ex-wife. They were from a prominent Boston law firm (she terminated Natalie earlier). The new lawyers, a male and a female, looked professional and had a very serious demeanor. The female lawyer was in charge, no doubt! She had no makeup, short hair, and wore a man's jacket and slacks. Her male associate had long-ish hair with sideburns, as was fashionable in those days. He appeared to be very humble—no wonder, when you work for a boss like that! The female attorney looked around and asked who represented me. I said, "It is me!" She frowned, and I could see that she felt the case was hers. The opposition lawyers started the proceedings by making a lengthy presentation and citing numerous examples of unpaid real estate taxes. It was intimidating because I did not know about any of these cases.

When it was my turn to speak, I implored the judge,

Your honor, I apologize for appearing in this courtroom and using your invaluable time, which could be better devoted to some just social cause. Before you stands a hard-working man whose life, for the past seven years, has been damaged by unscrupulous attorneys who have continuously harassed him without finding any wrongdoing. This man's earning power has been damaged, and now he has a new job with an uncertain career path. His ability to contribute to the welfare of his children and family is questionable and will be diminished. This process has consumed so much of his time that he has been unable to devote enough attention to his loving children, aging parents, and community service organizations, to which he has been committed for years. Everyone has unjustifiably suffered…"

and so on! As I continued in this vein, I was touched and felt genuinely sorry for this poor, suffering person. I wanted to shake his hand and maybe even give him a hug. Then I remembered the person was me.

As I looked at the judge, he did not seem to share my sympathies. He took off his thick, dark, horn-rimmed glasses, wiped the lenses, and gave me a penetrating look—not promising! He asked a few questions, and then the case was over. It did not look good, but I had given it my best try, and the amounts involved were not significant. My ego was bruised because I expected to do better—I had been admitted to Harvard Law School and turned it down to go to Harvard Business School instead. Perhaps I had no legal talent after all.

The next day, I called my friend, Ed, and told him about this experience. Ed said, "Do not bother, I know all about it! Did you not recognize the judge? He was one of your old Navy squadron mates; we all had drinks together at the Officers Club." I asked, "What was the verdict?" Ed replied that the judge had taken the case under advisement. As far as I know, forty years later, it is still there. I was relieved and thought I might have some hidden legal talent after all—or did I?

A few weeks later, at a gathering, I encountered the managing partner of the law firm that opposed me. I knew him socially. As one would expect, he was a proper Bostonian with a Harvard law degree, which entitled him to a condescending attitude and sanctimonious behavior toward us ordinary mortals. I could not resist saying, "If your firm encounters me again in the courtroom, please send the first team to make my life more interesting and challenging!" The man never spoke to me again—no loss.

With the legal distractions behind me once again, life in Boston became even more enjoyable. I continued to visit my friends, but my focus was on the children, who grew up rapidly. Lisa was now past her mid-teens, but Jay and his friends continued to spend their weekends with me. In October, the New England antique show opened, and it began with a private reception. I attended with my friends, Bill and Polly. While viewing the exhibit, Polly showed me a beautiful antique British grandfather clock and commented, "You almost bought one in England, and I know how much you like grandfather clocks." I liked the grandfather clock and nodded in agreement but could not judge its authenticity. Polly asked a nearby friend, Ned Johnson, who was not only an expert of American antiques but also had been extraordinary successful by growing his family's investment firm, Fidelity. Ned said, "While I know American antiques, I am less familiar with the British, but this looks very good." I was impressed with his assessment. Despite a very high price of the grandfather clock (almost as much as my Mercedes), I promised later to take another look. I had to leave to meet the boys (my son Jay and his friend Andrew) who were spending the weekend with me.

The next morning, due to my lack of culinary skills, I offered the boys donuts. They immediately turned breakfast into a donut-eating contest, and soon they were all gone. Andrew insisted on having more. I said, "Do you realize that I have to walk five blocks to get my car from the garage, and then drive to get you the donuts? It will take me almost an hour!" Andrew demanded, "We want more donuts!" So off I went. When I returned, he said, "Do you notice anything different in the apartment?" I looked around and noticed the grandfather clock I saw at the antique show. It was accompanied by a note from Polly indicating that it was a gift from her. I immediately called Polly and thanked her for this generous gift. She said,

> When you look at the clock, remember how quickly time passes and how precious every moment is—it's irreplaceable. Time inexorably moves on. While the clock can be turned back, life never can, so live and enjoy every moment! Have no regrets, and the future might be even brighter than you expect.

Friends continued to introduce me to single ladies, and eventually I met one whom I found interesting. Jan had recently moved to Boston and started an investment banking firm to finance small companies. She had an MBA from Columbia and a successful career at one of the large

Hartford insurance companies. Later, I found out that Jan was even featured in a two-page spread of *Life* magazine, as a shining example of the next generation of successful businesswomen. The photographs, which I saw much later, displayed her in rather skimpy garb. Jan had also been married briefly, but she had no children. She was a jogger who regularly exercised and was a fine representation of the successful modern woman. Months later, when I introduced her to my children, she immediately adored them. Because my children played a paramount role in my life, Jan turned out to be an excellent companion. She was bright, outgoing, athletic, and very hard-working. Unfortunately, Jan did not care much for social functions, and she wanted to devote her limited free time to study. She took graduate philosophy courses at Harvard and eventually received her Ph.D. She later taught at Yale and another university, while continuing with her investment business.

A telephone call from a friend added a new and interesting dimension to my life. The friend asked whether I would be interested in joining as an investor in a Broadway production. This appealed to me because in early childhood I was exposed to the art world. My parents had many artist friends and frequently entertained them at our country place. Now, I was ready to again enter this world! Assiduously, I attended the preliminary readings of the play and was impressed by the talent and plot. A few months later, the play opened in Boston and received good reviews. I started to feel like an important art patron and prepared for the Broadway opening, which would be followed by a formal reception with the cast. The play received favorable reviews, but it only lasted six months, and the forecasted breakeven point was at seven months. Even though my modest investment was gone, I had a lot of fun!

Months later, the same friend came and asked me to invest in a major musical. By now, I knew the preliminary routine and felt like a seasoned Broadway angel. After the tryouts, I thought the music and play were mediocre but decided to invest anyway. My prior experience implied that what I liked, the public disliked—therefore, I decided to invest in the production even though I thought it was not good.

I went to the Broadway opening with my daughter, who was at the Choate School. I also invited friends from Connecticut. The opening party was impressive, and there were many celebrities, none of whom I knew (except Ben Vereen, who I had heard of). The reviews were good, and the play won two Tony awards, but it lasted only eight months—one needed ten to break even. Another failure, but not a disaster.

Later, the same friend contacted me and asked me, for a third time, to invest in a play. This one featured Lena Horne. After two failures, I decided that my talent in picking winners on Broadway was poor, so I politely declined to participate. That show was a success and lasted for several years.

My relationship with the performing arts was not yet over. The Connecticut friends who I invited to the opening called me and told they were so impressed with Broadway that they now were major investors in a new musical, and I was invited to the opening. This reinforced my illusionary feeling that I was somewhat connected with the performing arts world. I asked my friend about the musical, and he said the title was *Onward Victoria*. I offered that Queen Victoria had become a popular subject and would attract audiences. My friend immediately corrected me and told me that the play was not about Queen Victoria, but the first woman stockbroker on Wall Street. I knew my tastes were not in sync with the public, but this was even further off than I anticipated.

On opening night, I found the music uninspiring, the plot boring, and felt there was nothing exciting about the play—even for those involved in the stock market. Later, I read the newspaper reviews of the play, and they were terrible—the theater critics were negative about the play, the music, the acting—it was the most scathing review I have ever read! I felt sorry for my friends but hoped for the best.

After returning to Boston, I checked the New York papers to see how the play was doing, but I found nothing. After several months, I asked my friend about the play. His reply was, "John, you saw the only performance on opening night!"

No doubt the performing arts world is exciting and full of surprises. When investing in plays, as in other endeavors of life, one must be realistic about one's ability to make sound judgments before making commitments, unless it is just for fun. From the experience, I concluded that it is better to be an observer than a participant! This healthy skepticism, however, did not deter me from later serving on the board of a Boston theater.

To be closer to the children, I bought a house on Beacon Hill, about a block from my prior residence. This made it easy to keep up with the family. I found the new home delightful and liked its unique features—it was on a private street and included two adjoining parking spaces beside a garage. On the third floor, there was a master bedroom with a small study that overlooked the roof. I hired a landscape architect to design a small garden with a water fountain. I could lie in bed, flip a switch, and see the lit fountain at night. It was a soothing feeling, like being in the country.

I also had the New Hampshire ski condominium, where I could spend winter weekends. I took many trips there with the children. I took them skiing in my favorite place (Zermatt, Switzerland), horseback riding on a Wyoming ranch with my west coast friends, and more. I remember well a rafting trip down the Colorado River through the Grand Canyon. It was quite an adventure. In June, the river's water level was still high, and as the rafts were going through the rapids, we got soaking wet. This did not bother us because the temperature in the Grand Canyon approached one hundred degrees and was only slightly lower at night. Evenings, we patched up the rafts and camped out next to the river. The trip ended in Las Vegas.

Earlier, I told a friend about our travel plans. He was an investor in Las Vegas casinos and knew their management, so he arranged for us to stay at Caesar's Palace, which at that time was the most glamorous hotel/casino in Vegas. All of us were assigned honeymoon suites, including my daughter, Lisa, and her girlfriend, my son, Jay, and his friend Andrew, and me. I had never seen accommodations like these before—the room had a heart-shaped bed next to a heart-shaped Jacuzzi with mirrors in the ceiling. I wondered what two teenaged boys would think, but they took it in stride.

In the evening, to end our trip, I planned a special treat by inviting everyone to the *Les Folies Bergère* performance. As a child, I heard about this performance from my parents when they visited Paris. Now I had a chance to see the show. Before going, I called the ticket office and asked whether there was nudity that would be inappropriate for young boys. The response I received was, "Everything is in good taste, and there's nothing to be concerned about." So, all of us went to the show, which, frankly, did not measure up to my expectations. I asked Andrew, "What did you like most about the show?" He replied, "The jugglers and the magicians!" I guess the show had no adverse effect on the boys after all.

After returning to Boston, we had a business meeting during which the managing partner and founder announced that he wanted to retire. I was asked to be the next president. I started to work on a limited-time basis but, shortly afterwards, put forth a significant effort in the firm. I enjoyed investment management and regularly brought my work home. I continued to work in the evenings at home because I had little social life, but I missed my friends who had been so considerate in the past. I joined an athletic club and, before going home, regularly exercised.

I saw Jan regularly over a year or so. She was extraordinary bright but disliked social life. Otherwise, she was wonderful and loved my son. Jan also worked long hours in her office—she was almost a workaholic.

As I assumed my new responsibilities at the company, I reviewed where we stood—and discovered that we had done little marketing, and the performance of our accounts was uneven; some of them had done exceptionally well, while others lagged. I could now understand why the former president wanted to retire! I looked at the overall performance of the company, personnel, financial controls, SEC matters, and more— none of which I found exciting. My primary interest had always been investment work. The choice we had now was whether to contribute more capital and hire additional personnel or continue to serve our existing client base with limited growth. My other partners did not have the funds to invest, and I was not going to carry the burden by myself. Frankly, even though I was working hard, my compensation at the new firm was minimal compared to what I had earned before. Still, I treasured the freedom and flexibility the job provided. After all these considerations, we decided to remain as we were and continue to better serve our existing clients. This fitted well with my personal plans, too, because it gave me more leisure time.

To expand my business horizons, I accepted election to the Board of Directors of two companies. One was a medium-sized automotive parts supplier in Canada, which required considerable travel to Ontario and other Canadian locations. The other, smaller company developed a new unique traffic-control product line that did not seem to do well against its entrenched competition. While not rewarding, it was an interesting experience.

I also looked at my personal life and realized that the children were growing up—I could not live my life through them. Jan had been a great friend and companion, but I knew there was no long-term future for us. While we shared much in common intellectually, our interests in an active social life were not close enough to spend the rest of our lives together. We ended our relationship, and she moved back to Connecticut and eventually married. Jan was a very fine, smart, and pleasant individual, and the children missed her.

I was again alone, but I was comfortable with this status. My children attended boarding schools and headed for college. I had more time for work and could spend time with friends. A friend, Sarah, who organized several Europe ski trips before, in which I participated, called and said, "We are planning a special trip to St. Moritz. Please join us!" The timing was perfect. A few months later, I was off to Switzerland with a dozen sophisticated acquaintances from New York and Connecticut. This was also an opportunity to celebrate Sarah's recent marriage to an acquaintance of mine.

Sheer joy! St. Moritz

Even though I had skied in Switzerland many times before, its winter beauty was unsurpassed, and the good company made it even more fun. My problem was that the others in the group were not good skiers and instead preferred the après ski parties. For more of a challenge during my trip, I decided to enter an amateur ski race, in which you are placed in a category based on your age. In some way, it was like the U.S. NASTAR races, except in St. Moritz, the course was longer and far more difficult. There were also more participants in the St. Moritz race. In the past, I entered NASTAR races and almost always won gold—probably not so much because of my skiing ability but because the others in my age group were not in good physical shape. To be prepared, the day before the St. Moritz race, I scouted out the slope and noticed a jump. In exuberance, I went off the jump, flew about a dozen feet through the air, and continued to ski down.

At the end of the day, I brought my skis to the local ski shop and, to practice my rusty German, explained that I wanted the bindings tightened for tomorrow's race. The next morning, to be ready for the race, I went early to the slopes for a practice run. While the jump was not on the race course, I tried it again, as I had done the day before. This time, when I took off, something was wrong. Both of my bindings came off, and I landed with a big crash—very embarrassing! Apparently, the ski shop, instead of tightening the bindings, loosened them. I should have given them the instructions in English instead of in my rusty German.

As I collected my gear, I noticed I could not move my right thumb, which already appeared swollen. I took the cable car down the mountain and headed directly for the local hospital (the *Krankenhaus*). Even though it was early in the day, the place was already crowded with more seriously injured skiers. I waited for a while, and then a young Swiss doctor came by. I told him my sad story and explained I was still determined to participate in the race. He invited me to his office and said, "There is a long wait for the X-rays, and you will miss most of the day. But I have another solution." He gave me a full bottle of Riesling wine and said, "If you can hold this bottle between your forefinger and thumb, it is only a sprain and not a break." I grimly managed to hold the bottle and insisted, "I still want to ski!" The doctor replied, "Do not worry—just show me how you hold your ski pole and I'll set the cast accordingly!"

In the afternoon, I was off to the race—and won silver. I still have the medal as a happy reminder of my St. Moritz experience. The real benefits of my minor injury came in the evening—I could not hold a wine glass in my right hand and had difficulty pouring it from the bottle, but there were quite a few attractive ladies who were compassionate and helpful. I did not refuse any of the favors they offered an injured skier.

A few days later, I flew to London, where I had a business commitment. Then, after returning to Boston, a friend called and said, "Remember, you promised to play with me in the round-robin tennis tournament on Sunday!" I looked at my right hand in a cast and then remembered that it only had to be on for two weeks. So, I immediately headed to the hospital to have the cast removed. After a brief wait, a technician came with a rotary saw-like instrument to remove the cast. He was funny and told me about his hot date from the night before. He did not seem to pay much attention to what he was doing. The cast came off and the only thing left on my arm was a burn mark from the saw. I went on to play a (bad) game of tennis and had fun. If you have a positive attitude and good health, you can accomplish almost anything!

After returning to Boston, I settled into my routine: for me, that meant work, spending time with the children, visiting my aging mother, enjoying the company of friends, and regularly working out in the gym. While this may seem like a dull lifestyle, my life was never dull for long! I continued to travel and combine business with skiing weekends in the Rockies or visits to California. I remember one such trip, which was quite an adventure.

I flew in from San Francisco and met the children and their friends at the Denver airport. We hired a Checker cab and told the driver to take us to Aspen, where we rented a large condominium with friends. On our way, the boys (Andrew and Jay) insisted on stopping for a hamburger, so we pulled over at a roadside joint. It was freezing, so the driver left the engine running while we ate dinner. Afterward, we continued to Aspen—but as we approached the town, the cab ran out of gas. Nothing is like being stuck in the middle of nowhere without gas while it snows at one o'clock in the morning!

Eventually, we reached Aspen and settled into our condo. Suddenly, both boys got violently sick and started throwing up. There was very little we could do to help them. In the morning, the boys seemed to feel better, but I asked them to stay in bed while Lisa and I went for a few ski runs. Upon our return, from some distance away, we heard a great commotion of shouting and laughing coming from the condominium's outdoor swimming pool. To no one's surprise, Jay and Andrew seemed to be completely recovered—they were running around in the snowbanks and diving into the heated pool. A miraculous recovery! One never knows what to expect when you travel with young, energetic people, but most of the time, they are a lot of fun.

At this time, my good friend, Polly, who had a complex blood disease, was now in the hospital. With her health deteriorating and no permanent cure, Polly spent long periods in the hospital. I regularly stopped by on my way home from work. Polly was an incredible person—regardless of her condition, one always walked away from a visit with her with an uplifted spirit.

Frequently, when I arrived at the hospital, I saw our mutual friend, Sarah, sitting with Polly and holding her hand. I had introduced her to Polly on one of the ski trips, and they became fast friends. It was not easy for Sarah to come to Boston from New York—plus, she was in the midst of a divorce. Despite her limited means and many obligations, Sarah never hesitated to help her friend. My initial impression of Sarah was as a gracious, fun-loving party giver, but I soon realized there was much more substance to her character behind the glamorous exterior. This experience showed me not to judge people based on their behavior when everything is going well—rather, see how they fare under adverse conditions. Based on my observations of her with Polly, my respect for Sarah grew significantly.

A few months later, Polly passed away, and I lost one of my best friends. Bill, her husband, remained a close friend for the rest of his life. I consider myself fortunate to have had friends like Bill and Polly, who made a positive difference in my life when I needed it most. They made my life much more enjoyable. In addition to family, one needs good friends to experience the full richness of all that life can offer.

I now had more free time, so I began looking for other challenges. In college, my major had been government, and I always wanted to be more actively involved in politics. I started to attend political gatherings, and at one of the dinners, the principal speaker was Ronald Reagan, who recently retired as governor of California. Reagan was a charismatic and inspirational leader with a human touch. I sat not too far from Mr. Reagan at the table.

After the dinner, Mr. Reagan inquired about my family, and I explained that I had discussed his old movies with my daughter, Lisa. Mr. Reagan asked, "How do I address Lisa?" I told him, and he scribbled a note on the program: "Lovely Lisa, it was a pleasure to meet your father. Good luck with your schooling!" Later, I gave the inscribed program to Lisa. Unfortunately, it was lost, but I will always remember Ronald Reagan as a wonderful and highly principled person who set high standards that seem to be difficult for other politicians to emulate.

Because I was a regular participant in the Republican party meetings, I was even asked to temporarily substitute as its treasurer. No one else wanted the job—there were hardly any funds in the treasury. At one of the meetings, we discussed potential candidates, but there were very few. Seldom did a Republican get elected to a federal office in Massachusetts. Nevertheless, I found the process fascinating.

One of the women considered for a position was an attractive, dynamic blonde. She had a non-political background, but her work in community service to homeless people was an asset. I thought this lady, Betty, was quite attractive, but she always had a male friend. I knew him somewhat, and after checking with friends, realized that he not a very high grade individual, so I dropped my interest.

Because my record of finding good lady companions was poor, I was ready for any advice I could find. One of my California Latino friends always had a slew of attractive ladies and freely offered his advice. He rattled something off in Spanish, which I did not understand, and then he handed me a note that read, "Dime con quién andas, y te diré quién eres." It sounded impressive, but I did not understand Spanish. My friend gave me the rough English translation: "Tell me who you walk with, and I will tell you who you are."

Based on my friend's proven and successful formula, I immediately and sadly took Betty off my list. However, a few weeks later, Betty came to a meeting without her friend and said, "He was only a temporary escort." That sounded good to me because I liked Betty and generally believed what attractive blondes said. From then on, I saw a great deal of Betty, and the more I was with her, the more terrific I thought she was. I admired her devotion to her children and that she moved from the Midwest to be near them while they attended boarding school.

I also continued to be with my children, who were now in college. Lisa studied in Paris at the Sorbonne extension. I flew there for a long weekend. It was terrific to be with her and visit the city she now knew so well. We celebrated with dinner at La Tour d'Argent, one of my favorite restaurants. During dinner, the restaurant lights dimmed so guests could view the illuminated Notre Dame across the Seine. That was a treat in itself! The ambiance brought back many happy memories. On several prior occasions, I celebrated in this same restaurant—after finishing graduate school, on my honeymoon, and with others. Now I was with Lisa, who was not only my daughter but also a good friend. What a blessing!

Back in Boston, I continued to see Betty. Once, as we walked to the far corner of the Boston Common, where many homeless people congregate, two dubious-looking characters came up and shouted, "Hello Betty baby, how are you? We've been missing you!" I did not know what to make of it. Betty smiled, waved to them, and then said to me, "These men are from the homeless shelter where I work, and I have not seen them for a while. It seems they're in good shape!" Frankly, I was impressed that her friendships reached across the spectrum of society. She certainly did better than me because I only had one homeless friend, Mike.

A year later, before Christmas, I invited Betty to a formal dinner dance, which is rare in Boston. A cold wave with subzero temperatures descended over the city, and there was light snow on the ground. I picked Betty up at her apartment, and she wore a fur coat over her elegant evening dress. I had on my black-tie outfit and a heavy topcoat. As we drove to the party, she turned to me and said, "I would like to look for a homeless woman whom I did not see at the shelter today. She is probably at her usual place on the street. On a night like this, she could perish from the extreme cold." So, instead of heading to the party, we cruised in my brand-new Mercedes through some of the less desirable sections of Boston, looking for the homeless woman.

Eventually, we found her huddled beneath blankets and the remnants of cardboard boxes. She did not want to come with us—she preferred to stay on the street. Finally, Betty persuaded the woman, and with the homeless person in the backseat, we began searching for shelter. It turned out that the place where Betty worked was full, but we eventually found another location. When I think back on this Christmas, it is not the gifts nor the parties that I recall; what stands out in my mind is that we were able to help the less fortunate. That is what the Christmas spirit is all about!

I was impressed with Betty's commitment to the homeless. Shortly afterward, I hired a man named Paul from the shelter to care for my house on Beacon Hill. He was cleaning, running errands, driving my car, and helping in other ways. Later, Paul helped Mother with her garden, too. Mother lived in the Boston suburbs, not too far from the city. With Paul's help, life was more comfortable for all of us. About a year later, however, Paul simply disappeared. It turned out that Paul borrowed significant amounts of money from Mother and her friends, in anticipation of future earnings. I was more cautious and had only advanced minimal amounts. Paul was a decent individual, but he was addicted to betting on horses. Apparently, Paul thought that by gambling more, he could repay his debts, but that is not how it worked out for him. It was sad to see how an addiction to gambling can ruin a person's life and future.

Betty and I continued to spend more time together. I grew more and more fond of her and liked her two children. Betty also loved my children, and it looked like this was the beginning of the family I had always wanted. I found Betty to be wonderful, outgoing, enthusiastic, and great company under almost any circumstances, except for her occasional bouts of melancholy. I attributed the latter to her prior marriage, which had been miserable and abusive. Betty's children had not seen their father for years and even changed their names to their mother's maiden name. A sad situation, but I was planning to be a part of their lives and was going to make it happy for everyone. So, on a trip to California, I asked Betty to marry me, and she enthusiastically accepted. We made plans for a wedding in Bermuda, where I previously owned part of a house and where I still belonged to a club—ideal for such a celebration.

In anticipation of the wedding, Betty mentioned we should have a prenuptial agreement. That was fine with me because I was more interested in the family—I considered the prenuptial agreement to be a peripheral matter. In principle, we agreed that what was hers would remain hers, and what was mine would stay mine. What we acquired together, we would split. This was important because Betty anticipated receiving an inheritance.

The day before we left for Bermuda to be married, Betty informed me, "I have engaged a new lawyer, and she insists that we modify the prenuptial agreement so that you guarantee me a very substantial annual income regardless of the length of the marriage." This last-minute change was an unexpected shock to me because everything had been agreed upon and settled before. The way I saw it, we were marrying for love and mutual affection, not material considerations. The fact that she brought up this issue at the last minute was unusual. The more I thought about it, the more I began to realize that perhaps my assessment of our relationship was wrong. The sudden changes to the terms at the very last minute was symptomatic of a deeper underlying problem. This situation probably reflected Betty's insecurities based on her last marriage. This was beyond my scope, however, because I was not privy to her prior life and relationships.

Frankly, I was mostly shocked because I thought I had finally found true love, but it looked like I was wrong again. Also, I felt that as far as material considerations went, that was not the key to our relationship. Betty had been generous in the past and even gave me a high-priced gold designer watch. Upon receipt, however, I insisted that it was too generous and showy of a gift and told her that a simple watch would do for me. I suggested she offer the difference to the children. Betty was upset, but she went along with my suggestion.

Even though Betty's behavior became unpredictable, and one could not know for sure what would happen next, we decided to go to Bermuda anyway. I hoped that everything would return to normal once we got there, but it did not happen that way. We had the most miserable trip. After we returned to Boston, I saw Betty a few more times. I explained to her that I visualized our relationship as a beautiful Steuben crystal bowl that sparkles and reflects the beauty of its surroundings—but once there is a large crack in the crystal, it is what one notices first. In other words, it is irreparable. I did not want to start a marriage on this basis.

We parted ways, and Betty returned to the midwest and happily remarried. I did not regret this outcome because I misjudged Betty's motivations for getting married. My ego was bruised because I again failed to understand a woman whom I adored. I wished for a book or manual I could study, like I had done in school, but there was none! I simply had to accept the fact that my judgment was not good, and all I could do was hope for better luck in the future. Deep down, I remained optimistic as always, convinced that happiness would eventually come my way.

Riga, Palm Beach, and Ski Trips

With my relationship with Betty behind me, I again began looking for new challenges and activities beyond work, which continued to progress well. Lisa and I decided to travel to Latvia, which recently opened to foreigners. The Soviet Union under Gorbachev was disintegrating, and there was hope that Latvia might regain its independence.

We flew first to Helsinki, the next day to Tallinn, and then traveled by bus to Riga, where we stayed at a hotel designated for foreign visitors. The once-beautiful Hanseatic city of Riga was drab, and the people looked depressed and avoided talking to foreigners. It was hard to believe that in the sixteenth century Riga had been one of the largest and most prosperous cities in the Baltic. It had also boomed before World War 1, especially during the country's independence (1918-1941). As we left our hotel, we were confronted by a huge statue of Lenin. In the city center, near the Freedom Monument that commemorated the country's independence, people gathered. I noticed several elderly men. One of them said, "I come here all the time in hopes of meeting some of my old friends, but they all seem to be gone, one by one." I am sure he did not mean gone due to old age, but rather the KGB. It was estimated that during Latvia's fifty years of Soviet occupation, more than twenty-five percent of the population escaped, was deported, or died under duress.

We were fortunate—a friend with a U.S. government connection arranged with a local official to provide us a car and driver. The locals knew the Soviet Union was nearing its demise and wanted to be on the right side of the United States. The next morning, a large black sedan arrived. We asked the driver to take us to Biksti, my family's country estate, where I had not been for more than fifty years.

After more than an hour of driving, we turned off the main highway and headed to Biksti on a dirt road that wound through fields, which appeared to be either neglected or abandoned. It was sad to see; this was one of the most fertile agricultural areas of Latvia. Biksti had always been important to my family—Mother took a great deal of pride in the expansive fields of wheat and rye, the herd of purebred Holstein cows, the dozen or more horses (which were quite valuable because, at that time, there were no tractors). Close to thirty people lived and worked on the estate. The daily operations were handled by a professional farm manager, but Mother made all the major decisions.

As we approached the buildings, I expected to see well maintained fields of wheat and rye, as they had been decades ago, but I saw only weeds and neglect. I was encouraged to see that only two to three buildings had been destroyed during the war. Those made of solid stone, dating as far back as the 1500s, survived. It was not easy to destroy buildings like that, but in some cases, the roofs were sagging. The flower garden in front of the house was gone, and so was the large formal English garden in the back, with its many pathways. There were still more than one hundred apple trees. It certainly did not look the way it had when I was there last. I was reminded of Margaret Mitchell's masterpiece *Gone with the Wind*— in the book, she describes how the culture and lifestyle of the south were destroyed during the Civil War, never to be brought back. Here, it was more than a culture or lifestyle. Many of the people who labored in the fertile fields were gone forever, replaced by Russians seeking a better life.

One could sense that people were in the buildings, but no one was outside—they were reluctant to greet us. I did see a child peeking through the curtains. Then it dawned on me—our large, black, official-looking car made the locals think we were KGB or someone from the government. Fear seemed to be ingrained into their character. We proceeded to the main manor house, which had been better maintained and now served as a school. The door was locked, and again no one came to greet us. As we walked around, we saw a young girl picking mushrooms in the forest—she was the only person to whom we could talk.

Overall, it was a sad visit, seeing the stark difference between the place of my memories, where I spent a happy childhood and what I saw that day. Before this trip, I had not dwelled much on my past, but it again came alive in my mind. It reminded me of my parents and their hope for an unfettered future for us—not all these hopes were fulfilled, but we managed to survive and prosper through our unexpected journeys. If the war had not come, my life would have been less stressful, likely devoted to the government and public service. Instead, I forged a different path and charted my own way. In that sense, it was good to return to the scenes of the beginning of my life—I could again face the future with renewed optimism. I felt confident that all obstacles eventually could be overcome.

In the afternoon, after our return to Riga, I had to make a few calls to the United States. It was almost impossible to complete a telephone call. Years later, I found out that the sixth floor of the hotel where we stayed was occupied by the KGB, and they monitored all communications, probably even tracking people. Not exactly a relaxing stay!

At night, I could not sleep. I thought, "Why I am still here, alive?" Looking at the odds, I should have been deported to a gulag with my family and perished there. If not that, then I would have been arrested later. There were also other, almost miraculous, circumstances through which I survived. We were fortunate to escape before the Soviet troops overran us in Latvia; we happened to be in a "lucky" ship that sailed for Germany. The Soviet advance stopped a few miles from us in Czechoslovakia, and again we escaped. What would have happened if the German policy toward Courland had changed during the last year of the war? I contemplated the mission and purpose of my life.

I recalled a passage from President Ronald Reagan's 1988 Moscow speech: "Every one of us put on this world has been put here for a reason and has something to offer." I also recalled a line from a sermon: "All things are done to God's plan and decisions" (Ephesians 1:11). I did not consider myself worthy of God's attention to all the details of my life, but I could not help but feel that His hand helped me at critical junctions. How else could I have survived and succeeded? I hoped this would continue in the future. I felt comforted and fell asleep.

We did not see any relatives because there were none left—all had either escaped abroad or met their end. While the trip was not always a joyful experience, it was a good reminder of my past and what happened to the rest of my family. I was lucky to have survived this fate and fortunate to live life in freedom.

During this unusual trip, the company of my lovely daughter, Lisa, made a significant difference. She was not only understanding but also very bright and uplifted my spirit. Lisa recently graduated magna cum laude, Phi Beta Kappa, and later got a master's degree from Smith College. On many other trips, I was accompanied by my son, Jay, who besides being an excellent athlete, could easily find solutions to most problems with his sharp mind (MBA from MIT) and winsome personality. His company made travel so much more enjoyable. I have been blessed with a family that serves as a legacy of those who perished during the war.

After returning to Boston, I received a call from my old friend, Sarah, who moved to Palm Beach, Florida. Sarah said, "I hear that you are again available and need some diversion! Come to Palm Beach and stay with us. My new beau and you have friends in common, and you could stay in our library. I will organize a party to introduce you to others." It could not have been a better-timed invitation! Earlier in my life, my former in-laws had a house not too far from Palm Beach, and I visited there. At that time, my preference was to spend vacation time skiing, rather than in Florida, but life had changed and I looked forward to the trip. It was fun to be in Palm Beach making new friends, playing tennis, and enjoying the sunshine. The visit was so successful that Sarah and her beau continued to invite me. From then on, whenever I had a business trip from Boston to California, I always detoured via Palm Beach.

I vividly remember a few of these visits. The first one relates to an elegant dinner to raise the initial funds for the Kravis Center for the Performing Arts. It was a spectacular event at The Breakers with excellent music, elegantly dressed attendees, and a performance by the Palm Beach Ballet. Sarah organized a table for ten. I was actively involved in my Boston charity, The Parents and Children's Services, and we were always trying to raise funds, so during intermission, I went to talk to Alex, the founder of the Kravis Center—we had common friends in Boston.

Alex directed me to one of the associates, who was responsible for the event. This man told me, "See the flowers on your table? They cost about the same as an airline round trip to Boston. We do not make much from a function like this, but it generates goodwill among our donors, which motivates major donations." I knew this would never work in frugal Yankee Boston!

After I returned to my table, one of the fellow guests said, "We think the performing arts center is a great cause, so we have decided that each of us will donate a seat." I thought it was an expensive proposition just to see your name inscribed on the back of a seat and engraved on some obscure part of the wall. Nevertheless, the Kravis Center was a great cause, and Alex, its organizer, deserved all the support. Not wanting to be an ungrateful guest from the provinces, when I returned to Boston, I sent them a check for the full amount. Only later did I learn that of my table of ten, I was the only one who donated! The lesson: I was a slow learner, assuming that others adhered to the same standards with which I was brought up. It would have been much wiser to find out beforehand the standards to which the locals adhered!

A few weeks later, I was invited to join another group of Sarah's friends at an elegant dinner dance in one of the private clubs. This time, Sarah also invited one of her girlfriends, who recently ended a long relationship with a man adored by many Palm Beach ladies. I never could understand what this man offered, but the ladies—regardless of their social status—were crazy about him. The man recently dumped Sarah's friend, and now she was escorted by another mutual friend. Sarah noticed that her friend's former lover was with his new lady friend, who was much older and more affluent. This did not mean anything to me, and I continued to enjoy the dinner dance.

After the party, all of us waited for our cars. Suddenly, Sarah left her beau, walked away, and started crying. I went up to her and asked, "Is there anything I can do?" Sarah replied that her girlfriend's former lover was behind us with his new lady and had come to her friend and said, "I will be with this woman [the older, richer woman] for an hour or so. Then I will spend the rest of the night with you." Sarah was crying and said, "This friend of mine is renewing a failed relationship that will lead nowhere. I am so sorry for her!" While I experienced a lot in my life, these values were beyond my comprehension. I decided then and there that I would avoid any close relationships in Palm Beach.

In all fairness, I have to say that the group with whom I associated was on the fringes of Palm Beach society and, I came to learn, did not represent its core. There are those in Palm Beach who hire publicity agents to get their photographs in the papers—they sponsor charitable events, and most of them are there to boost their own personal egos, rather than serve the causes they claim to support. The "real" Palm Beachers are low-key and belong to clubs that do not even allow photographers or news reporters inside. These individuals adhere to traditional values and love their families. One hardly ever hears about this segment because publicity is not their goal. Palm Beach hosts a highly diverse group of interesting individuals from all over the world, and it is fun to be here (I live part of the year here now).

I continued to accept invitations to visit Palm Beach and found them to be pleasant interludes, particularly when I could combine them with a business trip. On one visit, however, Sarah commented, "There is an auction on condominiums at one of the best buildings here. You should consider buying a unit." I realized that time was running out on the invitations, so with the help of a real estate agent, I attended the auction. This was a new experience for me—I had never been to a real estate auction before. The place was full of what appeared to be sophisticated buyers because the building was so desirable. I placed a few bids, but nothing happened, and I left the auction early because I had to fly to California to attend a business meeting. When I landed, there was a message that I had purchased a condominium. Because it was May, I had no interest in returning to Florida to inspect the property because the units required the finishing of the interiors before they could be occupied. This was a major project which I planned to undertake in the fall.

When I returned to Florida in October, to my surprise, it turned out that I had purchased the finished decorator's unit. While the furniture was gone, the interior was professionally designed. I started to think of myself as a real estate genius, but I must admit that this was the only successful real estate investment of my life. Even though I now had places in Florida, Boston, and New Hampshire, I was still actively involved in my business. I did not spend more than a weekend a month in Florida during the winter, but it was great to be there.

From the preceding, it might seem that I spent most of my time on fun activities, but that is not entirely true. I was very active in the investment business and, like everyone else, took four weeks of vacation each year, as well as occasional long weekends (when they could be combined with business). My work ethic was ingrained in me from my school days, when a superior academic record was necessary to maintain my scholarship. The reason my vacations left a lasting impression is because I enjoyed them with full zest, rather than passively staying at home. After a regular workday and a trip to the gym, my typical routine was to take my briefcase home and continue to work there. I would go to bed with a briefcase next to me and get right back to work when I woke up. It was not romantic, but practical. Fortunately, I enjoyed the investment business and would do it without pay.

My favorite leisure activity was skiing, particularly in Europe. While I skied in Zermatt, Switzerland, many times before, one special trip will always remain vividly in my mind.

With a group of Sarah's friends, we traveled to Zermatt from St. Moritz, where we had already skied for a week. Our journey was on the Glacier Express, one of the most scenic train rides in the world. The tracks snaked around mountains, passed through tunnels, and crossed many ski trails. Because the incline was so steep, occasionally the train had to engage its cog wheels. The surrounding alpine scenery was spectacular, and to enjoy it even more, the train attendant served us *kirschwasser* (cherry vodka). The drinks were poured in special glasses with stems bent at an angle because otherwise the liquid would spill—we were always on uneven ground. It indeed was a fun adventure.

At the Zermatt railroad station, we were met by an elegant horse-drawn carriage that resembled a Wells Fargo advertisement. On other occasions, when the streets were covered with snow, we were driven by a horse-drawn sleigh—no gasoline-powered cars are allowed in the village. It was a short ride to the comfortable, five-star Mont Cervin Palace, which offered magnificent views of the mountain that dominated the village. People appeared inconsequential compared with the majesty of the Matterhorn. The peak reflected and magnified the changing lights of sunset, and the scenery at night was even more spectacular. Snow covered the roofs, lights sparkled from numerous windows, and the whole town glittered like a well-polished jewel among a setting of mountain peaks. The sky was crystal-clear, and we could see numerous stars, as if they descended from their heavenly heights just to please us. We were mesmerized by the surrounding beauty and felt privileged to be there.

Initially, we skied with our group. Most of them were not serious skiers, but they were good company. The next day, with two friends, we hired a local guide and a helicopter to fly us to slopes not frequented by others. As we boarded the helicopter, we met our local guide, who had a climbing rope coiled around his shoulders. I asked, "Why the rope?" The guide replied that the best skiing was on nearby Mont Rosa, one of the highest peaks in the area at more than fifteen thousand feet, but it had unexpected crevices. Just in case we fell in, he had a rope to pull us out. Not wanting to spoil the day, I did not ask about the depth of the crevices or the length of the rope! It was a spectacular morning of skiing on slopes where no one had been for days. Around us were mountains and snowfields, but no homes nor people. In this setting, one's self is insignificant, but at the same time, for a moment, you feel as if it is your own world.

After half a day of skiing, we approached the tree line and came upon a charming Swiss inn. After lunch, we connected with the extensive Zermatt ski lift system, which covers about one hundred and fifty miles, and returned to the hotel. It was a spectacular experience! A few days later, there was an unexpected blizzard, and the mountains were covered with fresh powder. By now, we knew where to ski and found a slope with no one on it. As clouds rolled in behind us, we skied on untouched snowfields. As I glided through the powder, I sometimes did not know where I was—on the ground or suspended in the air. Skiing in those conditions in Zermatt is as close as anyone on this earth can get to heaven.

This feeling is pervasive and shared by many, regardless of age—I suppose it helps if they share the same gene pool. Years later, my twelve-year-old grandson, Will, expressed his feelings about skiing eloquently, writing:

I am happiest when I am skiing. I love the speed and the feeling of the wind blowing on my face. When I get up to a high speed, I start feeling an amazing sense of freedom and joy. I can only hear my heart thumping. Any distraction and worries get pushed aside as I race better down the mountain. The mountains are so peaceful and quiet; it becomes scary quiet once I get in my zone. There is no better feeling in the world!

I could not have said it better myself.

By this point, I had been a bachelor for several years, yet I still had not learned how to cook. I could prepare a good breakfast and use the outdoor grill, but that was the limit of my skills. Before marriage, I shared an apartment with three friends. My responsibility was to clean up, which I did effectively and did not mind. My housemate, Bill, professed to be a cook—in truth, his culinary repertoire was limited to fish sticks. To this day I still like fish sticks, but no one is willing to share this meal with me!

In the mornings, I often had early business breakfasts, but if not, I walked to work and stopped on the way at a private club on top of Beacon Hill. I began to have breakfast there when I first separated from Mary Ann and still lived in my Beacon Hill house. During that miserable experience, the quiet comforts of the club lifted my spirits. I developed a soft spot for the club and continued to breakfast there whenever possible. It was housed in a landmark historical mansion that had been the home of a prominent Boston family and still offered the same ambiance of peace and quiet. The elderly waitress, Ann, was a friend and knew how I felt and what I wanted. On one occasion, I mentioned something about the marmalade, and Ann said, "Please bring your own. I will keep it for you." The next time, at breakfast, there was my jar of marmalade—with a skull and crossbones drawn on it so no one else would try it. This club is still one of my favorite spots in Boston.

In the winter, whenever possible, Lisa, Jay, and I skied as a family, together with friends. Our trips ranged from the Alps to the Rockies, which created many great memories that all of us cherished. It did not matter if we skied across the Alps from Zermatt to Italy and back, or the New Hampshire mountains, or the Rockies. I have not forgotten one such trip to Vail. As we planned the trip, I overheard Jay's friend, Andrew, who was to accompany us, say, "Even though Mr. Livens taught us how to ski, this time we will ski him into the ground by taking double black diamond trails." That was quite a challenge, and I was not going to let this happen. In anticipation of the trip, I enrolled in a thrice-weekly aerobics class. Among all the attractive and flexible ladies, I was the worst in the class, but I persisted. One day, my daughter, Lisa, joined me and asked, "Why do you hide behind the plants when exercising?" The answer should have been obvious! It was all worth it because my results were satisfactory—I had no trouble keeping up with the boys.

When the children studied abroad, I visited them. I saw Lisa in Paris and London, and now I wanted to visit Jay, who was at the University of Freiburg in Germany. I mentioned my travel plans to a Boston friend, who—while she looked like a blonde model—was very prominent in the Boston legal community. We were good friends with no romantic involvement. She asked me to join her group of friends to ski in St. Moritz. The group consisted of sophisticated Europeans, who skied in St. Moritz only during the high season and stayed at Badrutt's Palace Hotel, which I knew quite well from prior trips. I called my son, Jay, in Freiburg and told him I would join him after first skiing a few days in Switzerland. Jay said, "Forget about coming to Freiburg—if you're staying at Badrutt's Palace Hotel, I am joining you!" Obviously, he had good taste, and all I had to do was bring his black-tie outfit.

During the first evening, I met the other members of the ski group and had an enjoyable time. As one would expect, the setting was elegant—men wore black tie attire, and the women were in sophisticated cocktail dresses, adorned with a lot of jewelry. There was soft music in the background. That first evening, I was seated next to an attractive German TV reporter and tried to practice my language skills. My companion was a charming woman, but unfortunately she was accompanied by her Swiss friend, who was twenty-five years older and a wealthy businessman. I guess wealth has its privileges! There were also several delightful Italian couples from Milan who had done very well in the fashion business and hinted about their relationships with Swiss banks. The Italians treated us to vintage wines and champagne—a very generous gesture.

I left the slopes early to meet up with friends who were going to a Christie's jewelry auction. I only went to tag along—while I liked beautiful jewelry, I did not want to buy any. Most of the jewelry came from the art deco period and was not my taste. When the auctioneer displayed a large, highly priced item, I could not resist—I covered my mouth with my hand and whispered to my companion, "That piece is absolutely ghastly." The auctioneer looked at me and said, "Sir, it is your bid!" For a few moments I was petrified, but then, fortunately, there was another bid. I learned to keep my hands still at an auction.

Before dinner that night, I told the hotel concierge that my son would be arriving at the railroad station. The concierge replied, "Do not worry. Normally, we pick up our guests in a Rolls-Royce or a similar car, but because there is snow on the ground, we will send a Jeep." It did not matter to me, so long as my son arrived in time for dinner. The elegant dinners at Badrutt's Palace Hotel always started around 9 PM.

The dinner started slowly, but by the time Jay, arrived dressed like others in a tuxedo we were ready to order. He studied the elaborate menu and lamented, "At the university, I have been eating a lot of wurst and spaghetti. This is an opportunity to get a solid meal. I would really like to have beef Wellington, but it is not on the menu." The waiter overheard and said, "Sir, we will prepare it for you right away, if you are willing to wait." One can never surpass the professional hospitality of the Swiss, particularly of Badrutt's Palace Hotel! After dinner, I looked forward to a good night's sleep so I could ski early in the morning. The other dinner guests retired to a disco called Three Kings. The reason behind the name was, supposedly, that three kings had danced there. Discos did not appeal to me, but Jay had fun dancing with the ladies (who were at least twenty-five years older!). All this activity did not handicap our skiing, and we spent several spectacular days together.

Before leaving, Jay wanted to take photographs of the opulent setting and the elegantly dressed people. There were quite a few from the Middle East—I doubted they came to ski, but instead came to enjoy the opulent social life. As Jay got out his camera and prepared to take a photograph, a black man suddenly materialized and politely requested, in perfect German, "Bitte *keine fotografieren.*" (Please, no photographs.) This man must have been a personal bodyguard of some famous person.

Altogether, it was a wonderful experience to spend those days with Jay in a unique and most enjoyable setting. It was sad to see him leave, but after a few more days, I too departed for Boston.

After the exciting trip to Switzerland, I was happy to return to my comfortable lifestyle. The circumstances surrounding my family were changing—Lisa had recently graduated from college, and she now worked for a consulting firm. Jay was finishing college. In anticipation of his graduation, we planned an early celebration and traveled during his spring break to Israel and Egypt—an incredible historical experience.

After graduation, Jay and I took a trip around the world. It would require pages to describe our adventures, but one stands out in particular. After almost two weeks in China, we flew to Thailand and visited Phuket. We went scuba diving around the island where the James Bond movie was filmed and stayed at the extraordinarily attractive Amanpuri resort. We had a private cottage in an incomparable setting, with a view that overlooked the Indian Ocean. After a gourmet dinner, we sat across a pool that reflected the graceful Thai dancers and their musical performance—a truly romantic setting with artistry that dated back centuries. An evening like that would be perfect to share with someone exceptional, but here we were, two lonely bachelors with just each other for company! Though a relationship with someone special was still missing in my life, it was nevertheless a great experience.

Work in Boston also proved to be exciting. Besides doing investment research and managing client portfolios, I participated in several venture investments on my own. The results were good, but not exceptional. One of my fellow investors, who was also a friend, asked me to invest in a major new startup serving the medical data industry. From prior research, I knew this field had great potential. The friend had a successful but spotty business record. He had been among the founders of a computer company that, within a few years after starting, was listed on the New York Stock Exchange—quite an accomplishment! The head of the new medical data company also had an impressive resume. He had an MD, an MBA, a professorship at a west coast university, and a record of other successful venture investments. After additional research, I decided that my new friends were probably right and that this company indeed had great future potential. As a result, I made a significant investment and was glad to see the company grow. In order to not diminish my ownership share, I continued to increase my stake. This undertaking added another exciting element to my work—but more on that later.

One day in Boston, Mother called, "Do you know that Latvia has regained its independence from the Soviets, and they are restoring properties to their rightful owners? We do not want to have our property in the hands of former communists!" After my prior trip, I had put Latvia out of my mind, but here it was again. What could I do but hire a lawyer in Riga and start the repossession process? I made several trips there, and the lawyer also flew to Boston. The result was that most of our properties were restored to us—we could not, however, evict the current occupants for at least seven years. In the interim, we were responsible for the upkeep and maintenance of the properties. It was not a great deal financially.

I flew to Latvia and met the government officials responsible for the Biksti region. When I entered their office, I saw a 1930s map of the Biksti estate posted on the wall. The officials pointed out that a large part of the land was now cultivated by "good" Latvian farmers, but on the corner of the estate, there was a new village inhabited mostly by Russians. I visited the place, and to my surprise, I was greeted warmly. The villagers were happy that the property was now owned by "a rich American" who would take care of the decaying buildings and neglected roads. That is the last thing I was interested in! With Mother's blessing, I gave away most of the land used by others.

My next stop was to visit our old Riga residence. The house there was like my place on Beacon Hill, except that it was larger and had two wooden apartment buildings across an open courtyard. These apartment buildings were in terrible condition, and I had no desire even to enter. I did meet the people who lived in the main house. When I walked into the largest room, which at one time had been a small ballroom, I saw it divided into two parts by curtains that hung from the ceiling—two families shared it. The dining room was in no better condition—on the floor, there were several buckets to catch dripping rainwater.

After seeing this, I had no desire to go up to the third floor. Frankly, I was glad when I was back out on the streets. It was sad to see a special place in this condition, especially because it had been beautiful and provided my family happy memories. It also served as a stark reminder of how the communist regime had not only destroyed lives but also the physical environment. We gave this complex to our attorney, and we were surprised later when the value of Riga properties quadrupled over the next three years.

Mother also owned several small apartment buildings in the second most important city, Jelgava. These buildings were destroyed during the war. In place of one of them, there was a supermarket, the other was replaced by a parking lot, and the third a movie theater. Technically, we owned the ground underneath, but we dropped the matter.

My late stepfather had owned an exemplary farm that specialized in raising seed crops. Mother gave this property to a distant relative. When I visited, I was not invited inside the house because they had to share it with Russian squatters. The interior was a disaster, and nothing worked. Being hospitable people, they treated us to a simple lunch in the garden. I am happy to report that this family eventually managed to evict the squatters and has since restored the farm to its former glory. Another farm, in a different part of the country, was given to my older sister. I contacted her in Wisconsin about it, but she had no interest in pursuing the matter. Fortunately, this spared me another unpleasant visit.

After the trip, I thought I had finally put Latvia behind me once and for all, but this did not turn out to be so. A little over a year later, Mother wanted to visit Latvia and see it for herself. Fortunately, I was able to limit our visit to Riga and Biksti. To stave off disappointment, I tried to explain to Mother what she might encounter when we arrived. Mother insisted, "I saw a lot of destruction after World War I, but I also saw how quickly the country recovered. If you sow good seeds in the fertile ground and cultivate them, the crops will be even better than before." What could I do but make arrangements for our trip to Latvia?

Our visit turned out better than expected. While in Riga, various people appeared, seemingly from nowhere, and greeted her. These were friends of friends whom I did not know existed. A few days later, we drove to Biksti. We were graciously welcomed by the locals, some of whom even kissed Mother's hand.

The headmistress of the school located in the Biksti manor house took us on a tour. Afterward, she handed Mother a large key to the main door and said, "Madame, this—and the surrounding area—is now yours!" I took a photograph of the occasion. Mother replied, "I have always believed in education—you can have what you need. It will serve your needs better than ours, so you can have it." Then Mother added, "By the way, my son will help you financially!" An unexpected commitment, but what can you do when your ninety-three-year-old mother says so?! Consequently, for more than twenty years, I gave financial prizes to the thirty best students of Biksti Elementary School and the teachers of their choice, in addition to helping the community with special projects. I have done my best to live up to Mother's expectations. Eventually, I established a small tax-exempt foundation to further foster these causes. Any contributions are welcome.[1]

---

[1] Should you so decide, you may make a tax-deductible gift to the Biksti Foundation, 529 S. Flagler Dr. 7H, West Palm Beach, FL 33401.

Time passed, and Mother approached her ninety-fifth birthday. As usual, we planned to spend Thanksgiving with my sister in Madison, Wisconsin, where she and her husband were both biochemistry professors. Mother liked to travel and enjoyed the anticipation of a trip. A few days earlier, she attended a Friday afternoon performance of the Boston Symphony Orchestra. She loved music, and my Christmas gift to her was season tickets with a car and driver to transport her back and forth. On some Friday afternoons, I joined her for the concert. Always meticulously attired, Mother visited her favorite hairdresser and packed her bags so we could leave early.

I arrived early in the morning to pick her up and drive us to the airport. Before leaving, I locked the front doors because we were going to exit through the back. Mother got up and said, "I have to double-check the multiple locks." While at the door, she said, "I feel faint." I quickly ran up, guided her to a chair, and put her in my lap while I searched for her heart medicine. After a while, I felt for Mother's pulse, and there was none—she peacefully passed away. She took a different trip with a far better destination than we planned.

At first, it was impossible for me to comprehend what had happened, even though we know that all life has an end. I lost a mother and a friend who, with unfailing faith, had guided our family through the chaos of war and led us to freedom and opportunity. Mother inspired us to believe that a brighter future lay ahead. If we failed, we knew that Mother was there to help, and her love was unconditional. This knowledge gave all of us confidence to reach higher and to realize our potential. My family and I were fortunate to have a mother like this, and I can only hope that her values will be passed to future generations.

The rest of the day was hectic. I contacted my sisters and received support from family friends. I remembered an invitation from a friend to attend her family's Thanksgiving dinner in Rhode Island. I turned it down because I would be out of town. I called up the friend and said I would be glad to attend, if she did not tell the others what happened. In the late afternoon, I drove to Rhode Island. I reached across the passenger seat to where Mother sat two weeks prior, when we drove to New Hampshire—but no one was there. My hand touched only a handkerchief that Mother left behind. Even though I was alone in the car, a feeling of peace descended upon me, and I felt Mother's presence. Mother seemed to convey the message that, although she was now in a better place, in spirit she would always be with me—just as it had always been when I needed her most. I firmly believe this, and it gave me a peace and respite from the sadness.

Later, at the funeral service, the minister commented, "Irma wanted to pass away in the presence of a family member, but her daughter lived far away, and her son traveled. Clearly, God was with her and granted her wish."

After Mother's death, my two sisters and I combined some of her assets and, in Mother's memory, gave a gift toward the restoration of the Latvian National Opera House—Mother always loved music. At that time, it was one of the largest individual gifts, but it has since been superseded by corporate donors. Mother's name is probably still inscribed in some obscure spot, but that does not matter because the cause is what is important. I followed this up with a personal gift to the Museum of the Occupation of Latvia, which depicts the horrors of the Soviet regime and reminds us all of the precious gift of human freedom. I hoped, like in my early years, I could put my whole Latvian experience out of my mind, but it seems to come up again and again. Perhaps the human mind is like an old DVD player—occasionally it replays scenes from the past, beyond your control.

I was glad to hear that Jay, after returning from our trip and graduating from college, decided to work at my firm as an investment analyst. Even better, he moved into the Beacon Hill home with me. The house had three floors and offered ample space and privacy. It was located on a private street and, besides a garage, had two parking spaces out front—a real treasure in Boston. It was a privilege to be with my son, who had been my close companion, especially because we shared many adventures together around the world. Later, Lisa also joined us in the house, and the family was together again.

A few years later, Jay went to graduate school (MIT Sloan School of Management), received an MBA, and chose to work in the technology industry. Initially, Lisa worked for a consulting firm and then later at an emerging technology company that seemed to have a great future but unfortunately failed. To pursue a different opportunity, Lisa worked for

Habitat for Humanity in Ecuador. At that time, Lisa had no plans to attend graduate school—so, to treat her equally, I bought her a beautiful piece of jewelry that I saw in the Sotheby's auction catalog. A few months later, Lisa told me, "Dad, I decided to go to Smith College's School for Social Work. I know you gave me this generous gift, and I am willing to sell it. I had it appraised, and its value is substantially more than before." I told her, "Keep it. A gift is a gift!" Lisa was always very fair and non-mercenary. A year later, I asked, "Lisa, why don't you wear the jewelry?" She replied, "There are not many occasions to do so in Boston. I do not want to pay the insurance!" That was fine with me—the gift was only a material representation of my feelings for a wonderful daughter.

Life for all of us continued to be fun. Some mornings, I walked halfway to work with Lisa and then saw Jay in the office. He mostly worked for another partner. Jay and I took several business trips together and often spent the weekends away. Working with Jay also gave me more free time to look after my personal investments.

One morning, I looked at the *Wall Street Journal* and saw that the privately held medical data company in which I made a substantial investment was to be sold to a leading company in the business. The acquiring company's stock was traded. Because I participated in several rounds of private financing, my holdings were substantial. I made a quick calculation and was surprised to see that my investment's worth was in the eight digits. An unexpected windfall! I felt I should share my good fortune with some of the organizations and people who helped me in the past. I almost felt like a philanthropist and even planned to sell half of my shares.

Before doing so, I contacted the friend who originally brought this investment opportunity to my attention. He was a director of the company and helped to negotiate the merger. I told him I placed an order to sell the stock. He immediately said, "I would not sell it now—more good news is coming! You will be able to give away much more if you wait a little longer. Hold out until year's end!" Because he had been right before, I canceled my order after having sold only a few shares. For a while, it looked as if my friend would be right again—the stock kept going up, and there were some days when my holdings increased by seven digits.

A few months later, I was surprised to see an announcement that the company that had acquired our private venture manipulated its accounting and hidden its liabilities. In one day, the stock dropped from the high seventies to fourteen and then to four. All my gains evaporated, and I hardly got back my original investment. Later, I learned that my "friend" and the other insiders could not sell their stock as early as I could, so they did not want me to sell it—though of course they made sure to unload all their shares before the bad news came out. This resulted in numerous lawsuits, but I had no desire to deal with lawyers.

Several years later, I had a condo in an upscale Florida building. The whole top floor—the grand penthouse—was occupied by my former "friend" who cashed out at the peak of the dubious investment while telling me not to sell. Nevertheless, I was very happy with my life and would not have traded places with him. This was a sad lesson, not so much because of the lost assets but because of my disappointment in people I trusted. I should have known that I was operating in a different environment and dealing with individuals who adhered to different ethical standards. The negative aspects of one's personality sometimes only become visible under stress, and greed is one of the worst. We should keep this in mind when judging people only in an favorable environment.

A Brighter Future

I had a comfortable lifestyle with places in Boston, New Hampshire, and Florida, but it felt incomplete because there was no special person in my life. My past personal relationships were not successful, and I had to accept that the future might not be different. One day, my good friend, Betsy, called and said, "I want you to meet someone very special." Betsy was one of the great hostesses on Beacon Hill and had introduced several couples who were happily married. This was not the first time Betsy tried to help me, but her prior efforts failed. I looked at my calendar and said, "Thank you for the invitation, but I cannot do anything for several weeks due to prior commitments." Betsy replied, "That is fine. The lady I plan to introduce you to is also quite busy. She just moved to Boston to serve as one of the Administrative Deans of Harvard Medical School." So, we set a date more than a month away.

As I pondered my conversation with Betsy, my hopes of meeting a compatible lady diminished. From prior experience, I knew that the academicians at Harvard believed that when the Good Lord allocated intelligence to mortals, the bulk of it went to Harvard, and only a few crumbs ended up at other, less deserving institutions. The university staff members, while basking in the brilliance of their academically minded colleagues, tried to emulate them. While this was less apparent among men, most of the women seemed to be in a race as to who could look dowdier. They avoided beauty salons like the rest of us avoid dentist's offices.

My hopes for a new and exciting date were slim. One redeeming feature was that Betsy had probably screened the lady. Also, because my date only recently arrived in Boston, hopefully she had not yet fallen into the Harvard mold. This lady came from Baltimore, known for its graciousness—the women there valued their appearances! Betsy's husband was a good friend of mine, and besides being one of the country's leading eye surgeons, he was also a professor at Harvard Medical School. I hoped his input was considered in arranging this date. Clearly, there were many unknowns, so I put the whole matter out of my mind and proceeded with my previous plans.

On the appointed day in November 1995, I arrived at Betsy's small cocktail party. After meeting the other attendees, including the special lady (Cush), I turned to the other guests, trying to assess the situation. I wanted to collect as much data as possible before making any moves.

No question—Cush was a very attractive, perky, blue-eyed blonde with a sparkling personality, great poise, and self-confidence to boot. She probably needed many of these attributes, in addition to intelligence, to be at Harvard Medical School. I thought, judging from Cush's appearance, she was too good for the job. Because her position was important, Cush probably had PhDs and MDs, carrying her briefcases around while attending important meetings. I did not have any of these degrees and, frankly, did not want to carry other people's stuff.

While I liked Cush at first sight, I did not pursue her immediately. Ladies with terrific attributes are accustomed to men gravitating to them like bees to honey at social gatherings. She certainly lit up the room and made the party interesting! Then I remembered what the father of a good friend of mine told me. This older gentleman had been married for more than sixty years, and when asked what his secret was, he answered, "Boys: pure luck!" So, all the data did not matter in the end, and I could only hope that luck would come my way.

By the time the cocktail party was over, I still had not decided what to do. As Cush was leaving, I helped her with her topcoat. On the spur of the moment, I said, "Let's have dinner." Cush accepted, and we walked to a restaurant. Later, I learned that the hostess had not told me, but I was expected to take Cush to dinner. Almost a missed opportunity!

As we walked across the Boston Garden, I took Cush's arm to guide her across the street. I noticed that she was short and casually mentioned, "You are one of the shortest ladies I've ever met." That was absolutely the wrong thing to say because I was over six feet tall and Cush was five feet two inches. I never realized how sensitive ladies are about their height. I tried for a comeback and said, "Your personality is so great that it overpowers everything else!" That seemed to work. I was going to add how wonderful she looked (which was true), but decided to save that for another occasion.

We had a delightful dinner, but having had poor judgment before, I decided to proceed cautiously and use the limited tools at my disposal. I remembered the advice of my beloved governess when I was only a few years old—I did not understand their meaning then, but I remembered her words: "Before you marry, insist on meeting your future mother-in-law. Your bride will eventually turn out like her mother!" I disregarded this advice when I first met Mary Ann because she insisted that she was entirely different from her mother and family. I thought Mary Ann's mother was a nice, low-key lady with a limited view of the real world, so it really did not matter. After the divorce, I regularly called my children, who were sometimes with their grandparents; during one of these telephone calls, my former mother-in-law answered the phone, speaking in her usual monotone, graveled, and unemotional voice. I politely asked to talk to my children. The answer was, "This is your ex-wife!" My governess was right!

I discreetly suggested that perhaps I could meet Cush's mother. My suggestion was probably not subtle enough, but I was invited to have tea with her. We immediately hit it off. I thought, *If Cush turns out like her mother, how lucky can I be!* Cush's mother was not only the favorite of the family but was liked by my children, too. I had already met Cush's three children. I could not have been happier knowing that all were going to fit well together into the new family. Cush probably had her children check me out, too, and I seemed to pass the test.

We were engaged a year later, in November 1996, and married shortly afterward, in June 1997. We have been married for more than twenty happy years now. It did not take me long to realize that Cush is a special person—not only attractive and intelligent, but she also has a sterling character. We share the same values. Cush is the kind of individual who, if she loves you, she will always be there, regardless of the circumstances. She is exceptional and has brought genuine and lasting happiness to my life. I could not have wished for more!

Wedding 1997

After our wedding, we continued to live on Beacon Hill. For weekends and holidays, we built a house on Squam Lake in New Hampshire, an area both of us knew and adored. Cush wanted our new combined family to be successful, and she spared no effort. Both of us still worked, but at Squam Lake, we could entertain all five children, only one of whom was married. Everyone enjoyed visiting us during the holidays. Their favorite time to visit was summer on

Squam Lake—for swimming, water skiing, and other daily outdoor activities. Besides that, one could enjoy the incredible view across the lake and the mountains. As in the movie *On Golden Pond*, the view could not have been more spectacular. The elevation rose rapidly from the shore and offered a panoramic view.

Ten years later, our family, including in-laws, grew to over twenty. During the Christmas season, family visited us, and sometimes we had more than a dozen staying. We built a larger house about thirty minutes away on Lake Winnipesaukee. This house was on the grounds of a private club that offered tennis, golf, swimming, and other activities. This was a more suitable environment for us because we did not work full time, and the place proved to be popular with our family. On some holidays, we had sixteen or more people staying with us! As time passed, it became more difficult to entertain so many. Fortunately, our children took over the responsibility of entertaining for most holidays, and we love to be there as guests.

My hope for a wonderful family has been more than fulfilled, but that would not have been possible were it not for the efforts of my beautiful, energetic, and sometimes too-well-organized wife. Our children do well in their careers and married lives. We love all of them and are particularly proud of the nine grandchildren. All of them are on honor or high honor roll, if their school has such a category. They have great potential to be contributors to society. Perhaps, in a way, they will help to repay my debt to the United States for the opportunities it provided. We are truly blessed, and I could not have asked for more.

Frequently, in the evenings, Cush and I stand on the deck of our New Hampshire house and look across the lake. It is a spectacular view of water shimmering through the trees. The tranquility is occasionally interrupted by a long, haunting loon call reverberating across the lake, the loon longing for his mate. I look at Cush, who stands next to me, and know that my search has ended. How fortunate I am to have found her! We glance at each other, give a hug, and say how lucky we are to be able to share our lives together.

For the sake of full disclosure, I must admit that I carry Cush's bags. When I first met her, I thought I would never carry her briefcase, like her PhD underlings had done. Now, when we travel, the airlines label Cush's bags "HEAVY," and I handle all of them. True love changes everything!

Family with spouses 2019

EPILOGUE

Visits to Latvia

Over the years, I have made several trips to Latvia and Biksti. Every time I travel there, the country looks more attractive and the people more friendly—as if they put their fifty years of Soviet domination behind them once and for all. Not an easy task—during World War II and two years of aftermath, the country lost more than a quarter of its population, either to the Soviets or to those who managed to escape to the west. Many of those who left were from the intelligentsia and represented the country's leadership.

In 2017, my family and I traveled to Latvia. For the grandchildren, this was their first trip there. I wondered how they would react to the places where our family originated. Altogether, it was a successful trip. It started in Riga, the nation's capital, with a population of about six hundred fifty thousand. This makes it one of the largest cities on the Baltic. Riga has a rich history, dating back to 1201, and is once again vibrant and attractive. It is not yet overrun by tourists, even though cruise ships make port calls there. The city has been cleaned up, and the drabness of the Soviet era is in the distant past. Art deco-style buildings, for which Riga is known, sparkle in a multiplicity of vibrant colors. No wonder Riga was declared a UNESCO World Heritage site and designated the European Capital of Culture in 2014.

During the summer, there are many charming outdoor restaurants and a variety of celebrations. The most noteworthy is the national Song and Dance Festival, which involves eighteen thousand singers and almost the same number of folk dancers. It is a national celebration that takes place every five years. Almost all communities, regardless of size, practice for months in advance and send participants to the festival. We were not there during the festival but still enjoyed the city. The grandchildren found the Museum of the Occupation of Latvia fascinating because it made the country's recent history come alive for them and illustrated the stark differences between freedom and oppression.

The next day, we visited Turaida Castle, located an hour away. It was a small fortress originally built in 1098 by the local pagan ruler Caupo. Burned down centuries later, it was reconstructed. My family traces its beginnings to Caupo and this location.

The following passage is recorded in Henry's Chronicle (*Henrici Chronicon Lyvoniae*), written in Latin circa 1229:

Caupo, who was a kind of king and elder of the Livonians, and, having traversed a large part of Germany, at length brought him to Rome and presented him to the apostolic father. The latter received him most graciously, kissed him, asked him many things about the status of the tribes dwelling about Livonia, and gave many thanks to God for the conversion of a Livonia people. After several days, the venerable Pope Innocent presented his gift to Caupo, namely a hundred gold pieces, and since he wished to go back to Germany, blessed him, bidding farewell with great and loving affection. By brother Theodoric, he sent to the Bishop of Livonia a Bible written by the hand of the Blessed Pope Gregory.

After returning, Caupo continued to wage a campaign against nonbelievers, but in 1212, his underlings rebelled. They supposedly jumped into the local river, Gauja, to wash off their baptism and reverted to their pagan religion, which was the worship of trees—quite an advanced concept! Caupo did not approve and, with sword, re-converted them to Christianity. He continued to spread the faith to neighboring regions with the help of the Livonian Knights.

In 1217, Caupo died in battle while fighting for Christian causes. Later, his descendants changed their name to a more Christian version, denoting their province. Their last name became Liewen, Lieven, or Līvens, depending on whether one uses the Swedish, German, or Latvian version, though the pronunciation remains the same in all languages (Leeven). A number of great powers, including Czarist Russia, at one time ruled the province.

On the way to Biksti, we visited the Mežotne Palace. It is an outstanding example of neoclassical architecture. It was built in 1797 for the Lieven (Latvian, Livens) family. In the late 1700s, a widowed Baltic German baroness was appointed the governess of Nicholas, Catherine

II's grandson, who was third in line for succession to the throne. Because there were two brothers ahead of him, his chances of becoming the czar were minimal. However—to everyone's surprise—years later, Baroness von Lieven's ward became Czar Nicholas I. The czar adored his former governess and respected her intelligence. After assuming power, he made her a countess and later a princess (this title is not quite comparable to the one by the same name in Western Europe). The Baroness built the Mežotne Palace but hardly ever visited. The palace was damaged during World War II, but it was beautifully restored and is open to the public. We enjoyed a tour and a delightful family lunch.

The next day we traveled to Biksti Manor. We were graciously received by the headmistress of the elementary school now housed in the manor house. It was designated as a National Cultural Heritage Site and is well maintained. While touring the house, I stood in the ballroom in the very same spot where I stood more than eighty years before, at the tender age of two. I remembered holding my father's hand while my younger

Biksti Manor - 2017

sister was christened. Since then, the room had been used as a private residence, a frontline military hospital, and half a basketball court. Now, it serves as an elementary school—the most worthwhile purpose of all!

As I walked around the well-maintained manor house, a story told by a former soldier came to my mind. During the war, when it was used as a frontline hospital, many wounded soldiers died and were buried nearby. Years after the war, the military-graves commission exhumed most of the bodies for reburial in a military cemetery. Because the graves were scattered, not all of the bodies were easily located. Former soldiers suggested leaving some of the earthly remains where they originally were buried. This was now part of the school's playground—the soldiers felt their comrades had died young, robbed of their future with its joy and promise. Why not take final rest under a playground and experience the laughter of happy children as they look forward to a bright future? Perhaps, in a way, the soldiers could share in the joy from their eternal resting place.

I looked at my grandchildren and thought about how fortunate they were to live in a society free from oppression, with equal rights and opportunities for all. It occurred to me that decades before, while standing in the same spot, my parents probably had high hopes for our futures, even after everything unexpectedly changed. That indeed was true for our material circumstances, at least—but character, values, and intelligence always stay with you, no matter what. My parents passed on these qualities and allowed us to overcome unexpected obstacles, which made us stronger. While I hope that hardships like these do not affect my grandchildren's lives, I know they will overcome whatever comes, as my family did. We should never give up hope for a better future because we can shape our own destiny.

After visiting the manor house, we did not want to spoil the favorable impression of the place, so we did not look at the six or more remaining buildings on the estate. Recently, these buildings were also designated National Cultural Heritage Sites; one of them dates to 1560. All the other buildings are in poor condition—hopefully, with help from residents, we will be able to improve their appearance, but it will be a major project.

To add a different dimension to the trip, we arranged an overnight stay at the Jaunpils Castle, located only three miles away. The castle was built in 1306. It had been occupied by the von der Recke family, who left for Germany in the 1920s. They were friends of my grandfather's. The local community took over the castle and opened it to the public. It is a small castle/fortress surrounded by a moat and a high wall. Its only noticeable changes from the original were modern plumbing, electricity, and probably the fastest Internet I experienced in Europe—everything else dated back centuries.

During our stay, we were treated to a candlelit, medieval feast in a room that resembled a dungeon. The grandchildren enjoyed the setting—particularly because there were no utensils except a spoon-like instrument and a knife. Typically, the management put on a skit that included a ghost, but it was unavailable at the time we visited. The help told me not to worry about it because there were genuine ghosts!

I ignored these comments and, after dinner, took two bottles of beer and went to my room. Every day, I texted my wife in New Hampshire about our trip. This time, I wrote, "I am spending the night in a garishly decorated room in the Jaunpils Castle, which previously was the baroness's bedroom. The color is pink, as are the curtains around the four-poster bed. The combination is tasteless... [etc.]!" I drank a beer and went to bed, but I left the window slightly open to get some fresh air.

At midnight, I heard a noise that woke me, and I felt that someone was in the room. When I reached for the beer bottles, they were knocked off my bedside table. There was a whoosh, as if someone was leaving, and the window was now wide open. I turned on the light and texted my wife what happened. She immediately replied, "I have been telling you to always be polite to your hosts and never be critical. No wonder the baroness had to visit and set you straight!" What could I say—most of the time, my wife is right!

The next morning, the grandchildren played unique medieval games, saw coin minting, and practiced archery. As we readied to depart, I saw a man loading gunpowder into an old cannon on the rampart. I asked, "What are you doing?" The man replied, "We are going to fire the cannon in honor of your visit." I commented, "The cannon looks very old." His reply: "Not really, we only captured it from the Swedes in 1703." Before I could say anything else, the cannon was fired with a big bang. The Swedes sure built solid cannons in 1703!

As we were getting into the car, a young lady came up to me and said, "I want to thank you for your support of the Biksti School. Years ago, when I graduated, I received one of your prizes for academic excellence. It encouraged me to continue my education and learn English." Comments like this, as well as my family's company, made the trip an especially meaningful experience.

The trip was memorable for all. After returning, my children said, "We would like to go on another family trip!" I thought that was a great idea but then remembered the cost of ten people, for more than two weeks, with airfare, guides, and other travel expenses, But then they chimed in, "We loved your company, and on the next trip, we will pay our own expenses." What an honor for my wife and me to be included! Our other children, who were not on this trip, were equally generous with their time and effort. How lucky we are! It seems that I have been able to pass along some of the family values to the next generation. That, all along, has been one of my goals.

Reflections

My life has been an unexpected journey. In the beginning, it looked like life would be an easy, comfortable voyage that would not require any major effort—nothing too different from what my family experienced before. It turned out to be entirely different and full of unforeseen challenges. Sometimes I wonder why, but I think that is beyond human comprehension. A casual observer might say my life represents "The American Dream"—the idea that everyone in the United States can realize his full potential, no matter his initial circumstances. It was not my choice to live this dream nor face its challenges—I would have been just as happy if the challenges had not come my way. Nevertheless, as the unexpected obstacles developed, I learned how to cope to the best of my ability.

My life shows that we as humans cannot always change or control our circumstances. We cannot anticipate all the obstacles in our path. We can, however, choose our attitude, our actions, and how to overcome the obstacles we face. This will define our character, values, and faith. William James, the famous American philosopher, said, "Change your attitude and you will change your life." We have a choice, but how do we make the right one?

As we travel the path of life, we are generally guided by signposts established before us by family or tradition. Along the way, we can modify our route, but these signs make the journey more pleasant. In my life, however, these signs were destroyed by war and its subsequent turmoil. It was a more challenging road to travel because I often had to forge my own path, never knowing where it might lead, but my journey was made easier by the support of family and friends. That said, no one can set our individual goals for us. I believe I was able to navigate the turmoil because of the Guiding Hand above, which at critical times nudged me in the right direction. I do not know why I deserved this attention, but without it, I would not be here.

Thank you for your patience in reading my story. I wish you a happy journey through life and a comfortable path to travel—but not too comfortable! Overcoming unexpected challenges makes you stronger and gives you self-confidence. Also, the well-trodden and predictable path can be boring. Genuine joy and happiness are even sweeter after enduring sadness and disappointments. I am sure that others will help you on your journey through life, but ultimately it will be up to you to decide which roads to travel. I was fortunate enough to enlist the help of the One above, who guided me at critical moments; I wish the same for you.